# Snapshots of School Leadership in the 21st Century

### Perils and Promises of Leading for Social Justice, School Improvement, and Democratic Community (The UCEA Voices From the Field Project)

D1225678

A Volume in
UCEA Leadership

*Series Editors:*
Michelle D. Young, *University of Virginia*
Liz Hollingworth, *University of Iowa*

# UCEA Leadership

Michelle D. Young and Liz Hollingworth, Series Editors

*At a Crossroads: The Educational Leadership*
*Professoriate in the 21st Century* (2011)
by Donald G. Hackmann and Martha M. McCarthy

*Snapshots of School Leadership in the 21st Century: Perils and Promises*
*of Leading for Social Justice, School Improvement, and Democratic Community*
*(The UCEA Voices From the Field Project)* (2012)
edited by Michele A. Acker-Hocevar, Julia Ballenger,
A. William Place and Gary Ivory

# Snapshots of School Leadership in the 21st Century

## Perils and Promises of Leading for Social Justice, School Improvement, and Democratic Community (The UCEA Voices From the Field Project)

Edited by

**Michele A. Acker-Hocevar**
*Washington State University Tri-Cities*

**Julia Ballenger**
*Texas Wesleyan University*

**A. William Place**
*University of Dayton*

**Gary Ivory**
*New Mexico State University*

Information Age Publishing, Inc.
Charlotte, North Carolina • www.infoagepub.com

**Library of Congress Cataloging-in-Publication Data**

Snapshots of school leadership in the 21st century : perils and
promises of leading for social justice, school improvement, and democratic
community : the UCEA Voices From the Field Project / edited by Michele A.
Acker-Hocevar ... [et al.].
     p. cm. — (UCEA leadership series)
   Includes bibliographical references.
   ISBN 978-1-61735-898-2 (paperback) — ISBN 978-1-61735-899-9 (hardcover) —
ISBN 978-1-61735-900-2 (e-book)  1.  School management and
organization—United States. 2.  Educational leadership—United States. 3.
Critical pedagogy—United States. 4.  Democracy and education—United
States. 5.  UCEA Voices From the Field Project.  I. Acker-Hocevar, Michele,
1948- II. UCEA Voices From the Field Project.
   LB2805.S681 2012
   371.2—dc23

                                                                    2012020196

Printed in the United States of America

# CONTENTS

# PREFACE

### Gary Ivory, A. William Place,
### and Michele A. Acker-Hocevar

This book is the product of years of work from dozens of scholars and the contributions of many superintendents and principals across the United States who between 2004 and 2006 gave of their valuable time to share their views with us in 27 focus groups. The book synthesizes the overall findings from *Voices From the Field: Phase 3 (Voices 3)*. It is the third stage of a University Council for Educational Administration (UCEA) project that began in the mid-1990s. Phase 1, *A Thousand Voices From the Firing Line* (Kochan, Jackson, & Duke, 1999), involved one-on-one interviews with principals and superintendents to document "their perceptions of their jobs, their most vexing problems, and their preparation to deal success-fully with their work and the problems they faced" (Duke, 1999, p. 10).

Barbara LaCost and Marilyn Grady led Phase 2 of Voices and used focus groups rather than one-on-one interviews (DiPaola, Acker-Hocevar, Grogan, Davis, & Ivory, 2002). Two of us (Michele and Gary) participated in this second phase of Voices and became excited about this research work and the focus on listening to voices in the field. So, when we were asked to lead Phase 3 of Voices, we accepted. We also continued using focus groups.

All three phases of the Voices project sprang from the hope that by looking through the lenses of practitioners, professors of educational leadership might be better able to see ways to strengthen our preparation programs, highlight policy-implementation issues, and better frame per-

*Snapshots of School Leadership in the 21st Century:*
*Perils and Promises of Leading for Social Justice,*
*School Improvement, and Democratic Community*, pp. vii–xii
Copyright © 2012 by Information Age Publishing

spectives of principals and superintendents as problems of practice in order to forge tighter systemic connections between the academy and the field around these problems.

In the book, we provide snapshots describing this critically important time in our nation when federal educational policy implementation has been at a level previously unheard of in the United States. We present a chapter on the design and method of Voices 3, eight chapters on analyses of the focus group discussions, and two invited chapters that provide a review and critique of our work. The chapters will be excellent resources for professors of educational leadership as we respond to the changing environment and improve preparation programs for superintendents and principals. We also see the book as a good resource for practitioners who desire to take the pulse of their colleagues in the field to see common concerns across various issues. Finally, it will be useful to policy makers as they consider the impact of their decisions on the implementation phases in districts and schools. With this book, you are receiving access to the 27 focus group transcripts on which the chapters are based. Instructors of qualitative research may find these data useful in their classes, for example, for students to practice different types of data analysis and coding.

http://infoagepub.com/snapshots_of_leadership

## CHAPTER OVERVIEW

### Chapters on the Method and the Data

Chapter 1 describes the design of the study and gives some feeling for the amount of collaboration it took from so many people to bring Voices 3 to fruition. We hope leaders of any future phases can learn from our experiences, both the positive and the negative ones.

In Chapter 2, Kristin Kew, Gary Ivory, Miriam Muñiz, and Fernando Quiz discuss No Child Left Behind (NCLB, 2002) as school reform. They review the arguments of House and McQuillan (1998) that any successful reform must deal with three components: the technological, the political, and the cultural. The authors then examine NCLB in terms of its accounting for those three factors. They present principals' and superintendents' descriptions of their own efforts to fill in the gaps in areas not adequately addressed by NCLB. They speculate on what more is needed for principals and superintendents to be successful in implementing inadequately designed reforms.

Bill Ruff and Sharon Geiselmann (Chapter 3) provide vivid pictures of school leaders torn between the unrelenting pressures from accountability systems to foster high student performance on standardized tests and their own awareness that children need more in their growth and development than good test scores. Ruff and Geiselmann point to new research in neurological and cognitive sciences to help guide school leaders in rethinking their roles in this time of split allegiances (both to good documentable results and to concern for children's healthy development). They close their chapter by urging educators and policy makers to broaden their views of school reform beyond improvement in test scores to a realization that it is important for schools to foster development in all the areas that are essential to being human.

In Chapter 4, Elizabeth Murakami-Ramalho and Mariela Rodríguez discuss the struggles of school leaders to adopt worldviews that commit to the academic success of all children. They highlight the facts that (a) any definition of success for all children is controversial and that (b) superintendents and principals must negotiate between views that urge tailoring programs to students' individual needs versus views that schools should be accountable for similar levels of success for all children.

Betty Alford and Julia Ballenger present leaders' views of the all-important role of quality personnel in ongoing school reform (Chapter 5). They note that to sustain reform, attention to personnel must be unrelenting. Decisions to hire are crucial, but so are decisions to terminate, and even to transfer. Furthermore, Alford and Ballenger provide specifics from the Voices 3 superintendents and principals on how professional development, in all its forms (and provided leaders consider carefully its purposes), is central to school improvement. The two authors weave the themes they see in leaders' focus groups into a set of recommendations for preparation and practice.

Sally Hipp and Jacquelyn Melin devote Chapter 6 to reporting on superintendents' and principals' experiences with assessment, particularly its relationship to teaching and learning. They show that annual standardized assessments in reading and mathematics (that on their face appear straightforward and benign and may have positive benefits) also do harm in a number of ways. After a thorough review of the literature on assessment and accountability, they share Voices 3 participants' views of the promise of assessment, as well as the ways in which it actually interferes with education. Hipp and Melin argue that we need to move to "productive assessment systems that balance classroom-level assessments, program-level assessments, and institutional accountability and policy-level assessments" (Chapter 6, Assessment).

In Chapter 7, Deb Touchton, Rosemarye Taylor, and Michele Acker-Hocevar maintain that leaders must deliberately choose how to negotiate between individual beliefs and organizational expectations within their school districts and schools to promote more democratic decision-making processes of giving voice, listening, and involvement. They identify two themes in the transcripts: (a) leadership decision-making perspectives and (b) factors that affect decision making. Leaders caught in top-down, hierarchical organizations where they are held accountable for decisions must wrestle with individual and organizational tensions that require letting go of control over decision making to adopt more democratic decision-making practices. Touchton et al. conclude leaders must articulate decision-making models, identify their philosophy of inclusive decision making, and select governance structures that promote democratic decision making.

Chapter 8, by Thomas Kersten and Julia Ballenger, presents education leaders' views of the key role of interpersonal relationships in leadership. The Voices 3 participants noted that positive relationships are frequently a *sine qua non* of leadership and require constant effort to maintain. Kersten and Ballenger show how superintendents and principals elaborated both on the importance of relationships and the obstacles encountered in sustaining them. The authors explore various factors: dealing with differing perspectives and values, grappling with the challenges of conflicting input, building collaboration, and using power, all of which come into play in human relationships.

Thomas L. Alsbury and Kathryn Whitaker provide vivid details in Chapter 9 of superintendents' and principals' struggles with recent changes in and stresses of school and district leadership. These external stressors come from many directions and seem to provide never-ending challenges for administrators who would really prefer to concentrate on the well-being of their students. Alsbury and Whitaker discuss the possible effects of these external pressures both on the work and well-being of current administrators and on the likelihood of recruiting new generations of principals and superintendents. They offer valuable recommendations to leaders, policy makers, and preparation programs on effectively addressing external pressures.

## Concluding Chapters

While we contributors were working on this book, we concentrated on remaining faithful to the specifics in the data. When one of us would catch another moving too far away from the data, we would call each other on it. That is one way to do good scholarship. Another way is to step back from among the trees and look over the entire forest from afar, taking a broader perspective in terms of history or geography, or coming at the research from different assumptions. So, we are fortunate to have two chapters by non-Voices scholars to comment on our efforts and put them into broader contexts.

To write Chapter 10, Ira Bogotch looked at transcripts and chapters through the lens of social justice. He points out areas where he thinks superintendents and principals, on the one hand, and chapter authors, on the other, missed opportunities to discuss and thereby to further social justice. He also points out how three parties who might come together to further social justice (prekindergarten through Grade 12 practitioners, academics, and policy makers) seem much of the time to be talking past one another. He suggests ways we might all begin to modify our communication and our work to progress toward an education system and a society that consistently and effectively look out for the welfare of all members.

Tony Townsend offers an expanded look at school improvement in Chapter 11, from the earliest days of the school effectiveness movement through the era of NCLB. He discusses education reform in other countries as well as the United States. He considers quotes from the superintendents and principals as well as the chapter authors in light of events in other places and times and gives his interpretation of why the effects of reforms have been so unspectacular in several countries. Finally, Townsend proposes his own model for considering and enacting school improvement and explains why he thinks it is likely to have more success than we have seen up to this point.

Throughout this book, we have cited transcripts in a standard way. We identify by number the superintendent or principal speaking, but we provide demographic information (size of district or level of school, region of the country represented, and year the focus group took place) only on the focus group as a whole. For example, though we tried to restrict each superintendent focus group to districts of similar size, on occasion a superintendent from a different-sized district participated. In such cases, the superintendent is identified by number along with the characteristics of the focus group (e.g., Superintendent 31, mixed medium-sized & small districts, Southwest & West, 2005).

## REFERENCES

DiPaola, M., Acker-Hocevar, M., Davis, J. E., Grogan, M., & Ivory, G. (2002, November). *Leadership perspectives of the superintendency: Perceptions, reflections, and observations from the field.* Paper presented at the meeting of the University Council for Educational Administration, Pittsburgh, PA.

Duke, D. L. (1999). Introduction: Origins and overview: Beginning the process. In F. K. Kochan, B. L. Jackson, & D. L. Duke (Eds.), *A thousand voices from the firing line: A study of educational leaders, their jobs, their preparation, and the problems they face* (pp. 10-13). Columbia, MO: University Council for Educational Administration.

House, E., & McQuillan, P. J. (1998). Three perspectives on school reform. In A. Hargreaves, A. Lieberman, M. Fullan, & D. W. Hopkins (Eds.), *International handbook of educational change: Part one* (Vol. 5, pp. 198-213). Boston, MA: Kluwer.

Kochan, F. K., Jackson, B. L., & Duke, D. L. (1999). *A thousand voices from the firing line: A study of educational leaders, their jobs, their preparation, and the problems they face.* Columbia, MO: University Council for Educational Administration.

No Child Left Behind, Pub. L. No. 107–110 (2002).

# ACKNOWLEDGMENTS

We acknowledge here with gratitude the many UCEA scholars who conducted Voices 3 focus groups and the superintendents and principals who gave of their time to share their perspectives. We thank the chapter authors who brought all of their scholarly abilities as well as their persistence to contribute their chapters to this book. Seven graduate assistants, Amneh Al-Rawashdeh and Sanaa Shindi of New Mexico State University and Amy McGuffey, Sherry McAndrew, Nancy Silverman, Curtis Nash, and Rick Ferris of the University of Dayton, did considerable work coding transcripts, working on the website, editing manuscripts, or managing miscellany.

Without the support of UCEA leaders, this book would not exist. So we thank Executive Director Michelle Young; Gerardo López, who was publications director at the time we vetted the book to UCEA; and all the others who have served on UCEA's executive committees over the past decade. We especially note our dependence on the original researchers and writers of *A Thousand Voices From the Firing Line*, especially Fran Kochan, Barbara Jackson, and Dan Duke, whose vision inspired the Voices projects. May the efforts of all these people make us better informed and wiser scholars of education leadership.

*Snapshots of School Leadership in the 21st Century:*
*Perils and Promises of Leading for Social Justice,*
*School Improvement, and Democratic Community*, p. xiii
Copyright © 2012 by Information Age Publishing

CHAPTER 1

# VOICES FROM THE FIELD, PHASE 3

## Design and Method

**Gary Ivory, A. William Place,
and Michele Acker-Hocevar**

Acker-Hocevar and Ivory began Voices: Phase 3 with careful consideration of a review by Salsberry (1999) of the Phase 1 (Thousand Voices) project. They hoped Voices 3 could build on and go beyond A Thousand Voices by drawing on its strengths and minimizing the weaknesses noted by Salsberry. Then, through 2001 and 2002, they led conversations with colleagues at national conferences to consider how to design Phase 3 (Ivory & Acker-Hocevar, 2003). They decided to target focus-group interviews on superintendents' and principals' perspectives on school improvement, social justice, and democratic community (Murphy, 2002). Ivory and Acker-Hocevar (2003; see also Acker-Hocevar & Ivory, 2004, 2006) selected the Murphy framework for Voices 3 because it provided a broad framework in three areas of interest to UCEA researchers. In addition, the framework was expansive enough that they felt that it allowed for researchers to use their own preferred frame-

*Snapshots of School Leadership in the 21st Century:*
*Perils and Promises of Leading for Social Justice,*
*School Improvement, and Democratic Community,* pp. 1–12

works in their analysis of findings from the data. They drafted focus group questions, one set for each of Murphy's (2002) anchors (school improvement, social justice, and democratic community), and colleagues piloted them with principals and superintendents. Interested scholars discussed outcomes and implications of the pilot study at the 2003 UCEA Convention in Portland, Oregon (Ivory et al., 2003). Acker-Hocevar and Ivory (2006) wrote of this discussion:

> Our reading of the pilot study transcripts revealed that participants' responses tended to be normative and not particularly informing. Symposium participants reported that some questions had not elicited good discussion, and that some terms popular in the academy, for example, "social justice," did not seem to resonate with practitioners. In addition, we found from the pilot study transcripts that some focus group moderators had used questions or comments that might have lead to particular responses, and that some participants seemed to want to give "pleasing" responses. Symposium participants called our attention to the fact that some participants may have deferred to others, for example, superintendents with less experience tended to defer to their senior colleagues. Ironically, some questions we had intended as ice breakers, to get only brief responses, elicited lengthy ones.
>
> We found also from one focus group that particular kinds of probes elicited more useful responses. That is, when the moderator used probes asking for specifics (e.g., "Tell me about an experience you had with that," "Tell me about a time when that issue came up," and "Would you give me an example?"), participants contributed more useful information. We also realized that some data had been lost due to equipment malfunction.
>
> Symposium participants suggested we separate principals by level of school (e.g., elementary, middle, and high) and seek more gender and ethnic diversity in participants. These findings guided our re-design of the protocol for the actual *Voices 3* study. (pp. 22–23)

After the UCEA meeting in Portland, Acker-Hocevar and Ivory (2004) finalized the choice of questions, combined questions from the three separate protocols into one protocol, wrote very specific instructions for focus group moderators, taking into account the findings from the pilot, and began recruiting focus group moderators from UCEA and the National Council of Professors of Educational Administration. All moderators were required to participate in training on the instructions, either at meetings of UCEA, the National Council of Professors of Educational Administration, or the American Educational Research Association or via telephone.

## FOCUS GROUP QUESTIONS

Acker-Hocevar, Miller and Ivory (2009) noted, "The study's protocol was built on Krueger and Casey's (2000) approach, specifically working to establish rapport at the beginning of the dialogue and then summarizing what was heard at the end to verify participants' responses" (p. 2). The first key question targeted leaders' perspectives on social justice. Since the pilot study had revealed that the term *social justice* did not elicit informative discussion, they phrased the question in terms of doing what is best for students. The second key question asked participants to discuss NCLB as a proxy for school improvement. The third question asked about "other people" wanting a voice in decision making, as a way to invite participants to talk about democratic community. Questions 4 and 5 were asked if time permitted. Table 1.1 presents the focus-group protocol questions.

## SELECTING FOCUS GROUP PARTICIPANTS

In a workshop at the UCEA Convention in 2003 (Scheurich, Acker-Hocevar, & Ivory, 2003), James Scheurich pointed Voices 3 researchers to the work of Ritchie and Lewis (2003), whose instructions then guided much of the design of Voices 3. Ivory and Acker-Hocevar drew on Ritchie and Lewis's advice that a group-discussion study be restricted to about 100 participants and that researchers carefully select the variables on which the sample would be stratified. For each population (superintendents and principals), they aimed to conduct 16 focus groups (of approximately six members each, for a total of 96 interviewees), stratifying each group on two variables. They stratified superintendent focus groups on student enrollment of the district (Snyder, Dillow, & Hoffman, 2008b) and U.S. region (Glass, Björk, & Brunner, 2000). They stratified the principal groups on level of school: elementary, middle, and high (Snyder, Dillow, & Hoffman, 2008a) and number of accountability sanctions in place in their state ("Standards and Accountability," 2002). At the time, they did not foresee that the No Child Left Behind Act (NCLB) would largely equalize accountability sanctions and pressures across states and that, consequently, that factor would become less important to getting a picture of the variety of principal experiences. In all cases, they sought to keep the numbers of focus groups proportional to the number of superintendents or principals in that district size or school level (Acker-Hocevar & Ivory, 2004). One gap in the data collection was with large-district superintendents. As only 6% of districts

## Table 1.1.   Focus Group Questions

| Question Number | Question |
| --- | --- |
| Opening question | Each of you please, tell me who you are, where your district is, and one of your interests outside school. |
| Transition question | Think back to an experience with school leadership that made a strong impression on you, either positive or negative. Please share it with us. |
| Key Question 1 | Superintendents/principals talk about doing what's best for students. Tell me about your experiences with that. |
| Key Question 2 | What has No Child Left Behind meant for you as a leader in education? |
| Key Question 3 | There is a piece of paper in front of you. Write an answer to this question and then we'll share our responses with one another: What does it mean that other people want to have a voice in decision making? |
| Key Question 4 (if needed and if time permits) | Think back to an experience you've had with doing what's best for students or school accountability or other people having a voice in decision making that was outstanding. Describe it. |
| Key Question 5 (if needed and if time permits) | What has been your greatest disappointment with doing what's best for students or school accountability or other people having a voice in decision making? |
| Ending question (Summary question) | Moderator gives a 2- to 3-minute summary of the major issues covered and then asks, "How well does that capture what was said here?" |
| Ending question (all things considered question) | Of all the issues we discussed here today, which one is most important to you? |
| Ending question (final question) | Is there anything about educational leadership that we should have talked about but did not? |

nationwide were larger than 9,999 students, they sought only one focus group with superintendents of districts of that size. Despite their efforts, no focus group with those superintendents was conducted. Within each stratum is a convenience sample, because moderators' access to participants depended on their accessibility and their willingness to participate.

They also decided not to devote separate focus groups to each of Murphy's (2002) anchors—school improvement, social justice, and democratic community—as they had in the pilot. That decision was motivated by Gross and Shapiro's (2005) argument that it is difficult to tease out school improvement, social justice, and democratic community as separate constructs because the three seem interdependent.

## DEMOGRAPHICS OF THE STUDY

Data on superintendent focus groups completed and participant demographics appear in Tables 1.2 and 1.3. As Acker-Hocevar et al. (2009) reported, "At the time we designed the sample, Brunner and Grogan (2007) reported that women comprised 12% of U.S. superintendents and ethnic minorities 5%. Our focus groups, with 22.2% women and 1.2% ethnic minority participants, over-represented women and under-represented ethnic minority superintendents" (p. 2).

Principal focus groups completed are shown in Table 1.4. At the time of the study design, 56% of U.S. principals were male and 44% female; 84% percent were White, 11% Black, and 5% Hispanic (Snyder et al., 2008b). The focus groups in this study contained 85 principals. Principal demographics are shown in Table 1.5. The focus groups slightly overrepresented women. Specific ethnicity data are lacking on 19 principals (22.3%), so it is impossible to tell how closely ethnicity of focus group principals coincides with national figures.

**Table 1.2.   Numbers of Superintendent Focus Groups Completed**

| School District Size and Student Enrollment | New England & Mid-Atlantic | Midwest | Southeast | Southwest & West |
|---|---|---|---|---|
| Small: student enrollment 1–999 | 0 | 2 | 1 | 1 |
| Medium-sized: student enrollment 1,000–9,999 | 2 | 1 | 1 | 1 |
| Medium-sized: mix of participants. Superintendents and board members from medium-sized school districts | 0 | 0 | 0 | 1 |
| Mixed: small and medium-sized school districts | 0 | 2 | 0 | 2 |

**Table 1.3.   Gender and Ethnicity of Superintendents: Number (Percentage)**

| Gender | African American | European American | Other | Ethnicity Not Reported | Totals |
|---|---|---|---|---|---|
| Female | 1 | 15 | 0 | 1 | 17 (22.2%) |
| Male | 0 | 47 | 4 | 8 | 59 (71.6%) |
| Gender not reported | 0 | 0 | 0 | 5 | 5 (6.2%) |
| Totals | 1 (1.2%) | 62 (76.5%) | 4 (4.9%) | 14 (17.3%) | 81 (100%) |

**Table 1.4.   Number of Principal Focus Groups Completed and Number of State**

|  | *Number of State Accountability Sanctions* | | |
| --- | --- | --- | --- |
| *School Level* | 0–1 | 2–3 | 4–6 |
| Elementary schools | 3 | 2 | 3 |
| Middle schools | 0 | 0 | 2 |
| High schools | 1 | 1 | 1 |

**Table 1.5.   Gender and Ethnicity of Principals: Number (Percentage)**

| *Gender* | *African American* | *European American* | *Hispanic* | *Other* | *Ethnicity Not Reported* | *Total* |
| --- | --- | --- | --- | --- | --- | --- |
| Female | 7 | 18 | 5 | 7 | 6 | 43 (50.6%) |
| Male | 3 | 29 | 4 | 3 | 2 | 41 (48.2%) |
| Gender not reported | 0 | 0 | 0 | 0 | 1 | 1 (1.2%) |
| Total | 10 (11.8%) | 47 (55.3%) | 9 (10.5%) | 10 (11.8%) | 9 (10.5%) | 85 (100%) |

## RESEARCH ON VOICES 3 TRANSCRIPTS

As Voices 3 scholars around the country conducted their focus groups and transcribed them, they sent them to Ivory and Acker-Hocevar, who edited them to eliminate identifiers of individual persons, schools, districts, and states and to standardize some formatting and punctuation. Sessions at UCEA and the American Educational Research Association had been devoted to the design of Voices 3, but now those sessions were devoted to analyses and presentations on the data emerging from Voices 3. Simultaneously, Ivory and Acker-Hocevar (2007) secured a contract for a book of leadership advice for school board members based on interviews with superintendents in the first two phases of Voices and the pilot for Voices 3. Seventeen researchers worked on chapters for that book.

Researchers also developed several articles including ones for a special themed issue of *Educational Considerations* (Acker-Hocevar et al., 2009). The richness of these two data sets (one on principals and one on superintendents) was becoming obvious to all involved with them.

While various individual efforts were proceeding, Acker-Hocevar and Ivory issued a call for two additional coeditors for this book that would present the comprehensive findings from the study. At the UCEA conference in 2007, they announced that Julia Ballenger and A. William Place would assist with the project, and the collaborative work began on this edited book. Initially, we (now four) coeditors proposed organizing the book around the two role groups and the various demographic variables such as level of school and the size of school district.

However, feedback from UCEA's Executive Committee guided us "to arrange these chapters by theme ... as opposed to respondent (principals/ superintendent)" (G. López, personal communication, February 3, 2010). We agreed. We coeditors had spent 2 years individually and then collectively analyzing the transcripts. During this process, the four of us individually read and analyzed the transcripts. Michele came up with the initial six or seven groupings of topics while the other three coeditors read transcripts to compare and contrast their coding schemata with hers within and across these groupings. This was a laborious process in which the groupings initially developed were later modified and finally revised. We four had numerous phone conferences in which particular examples of quotes were considered to see where they fit within the groupings. We were especially concerned about potential overlap among different groupings and spent considerable time and effort hashing out our varied perceptions of these groupings to achieve consensus around the final groupings that would comprise the chapters.

We further validated the groupings through the help of two of Gary's graduate assistants, Amneh Al-Rawashdeh and Sanaa Shindi from New Mexico State University. Gary guided these two students to use QSR's N7 software, instructing them to code the transcripts according to the themes we had developed. As they analyzed transcripts, they added themes and raised questions for us to consider to avoid overlap.

The work of the two graduate students, the contributions of the many fine scholars to this Voices project, and our initial work lead us to feel confident that the themes presented in these chapters are well grounded in our data. To us, this book provides a snapshot in time of education leadership during the historically significant period of NCLB (2002). In Spring 2010, as the last phase of the book preparation was underway, we sent a formal call for chapter proposals to all Voices 3 researchers. We also invited scholars renowned for their work in school improvement, social justice, and democratic community to read draft chapters and write responses to them. Due to time pressures and other commitments, not all have contributed chapters. We are fortunate to have at the end of this book a chapter by Ira Bogotch and one by Tony Townsend to comment on our study and our findings. We are grateful to each of them for their contributions.

## STRENGTHS AND WEAKNESSES OF THE UCEA VOICES PROJECTS

Voices 3 has felt sometimes like an Andy Hardy movie, one where all the kids get together and decide, "Let's put on a show." The difference from

Voices is that the kids were not concerned by the details of conceptualizing their show and getting everyone working together. It just happened magically, from one scene to the next. They knew they could pull it off because of their considerable individual talents.

There are considerable individual talents in UCEA as well. But researchers do not often get together in large groups and "put on" a project like Voices. Diana Pounder (1999), UCEA president at the time Voices was conceived, expressed her concern about that very issue, the challenges of a "project that requires the coordinated efforts of so many researchers and participants" (p. 5). Indeed, Voices has demanded considerable coordination, and it has not always been clear that the rewards would be proportionate to the effort involved. Michele and Gary, in planning Voices 3, had benefited greatly from Salsberry's (1999) review and critique of the original Thousand Voices project. In similar fashion, conceivers of any future collaborative research projects can benefit from Voices 3 scholars' thoughts on this one. So, as we brought this book to completion, we thought we should solicit input from Voices scholars about the positives and negatives of this large-scale collaborative project. We invited contributors to this book and to Acker-Hocevar et al. (2009), a total of 28 people, to respond to three questions:

1. Describe any positive outcomes you have seen emerge from the UCEA Voices project, from the 1999 Thousand Voices book until now.
2. Describe any challenges or drawbacks you have noted, or make suggestions for improving the project, or both.
3. Is there anything else you would like us to know about this collaborative work?

Twelve people responded. Our selection process left out, of course, those who were not involved in these two publications, perhaps because of their dissatisfaction with some aspects of the project. So, we may be missing the most negative possible responders. Still, the perspectives of the 12 respondents are helpful because they illuminate some benefits and some challenges of large-scale, collaborative research projects.

## Networking and Learning

Clearly, collaboration is often messy, and those who work with others lack total control of the direction of a project and of its fruits. This can make projects take longer and produce work that perfectly fulfills the visions of none of the collaborators. The upside of the lack of control is encountering new perspectives, chances to learn from others, and networking opportunities. One respondent described his previous experience with collaboration and noted, "The depth and breadth of collaboration in the Voices project is what I would call a quantum leap beyond what I had previously experienced." Another wrote of her "getting to know other colleagues from different disciplines," "tighten[ing] the bond" with colleagues, and networking "with other writers for future writing opportunities." A third referred to "collaboration among many colleagues throughout the U.S. at many different institutions." Another told of his beginning "to establish a network of scholars and friends ... with whom I maintain contact today." Finally, one of the leaders of Voices 3 wrote, "This work has been a form of ongoing professional development for me.... I learned a lot about project management and how to provide clear directions.... I have learned to stay fluid and to involve others in sharing common understandings early." Others told of learning to be better editors, learning to conduct focus groups, and even learning to mentor junior faculty.

## Benefits to Participants

An unanticipated positive from Voices 3 was the effect on the principals and superintendents who participated. Sharing their perspectives with one another seemed rewarding to them. One researcher wrote,

> I sense that just the process of asking principals and superintendents to reflect on their work has had a positive impact in the field. Although there is not hard evidence of this, informal comments after focus groups have always alluded to this. School leaders have always been thankful to us for asking questions (researchers are not always accustomed to this).

Another wrote, "Locally, it enabled a team of us to elicit views from principals and superintendents who were inspired by the act of participating in the focus groups. They exited with ideas to take to regional councils for the improvement of leadership." A third said of those she interviewed,

> The project allowed for principals in our area to come together to reflect and brainstorm about significant issues that were impacting their work. The focus group format was highly beneficial to those involved, providing much shared input. Each principal learned from the experience.

## The Value of the Findings

The Voices projects have, after all, been research endeavors, designed to illuminate, as Pounder (1999) wrote, the "complex and pressing problems that [practitioners] must routinely face in the field" (p. 5). So, it is gratifying that Voices 3 scholars have found the findings valuable. Recall that we said above that the Voices 3 pilot focus groups yielded responses that were not particularly informative. In contrast, with reference to the actual study, we heard this from the Voices 3 scholars we polled: "Rarely does a more in-depth study provide so many perspectives." "The project's strength is in its broad reach throughout several states." "The breadth of coverage for the work is positive as well: small districts, large districts, middle-sized districts from across so many regions in the nation. What an undertaking and wealth of information." Qualitative research often aims to get deep understanding of rather narrow situations. So, Michele and Gary worried throughout this study if we were not going to be guilty of overkill, asking the same questions again and again of different administrators in different roles in different parts of the United States. We are gratified to see this comment:

> I believe the depth of comments from individuals involved in school leadership across the country provided an accurate account of successes and challenges that those in the field face day-to-day. If the project wasn't so broad, I think we might have missed some of the challenges or successes faced by school administrators.

One respondent noted the "serendipitous" timing in that we launched Voices 3 just as principals and superintendents were beginning to deal with NCLB. This gave us an intimate understanding of administrators' perspectives on this important legislation.

Some Voices 3 researchers suggested directions for future Voices-like research: "Keep the project going," include large-district superintendents (we had missed them in this study), and go back to reinterview some respondents to assess their takes on NCLB's success at "improving the quality of education in the country."

## Leading and Managing Collaboration

A challenge of any leadership role, how to provide direction and yet allow creativity and problem solving to emerge from group members, was writ large in this project. One Voices 3 leader wrote,

> The challenges and drawbacks are in the coordination efforts that ensure there are shared and common understandings about the purpose of the research, the use of the protocols, how to report the data, and how and what the processes are ... for reporting findings and publishing results. The big-

gest drawback to this work is the complexity of taking a leadership role and managing the process in a productive manner.

Another wrote soberly, "Concern for quality required that time be taken to discuss and come to consensus about a number of issues." He called attention to "the time that it took to do this right. It was well worth the time, but at some points in the work it was still a frustrating experience."

A participant described her concern that in an earlier phase of Voices "few guidelines were being enforced." She wondered if Voices 3 had the opposite problem, "the strong vision of the editors" that left potential authors with less freedom to make contributions. On the contrary, another thought more direction might have been beneficial: "Possibly a video conference or more face-to-face training would have helped." A final researcher referred to "logistical problems" and the lack of even minimal funding for the project.

On the positive side, one researcher wrote, "Your leadership (and others') has been great and has kept everyone moving along. I think leadership is the key to a smooth process." Another wrote, "The project coordinators were so organized that it made it relatively simple to complete. You all have done a fantastic job!" The reader can judge from this book whether the rewards have outweighed the challenges.

## REFERENCES

Acker-Hocevar, M., & Ivory, G. (2004). *Voices From the Field Phase 3: Principals' and superintendents' perspectives of school improvement, social justice, and democratic community instructions for focus-group moderators.* Unpublished manuscript. Retrieved from http://education.nmsu.edu/emd/documents/ voices-from-the-field-phase-3-principals-and-superintendents.pdf

Acker-Hocevar, M., & Ivory, G. (2006, Winter). Update on Voices 3: Focus groups underway and plans and thoughts about the future. *UCEA Review, 48*(1), 22-24.

Acker-Hocevar, M., Miller, T. N., & Ivory, G. (2009). The UCEA project on educational leadership: Voices From the Field, Phase 3. *Educational Considerations, 36*(2), 1-7.

Glass, T. E., Björk, L., & Brunner, C. C. (2000). *The study of the American school superintendency: A look at the superintendent of education in the new millennium.* Arlington, VA: American Association of School Administrators.

Gross, S. J., & Shapiro, J. P. (2005, Fall). Our new era requires a new DEEL: Towards democratic ethical educational leadership. *UCEA Review, 48*(3), 1-4.

Ivory, G., & Acker-Hocevar, M. (2003, Summer). UCEA seeks superintendents' and principals' perspectives in "Voices 3." *UCEA Review, 45*(2), 15-17.

Ivory, G., & Acker-Hocevar, M. (2007). *Successful school board leadership: Lessons from superintendents*. Lanham, MD: Rowman & Littlefield Education.

Ivory, G., Tucker, P. D., Taylor, R., Touchton, D., Acker-Hocevar, M., Alsbury, T. L., … Piveral, J. (2003, November). *Researchers focusing on superintendents' and principals' conceptions of educational leadership*. Symposium conducted at the meeting of the University Council for Educational Administration, Portland, OR.

Murphy, J. (2002). Reculturing the profession of educational leadership: New blueprints. *Educational Administration Quarterly, 38*, 176-191.

No Child Left Behind Act, Pub. L. No. 107–110. (2002).

Pounder, D. G. (1999). Forward. In F. K. Kochan, B. L. Jackson, & D. L. Duke (Eds.), *A thousand voices from the firing line: A study of educational leaders, their jobs, their preparation, and the problems they face* (p. 5). Columbia, MO: University Council for Educational Administration.

Ritchie, J., & Lewis, J. (2003). *Qualitative research practice: A guide for social science students and researchers*. Thousand Oaks, CA: SAGE.

Salsberry, T. A. (1999). Uncovering the mysteries of educational administration through collaborative research: A review of the process. In F. K. Kochan, B. L. Jackson, & D. L. Duke (Eds.), *A thousand voices from the firing line: A study of educational leaders, their jobs, their preparation, and the problems they face* (pp. 111-121). Columbia, MO: University Council for Educational Administration.

Scheurich, J. J., Acker-Hocevar, M., & Ivory, G. (2003, November). *Voices 3: Qualitative research workshop*. Conducted at the meeting of the University Council for Educational Administration, Portland, OR.

Snyder, T. D., Dillow, S. A., & Hoffman, C. M. (2008a). *Digest of education statistics 2007* (NCES 2008-022). *Table 82. Principals in public and private elementary and secondary schools, by selected characteristics: 1993-94, 1999-2000, and 2003-2004.* Retrieved from http://nces.ed.gov/programs/digest/d07/tables/dt07_082.asp?referrer=list

Snyder, T. D., Dillow, S. A., & Hoffman, C. M. (2008b). *Digest of education statistics 2007* (NCES 2008-022). Table 90. *Public elementary and secondary schools, by type of school: 1967-68 through 2005-06.* Retrieved from http://nces.ed.gov/programs/digest/d07/tables/dt07_090.asp

Standards and Accountability. (2002, January 10). *Education Week*, p. 76.

CHAPTER 2

# NO CHILD LEFT BEHIND AS SCHOOL REFORM

## Intended and Unintended Consequences

Kristin Kew, Gary Ivory,
Miriam Muñiz, and Fernando Quiz

In this chapter, we consider No Child Left Behind (NCLB, 2002) as a school reform. We bring to bear on our consideration House and McQuillan's (1998) prescription that to be sustained, any reform must take into account political, technological, and cultural factors. They argued that reform neglecting any of the three would likely fail. We analyze NCLB in terms of these three factors. Then we present the perspectives of superintendents and principals and convey how they have bought into the egalitarian values promoted by NCLB but have had to struggle to implement it in the face of its inadequacies, internal contradictions, and unintended consequences. We end with the consideration that the next step should be providing more support for leaders to sustain school reforms that do not adequately address all the necessary factors.

*Snapshots of School Leadership in the 21st Century:*
*Perils and Promises of Leading for Social Justice,*
*School Improvement, and Democratic Community*, pp. 13–30
Copyright © 2012 by Information Age Publishing

## METHOD

We began by reviewing the data relevant to the five main themes uncovered by the book editors for our chapter: (a) NCLB, (b) superintendent voices, (c) principal voices, (d) intended consequences, and (e) unintended consequences. The editors discovered these initial codes using an inductive approach and analysis (Patton, 1980). Keeping the five major themes provided to us in mind, we continued to allow themes and categories to emerge from the data. As qualitative analysis is enhanced if conducted as a group activity, we recorded emerging patterns and trends and met as a group multiple times in person and online to discuss and compare our individual codings. We chose this form of triangulation to ensure that one view would be tempered by another (Armstrong, Gosling, Weinman, & Martaeu, 1997) and to increase reliability of results and transparency of methodology technique. We then agreed upon a more concise group of generalizations (Miles & Huberman, 1994). We disaggregated the core themes using axial coding (Strauss & Corbin, 1998) and made final inductive inferences analyzing both the Voices 3 data and relevant literature on change and reform.

## THREE DIMENSIONS OF SCHOOL REFORM

Our initial reading of the transcripts alerted us to the significance of superintendents and principals dealing with political aspects of NCLB and the struggle to balance the many requirements of the reform within their individual cultures and contexts. From here we searched for literature that would elaborate the role of politics and context in large-scale reform. We found House and McQuillan's (1998) three perspectives on school reform (technological, cultural, and political) helpful and used this framework to guide our subsequent readings of the transcripts and to structure our coding.

House and McQuillan (1998) maintained that to sustain school reform, leaders must attend to three dimensions: (a) the technological, (b) the cultural, and (c) the political. They argued that initiatives often fail because reformers focus on one of the three perspectives and either ignore or are unable to control the other two.

Reform from a technological viewpoint considers the technical and systematic execution of reform. "The technological perspective takes production as its root image or metaphor. Examples include concepts like input–output, specification of goals and tasks, flow diagrams, incentives, and performance assessment. How to do the job is the dominant concern" (House & McQuillan, 1998, p. 198). Purely technical reforms that spotlight the systemic aspects of implementation may fail because they have not sufficiently taken into account the culture of the community or the contextual differences between schools. They may also have underestimated political forces and movements.

The cultural perspective "rests on an image of community. Central concepts include culture, values, shared meanings, and social relationships ... the primary concern is cultural integrity" (House & McQuillan, 1998, p. 198). A reformer who emphasizes the cultural viewpoint addresses the human side of change, such as habits, meanings, values, and perspectives and how they relate to factors such as changing teacher demographics and their impact on teachers' generational missions (Goodson, Moore & Hargreaves, 2006; Huberman, 1989) and years of teaching experience (Hargreaves & Goodson, 2003). Change agents who embody solely a cultural frame of reference may focus on what is most important to their community, such as what a particular community desires of its schools, but may overlook or ignore the technical and political aspects of implementing a reform.

The political perspective "takes negotiation as its underlying image. Key concepts include power, authority, and competing interests ... and the primary concern [is] the legitimacy of the authority system" (House & McQuillan, 1998, p. 198). House and McQuillan (1998) pointed out that reformers subscribing to mainly political ideals may not necessarily agree with one another on solutions. For example, reformers who interpret educational change and reform in a school or system from a political perspective may frame problems or successes as an issue of centralization versus decentralization but may disagree as to which of the two is the most promising strategy. Highly political reforms may fail because they do not address technological needs such as time, resources, and professional development to build the capacity to achieve desired outcomes (Bailey, 2000; Elmore, 2003). They also may not reflect the many cultural and contextual aspects that affect reform (Hargreaves & Fink, 2006).

House and McQuillan (1998) illustrated the validity of their claims by providing three examples of successful school reform: (a) Central Park East Secondary School in East Harlem, (b) Green Valley Junior/Senior High School in the rural Northeast, and (c) the Dubuque Public School System in the Midwest. These ideal cases embodied an appreciation of all three perspectives of reform. They also were small schools of choice; enjoyed great autonomy to pursue their goals; and had leaders with the moral vision, determination, and foresight for long-term sustainable change.

In contrast to the three examples provided by House and McQuillan (1998) are the majority of U.S. schools that do not operate in such ideal circumstances. Few American public educators have ever had or will have the opportunity to work in schools of choice or in relatively autonomous small schools. We suspect there are shortages of leaders (that these three schools had) with the charisma, assertiveness, and tenacity to lead schools through the ups and downs of breaking the mold of traditional grammars (Tyack & Cuban, 1995) and sustaining innovative practices. As the Wallace Foundation (2006) noted, "Superhero leaders ... are, by definition, in short supply" (p. 5). Most schools face difficulties in implementing and sustaining a large-scale reform such as NCLB, in situations less auspicious than House and McQuillan's schools. Thus, we found ourselves at the same time enlightened and nonplused by their conclusions. They convinced us that attending to the three dimensions (technological, cultural, and political) of school reform is the best and perhaps the only way to sustain change. We were inspired by their three examples of successful reforms. Yet, we wondered what the implications of House and McQuillan's claims were for the reforms set in motion by NCLB. NCLB has arguably not fully taken into account all three perspectives. Furthermore, it affects schools across the nation, of varying sizes, whether public or choice, amid varying cultural and political contexts, and where there is no guarantee that every superintendent or principal is a larger-than-life dragon slayer. Many of them do not match the conditions of House and McQuillan's ideal schools. Yet, schools and districts must meet the requirements of NCLB or lose the federal funding on which they depend.

What are the consequences of this large-scale reform on superintendents and principals, particularly in situations where leaders and school conditions do not live up to the examples set by House and McQuillan (1998), and the reality that NCLB may not sufficiently address the three components necessary to sustain reform? The Voices 3 project provided a wealth of data detailing the perceptions of principals and superintendents living and working in response to NCLB. As we monitored how this legislation played out in the minds of these education leaders, we noted their struggles in areas where NCLB fell short of House and McQuillan's model and where it had consequences not intended by its framers. We believe at least some of the unintended consequences stemmed from its failure to attend adequately to the three perspectives of school reform.

Understanding the intended and unintended consequences of the NCLB (2002) legislation not only increases our knowledge of top-down, large-scale reform on school and district leaders but also uncovers the positive and negative pressures on those charged with the most responsibility for implementing it: superintendents and principals. It also reveals promising aspects of top-down reforms and where they fail to live up to their promise.

## FINDINGS

We present our findings, beginning with a short explanation of the intentions of NCLB. We then share superintendents' and principals' perceptions of the intended and unintended consequences of NCLB.

Politics was the first of the three perspectives on school reform to emerge from the Voices 3 data. From the very first pages of the transcripts, administrators spoke of the effects of top-down reform, accountability to constituents, competing power structures, and economics. Technological issues also surfaced, as interview participants also spoke about finding and hiring highly qualified teachers, completing extensive paperwork, and lacking time and funding to complete the tasks required of them by NCLB. We identified the final theme of school and community culture as the most important to school leaders. Superintendents and principals spoke of their roles and responsibilities to children, community trust, teacher empowerment and creativity, creating a culture of student achievement, and isolation amid reform. These constructs proved to be more difficult to code, as many of them related to more than one theme. For example, the role and responsibility to children was coded as cultural by two authors and as political by the others. We conversed to determine where best to place these constructs in relation to the Voices 3 data. We decided that school and community culture was more relevant because principals and superintendents spoke of their responsibility to stakeholders as an issue of building and maintaining trust, as opposed to a power struggle for competing interests.

### Intended Consequences of NCLB

NCLB is comprised of four pillars: "stronger accountability for results," "more freedom for states and communities," "proven education methods," and "more choices for parents" (U.S. Department of Education, 2004). The stated main intention is to create equity and "close the achievement gap and make sure all students, including those who are disadvantaged, achieve academic proficiency" (U.S. Department of Education, 2004, para. 2). Test scores are published through annual state and district "report cards" to ensure accountability, increase transparency of school and district practices, promote competition, and provide choice to unsatisfied parents and students. Schools that do not make Adequate Yearly Progress (AYP) are subject to corrective actions and possible school takeover by the state.

Many of the administrators in the Voices 3 project supported the concept of NCLB, particularly the need to disaggregate data to find inequities among groups of students in their schools and districts. Superintendents in particular felt that the government mandates gave them clout to push accountability for results in their districts. Superintendent 22 told us,

> If there's one good thing out of NCLB, that it forces the schools to reform, I don't think that's a bad thing. I know I would be crucified by people for saying that in a large group, but we just are not willing to change. And communities don't want their schools to change, because "it was that way when I was a kid," but we're not cutting it with kids anymore. We just are not, and I think that's wrong, wrong, wrong, and we need to do whatever it takes to change it. (small districts, Midwest, 2004)

Many principals also supported the fact that a sense of urgency was needed in their schools to pressure teachers to move beyond the status quo to examine the quality of instruction for all students in their classrooms, and that NCLB provided that sense of urgency. Principals at all three levels (elementary, middle, and high school) noted this. Elementary school Principal 21 said,

> I think one of the very positive things about it ... we're coming in on a collegial manner to talk about and look at what we are doing, the strategies that we are doing, and "This may have worked 10 years ago, but the children we are getting today, it isn't working. That doesn't mean we are a bad person, this isn't working." So they are going to be looking at the data, to figure out, "Let's try some other things and see if the data shows it working." So that has been very positive. (Southeast, 2005)

Middle school Principal 66 told us,

> Well in many aspects, I see it as a very good thing. We can't ignore the subgroups.... It is always good to look at how kids are achieving and "what can we do better?" I think in that aspect it is very good. (Midwest, 2005)

High school Principal 81 saw NCLB as supporting her efforts: "In some ways, it has made life simpler as a leader, because you can look at your staff and say, ... 'No choice; it's in there; gotta do it'" (Midwest, 2006).

## Unintended Consequences of NCLB

We maintain that NCLB's failure adequately to address technological, political, and cultural aspects of reform led to superintendents and principals experiencing a number of negative consequences that work against the very objectives intended by the framers of the policy. These include undue pressure to achieve results quickly, a sense of being set up for failure, lack of responsiveness to local issues, narrowing of the purposes of education, and internal inconsistencies.

### Pressure for Quick Results

Although many administrators were in support of accountability and creating equity among all students, they found one political aspect, the need for quick results, daunting and even dysfunctional. The well-meaning intention of NCLB to create urgency for results through both annually published test scores and sanctions placed on underperforming schools had negative unintended consequences in those districts that needed the most investment and patronage from external sources. Superintendent 4 lamented, "I think we'll see improvements as far as our students are learning. The sad thing about that is it takes so long for that to start showing up on the test scores" (mostly small districts, Midwest, 2006). Principals referred to this time pressure far more than superintendents did. For example, elementary Principal 21 said,

> If there was more time to develop and nurture over time and finesse things along it might ... they could buy into it a little easier, with time.... How do you relieve some of the stress? ... I don't know what you do because there is only so much time in a day. (Southeast, 2005)

Elementary Principal 20 disclosed,

> I think that is the biggest way that I have seen myself change, is that rather than taking months or even years to instill a concept and nurture it and get it to grow and get people to buy in, we don't have that time. So there are too many things that I may spend a couple of meetings trying to get you to buy into it, and then I'm going to tell you that that's the way it's going to be. (Southeast, 2005)

Some leaders talked about how the stress could limit, rather than enhance, productivity. The quotes appear in other chapters in this volume, referring to the standard being "ridiculous" (Superintendent 6, mostly small districts, Midwest, 2006), the stress being "damaging" for teachers (elementary school Principal 23, Southeast, 2005), and the process of labeling schools as unacceptable being "incredibly demoralizing" (middle school Principal 66, Midwest, 2005).

Principals were responsible for meeting the immediate requirements of the reform and were ultimately responsible to their school communities. Just as it is the nature of the superintendent's role to be closer to legislative and policy makers and to see things from their perspectives, it is the principal's role to interact constantly with students, teachers, and community members and to focus attention on their concerns. This may explain why principals reacted more negatively than superintendents to this aspect of the policy.

### Set up for Failure

Some leaders felt they were "set up for failure" (Superintendent 24, small districts, Midwest, 2004) due to the unreasonable expectations and pressure for compliance. We see this as NCLB's lack of attention to technological details. Administrators were not given the funding, training, time, or opportunity to make choices for their individual schools. They were told that they needed to show improvement but left to their own devices. As noted in Chapter 6 (Assessment, this volume), Superintendent 4 speculated that NCLB had been "set up to make public schools fail" (mostly small districts, Midwest, 2006). Superintendent 22 described the situation this way: "Even though we have the legislation and we're accountable for it, nothing else has changed to help us, help teachers be successful in meeting the [legislation]. So I think that's a real big dilemma" (small districts, Midwest, 2004). Those in poorer and more remote districts were particularly disillusioned.

> We can't get teachers that are highly qualified out there. We can't pay them enough. There is no way. We cannot compete with the districts here. So for us, it is an ongoing battle daily just to try to meet the minimum requirements that we can for the feds and then still keep that focus where it needs to be, and that is on the kids. I think the teachers do step up. I think they do that. (Superintendent 32, mixed medium & small districts, Southwest & West, 2005)

Both superintendents and principals saw funding as inadequate to meet policy requirements. Superintendent 16 told us,

> We've started a lot of new programs like Saturday school and after school, extended summer school, and remedial through the high school, but I'm not sure we're going to be able to keep those up because we're not going to get the funding I understand this year.... I've got to make the choice of either keeping those programs or giving teacher increases. And, if I don't give teacher increases in the era of teacher shortages, then I'll lose them. I don't know how much longer we can keep doing all of these things to meet NCLB with no money. That's a real problem. (small districts, Southeast, 2006)

Elementary school Principal 22 noted,

> We know that teachers need ... new strategies, new ways of teaching, new ways of doing things, but ... as a leader, there is only so much you can do

without money. You know you can team, have people collaborate and coach and do all that, but sometimes you are going to need funding for some staff development, and you know, they put that out there, but the funding is just not there to back it up. (Southeast, 2005)

### Lack of Responsiveness to Local Issues

Some leaders were troubled by the one-size-fits-all culture that many of them had to embrace. Due to the need to focus on gaining high test scores in core subject areas, many administrators felt pressure to gear their curriculum, teacher professional development, and in many cases the entire focus of the school on test preparation. Superintendent 17 noted,

> We end up in small school divisions focusing such an inordinate amount of our resources, our time and money, on meeting those standards that we have so many other things that get left in the dust. And so, I think it's a mixed bag. It's a good thing, but there are some costs. (small districts, Southeast, 2006).

Superintendent 69 (whom we quoted above as supportive of NCLB) worried about its side effects as well:

> The negative way I think that it's impacted the districts is that it's put a stigma on some of the schools. They were doing some real high social things that the students really needed as well, that they had to pull back on. For instance, maybe music, art, you know, cultural things…. You know, in some of the places they've eliminated field trips because…. they did not have that academic situation…. So you're no longer looking at as much as well-rounded students any more, but how they're going to produce on a test or how they can do academically. (medium-sized districts, Southwest & West, 2006)

Superintendent 20 said,

> I hate to hear someone say, "Are you teaching toward the test?" They'd better be teaching toward the test nowadays. It's not right, because I think they lose a lot of very important issues by teaching toward a test. And that's what we're being [forced] to do—our teachers are being forced to do, because our teachers are accountable.

Principals had more complaints. High school Principal 75 stated, "It is so superficially imposed upon test scores that it doesn't really provide for some of these really important issues that allow a structure of school, individual students, families, communities to actually build an academic base" (Midwest, 2005). High school Principal 85 asked,

What does No Child Left Behind mean? And does it mean no children left behind in your community? Because in our community we're educating kids for work and life in our community—then it means very different things in [Community 1] ... than it does in [Community 2] ... than it does in [Community 3].... There are communities where that's not going to be the focus of the education because those kids are not going to need that to be successful in those communities. So, really what does No Child Left Behind mean for given communities? And I think we don't—we haven't answered that question. (Midwest, 2006)

Principals, particularly in failing and struggling schools, had to master a balancing act between the top-down technological requirements of NCLB and either preserving their individual school cultures from mono-standardization at the risk of failing to meet AYP or joining the singular culture of back to basics. Many were compelled to shape their individual school cultures and practices to the one-size-fits-all reform. Administrators were successful in balancing the external technological obligations of the policy with their school cultures in varying degrees. High school Principal 85 spoke of the difficulties of maintaining relationships and a healthy school environment while implementing policy requirements:

One of the things we struggled with the high school reform this past year was not only to adopt the benchmarks but to adopt the relationships and relevance piece that [name] put forth as a part of our overall mission. And we structured the counseling center, and we structured some other things in the building to make sure that the relationship piece was not lost and that we would not sort of just say, "Okay these are the benchmarks by which we're gonna be measured." And that's not the only benchmark, but there's another benchmark, which is: How are you dealing with those students on a day-to-day basis? What does that mean? How does that look? And it may not have tangible sort of results, but it does have good-spirited meaning in the high school environment, and you can feel it. It feels a whole lot more wholesome and complete for kids. (Midwest, 2006)

### Internal Inconsistencies

Some leaders identified conflicts within NCLB and explained how complicated it was to comply with some of the technological requirements in their districts and schools. For instance, special education law required students to have individualized educational plans to accommodate their uniqueness, and NCLB required nearly all students to meet the same learning goals at the same time (Superintendent 24, small districts, Midwest, 2004; Superintendent 36, small districts, Midwest, 2004; Superintendent 72, medium-sized districts, Midwest, 2005).

In another example, middle school Principal 72 (Midwest, 2006) described his frustration with teachers' resistance to teaching reading skills across the curriculum. Mathematics teachers, specifically, did not want to do this. He considered experimenting with assigning every teacher to teach a section of reading but was unable to sustain the experiment because it would violate the tenet of highly qualified teachers.

Even though NCLB stated that schools could detail their own plans to meet AYP, it was requiring a one-size-fits-all traditional schooling with a focus on core subjects and testing. Principals felt pressure to focus on basics at the expense of other subjects such as music, art, drama, and foreign languages. Others felt that NCLB stifled creativity in their schools and classrooms.

## ANALYSIS

NCLB does not fit neatly into any one of House and McQuillan's (1998) three concepts. We have argued among ourselves as to whether it is primarily political (because it has clear mandates and sanctions from above) or primarily technological (because of its reliance on standardized tests and accountability systems, definition of highly qualified teachers and requirement to hire them, emphasis on research-based findings, technical definitions of acceptable performance, and schedules for compliance or sanctions for noncompliance). We doubt any intervention at the federal level could be primarily cultural, but we have learned from superintendents' and principals' conversations that the political mandate for subgroups of students to make AYP lead in some instances to a cultural shift toward a new concern for the achievement of those subgroups, as we stated above.

We began viewing our data through the three perspectives on school change by considering the explicit intentions of NCLB: stronger accountability for results to close the achievement gap, increased transparency in practices, competition among and between schools to provide an impetus for improvement, and school choice for discontented parents and students. Through conversation and detailed comparison of our codings, we determined that the goals of NCLB rest primarily on political and technological underpinnings.

We were concerned however, that although House and McQuillan (1998) provided us with a lens with which to view educational change on a large scale, their framework did not appear to be developed fully enough to explain NCLB from the perspectives of school leadership, teaching, and learning. One of the explicit goals of NCLB is demonstrated improvement in teaching and learning of all subgroups of students. The House and McQuillan framework, although illuminating, did not seem detailed enough in this respect for a thorough analysis of our data. We found assistance with our perspectives on NCLB and understanding of the data with Darling-Hammond's (2009) explanation of the four contending theories of action for systemic school reform. This secondary framework is more specific to the business of teaching. Moreover, it addresses how we treat the people who are leading change efforts and most directly influencing student learning. It is in line with the three perspectives on school reform in that it clarifies not only our claim that NCLB embraces the political and technological paradigms of educational change but also the need for and importance of the neglected cultural perspective.

Darling-Hammond (2009) described four approaches to large-scale change: (a) bureaucratic, (b) professional, (c) market, and (d) democratic. The bureaucratic approach, like House and McQuillan's (1998) technological perspective, relies on top-down management of schools with detailed procedures for educators to follow, such as prescribed curricula, standardized rules and practice, and accountability. Subscribers to this type of reform believe that unsatisfactory outcomes such as lower than expected test scores demonstrate the need to rework the implementation process. The technological perspective is exemplified in "more precise regulation of educational or management processes: a more tightly specified curriculum, more frequent and intensive testing, more standardized approaches to teaching behaviors, and more regulations over the uses of funds and the design of school organizations" (Darling-Hammond, 2009, p. 47). Major decision making and planning are done by administrators and specialists.

NCLB includes aspects of the technological aspects of the bureaucratic approach, such as hiring highly qualified teachers, completing large amounts of paperwork, and using prescribed interventions in failing and sinking schools. However, the bureaucratic elements of this top-down reform are mainly political rather than technological in nature. Districts must comply to receive necessary funding, and school decisions become hierarchically administered if schools do not make AYP. Short-term benchmarks are key components of NCLB, and failure to reach these goals over time could result in school takeover. Although the requirements and actual implementation of the policy are technical, the reform and its anticipated result are politically motivated with the purpose to both maintain and challenge existing structures. That is, NCLB maintains the narrow emphasis on academics, primarily academics that can be assessed with standardized tests, and simultaneously challenges the schools that are unsuccessful with that narrow focus. Ironically, NCLB simultaneously disparages traditional ways of running schools (Tyack & Cuban, 1995) and upholds traditional narrow views of the purpose of schooling.

Darling-Hammond's (2009) second paradigm for systemic change is the professional approach. Supporters of this type of reform embrace the cultural perspective. This theory of action entrusts teachers to do what is best for students,

> not what is most expedient, and to base decisions about what is best on available knowledge—not just on knowledge acquired from personal experience, but also on clinical and research knowledge acquired by the occupation as a whole and represented in professional preparation, journals, and licensure systems. (Tyack & Cuban, 1995, p. 49)

NCLB enforces the hiring of highly qualified teachers. It also states that schools and districts may utilize the curricula and practices that they feel are most efficient and effective for student progress. However, it does not embrace the professional approach beyond freedom of curricular and structural choice. Again, this implies challenging existing structures and skepticism about the education occupation as a whole, including critiques of professional preparation, journals, and licensure systems. It replaces the conventional wisdom of educators with the requirement that failing schools use a small number of "proven" techniques, limiting creativity and innovation. Administrators and teachers are not given the extensive training, professional development, and input into reform decisions that is representative of a cultural or professional approach to school reform.

The third approach to large-scale reform is the market approach. Advocates promote choice and competition among schools to encourage schools to strive to become more effective; to keep their students or gain new ones; to introduce innovative practices; and to increase feedback among schools, policy makers, and parents. NCLB (2002) allows school choice for students in schools that do not meet AYP. This highly political aspect of the legislation has a dual purpose: to pressure schools to "work harder to provide services that parents or students want" (Darling-Hammond, 2009, p. 51) and to "make dramatic changes to the way the school is run" (U.S. Department of Education, 2004, para. 2).

The fourth approach, the democratic, incorporates governance at the school and community that involves participation and consensus among all stakeholders. Central to this theory of reform is that decision making is "grounded in principles ... of trust, openness, and equity" (Darling-Hammond, 2009, p. 53). Darling-Hammond (2009) explained that successful implementation of this cultural and community approach requires building professional knowledge and an understanding of moral and ethical responsibilities to all students, including those traditionally underserved. The inherent goals of NCLB are couched in terms of equity for all students, but the enactment has involved little input from local communities or consideration of local culture.

Darling-Hammond's (2009) recommended reforms draw on both professional and democratic approaches so that decisions can be granted to those in the schools. This restructuring would require support from the top, including capacity building, funding, and continued support for professional development. It would necessitate shared responsibility and purpose between governments and schools. This type of reform would encourage intrinsic motivation among administrators and teachers to practice thoughtful consideration of the moral and ethical responsibilities of schools to protect the interests of all students.

The application of the four contending theories of action (Darling-Hammond, 2009) to House and McQuillan's (1998) three perspectives reveals NCLB as a highly political movement with technological traits. Using a combination of the bureaucratic and market approach, the federal government used its political power to require technological changes in schools through accountability measures such as testing, paperwork, and increased transparency of practices through the public reporting of scores. Whether intended or unintended by the legislature, these measures led many districts toward mono-standardized practices, leading them toward a shift in culture. The law has pressured superintendents and principals to enact reforms that run counter to their accumulated wisdom, and that of teachers, and treats the preferences of their communities as idiosyncratic and of little concern, in fact, as irrelevant. This seems to have been an aspect of school reform that predated NCLB. Cronin and Usdan (2003) reported, "International reports that placed the U.S. as 15th or 20th in mathematics and science education were viewed as indictments of local control" (p. 185).

The superintendents viewed NCLB more globally than the principals. They experienced stress from it but were not as directly responsible for implementing the technical aspects of the reform on a daily basis. They also did not give as much emphasis to the pressures of retaining individual school culture, good relationships, and high morale amid standardization. Our analysis of NCLB and the Voices 3 data supports the claims of House and McQuillan (1998) that consideration of all three perspectives is important to understanding and sustaining reform. The outcome of reform that either ignores or is unable to control the political, technological, or cultural is more likely to result in unintended consequences. In this case, we believe undue stress on those carrying out the requirements was unintended.

Educators are often not given the time, resources, or professional development to build the capacity to achieve desired outcomes. This is especially the case in large-scale reforms with compulsory standards and high pressure for compliance. According to Elmore (2003),

Stakes, if they work at all, do so by mobilizing resources, capacities, knowledge, and competencies that by definition are not present in the organizations and individuals whom they are intended to affect. If the schools have these assets in advance of the stakes, they would presumably not need the stakes to mobilize them. (p. 18)

Until the preconditions for reform are in place and there is a fundamental investment in and restructuring of teachers' work (Seashore Louis & Smith, 1991) so that they are given the time, opportunity, and training to make choices for their own schools and students, it is likely that schools will continue to be intractable to change.

## CONCLUSION

In the years since we collected the Voices 3 data, major studies have yielded lists of components of sustainable school reform (Honig, Copland, Rainey, Lorton, & Newton, 2010; Knapp, Copland, Honig, Plecki, & Portin, 2010; Leithwood & Jantzi, 2008; Rorrer, Skrla, & Scheurich, 2008; Seashore Louis, Leithwood, Wahlstrom, & Anderson, 2010; Wallace Foundation, 2006). These sources confirmed House and McQuillan's (1998) advice that sustainable school reform involves more components than the mechanistic, big-stick approach, which seems to be school leaders' main sense of NCLB. Furthermore, the research conducted by the authors we have cited greatly elaborated on House and McQuillan's three concepts, demonstrating what the components look like and how they play out in districts (not merely isolated schools) that have sustained reform. Space limitations do not permit us to reproduce the lists here, but we must note that the findings of these studies are promising.

What are the implications of the intended and unintended consequences of NCLB, a reform that arguably does not sufficiently address all three perspectives on school reform, particularly in schools that do not fit the ideal circumstances of House and McQuillan's (1998) examples? We are convinced from our findings and the educational-change research that a lack of consideration of all three perspectives on school reform makes both the implementation and sustainability more taxing and difficult on those in the fray, particularly leaders in struggling districts and schools. These individuals spoke consistently of the undue stress they experienced as they struggled to reach short-term benchmarks imposed on them. Chapter 9, Pressure of Outside Forces, Stress, and Finding Balance, elaborates on this issue.

Our consideration of the words of the Voices 3 superintendents and principals suggests the following: Superintendents and principals see benefits in NCLB having focused attention on the academic success of all children. It gave school leaders legitimacy to talk about equity in terms of not only equality of opportunity but also equality of outcome. It gave them leverage over individuals and groups who resisted change. In other words, the political power of NCLB indirectly influenced changes in school and district culture. But it failed to give them all the support they needed to sustain reform, and some of its unintended consequences actually work against leadership for reform.

Seashore Louis, Toole, and Hargreaves (1999) wrote of the difficulties of working "to better manage a change process that inevitably takes place in rather chaotic, unpredictable, and often nonrational contexts" (p. 253). NCLB has added to these contexts pressures for quick results, a climate in which people feel set up for failure, lack of responsiveness to local issues, and internal inconsistencies. Superintendents and principals see at least as well as anyone the "chaotic, unpredictable, and often nonrational" conditions in which they must work, and they are frustrated by these characteristics of NCLB that seem to interfere with sustaining reform.

We do not question that all children deserve the educational successes that NCLB was ostensibly designed to bring to them. We did not see our Voices 3 superintendents and principals questioning that, either. We believe, though, that the education system in general and this legislation in particular need adjustments to be able to sustain the reform. In order for reform to last over time, leaders and their teachers must be encouraged to sustain themselves (Hargreaves & Fink, 2006) through capacity building through professional development, time to plan and reach the standards expected of them, and trust to promote equitable and moral practices in their schools and districts.

One of us (Gary) was educated throughout his adolescence largely by Irish priests. A saying from one of those priests was, "Your whip and another man's horse—and you can go like hell!" The humor, of course, stems from the fact that if the horse belongs to another, you need worry only about getting expeditiously to your goal, not about the wear and tear on the horse. Furthermore, if all you require is speed (and not comfort, a meaningful and enriching journey, or a horse who will be fit and eager to carry you another day), then all you need is a whip.

We think the witticism makes an apt metaphor here: Superintendents and principals see NCLB as the whip urging them on to the goal of educational success for all children. They see themselves as the horses (at least, we see them as the horses) who, along with the teachers, students, and communities, must endure the wear and tear of the trip toward the destination of educational success for all children. We are not proposing to give up on the destination. But we worry that in the current context, the educational journey is stressful, less meaningful and enriching than it should be for educators and students, and wearing on the fitness and spirit of superintendents and principals. Our next step as a nation should be to find better ways to equip the horses for the trip and keep up their strength and spirit along the way.

## REFERENCES

Armstrong, D., Gosling, A., Weinman, J., & Martaeu, T. (1997). The place of inter-rater reliability in qualitative research: An empirical study. *Sociology, 31,* 597-606.

Bailey, B. (2000). The impact of mandated change on teachers. In A. Bascia & A. Hargreaves (Eds.), *The sharp edge of educational change: Teaching, leading and the realities of reform* (pp. 112-128). London, England: Routledge Falmer.

Cronin, J. M., & Usdan, M. D. (2003). Rethinking the urban school superinten-dency: Nontraditional leaders and new models of leadership. In W. L. Boyd & D. Miretsky (Eds.), *American educational governance on trial: Change and challenges* (pp. 177-195). Chicago, IL: University of Chicago Press

Darling-Hammond, L. (2009). Teaching and the change wars: The professional hypothesis. In A. Hargreaves & M. Fullan (Eds.), *Change wars* (pp. 45-70). Bloomington, IN: Solution Tree.

Elmore, R. (2003). The problem of stakes in performance-based accountability systems. In S. Fuhrman & R. Elmore (Eds.), *Redesigning accountability systems* (pp. 274-296). New York, NY: Teachers College Press.

Goodson, I. F., Moore, S., & Hargreaves, A. (2006). Teacher nostalgia and the sus-tainability of reform: The generation and degeneration of teachers' missions, memory, and meaning. *Educational Administration Quarterly, 42,* 42-61.

Hargreaves, A., & Fink, D. (2006). *Sustainable leadership.* San Francisco, CA: Jossey-Bass.

Hargreaves, A., & Goodson, I. (2003). *Change over time? A study of culture, structure, time and change in secondary schooling* (Project No. 199800214). Chicago, IL: Spencer Foundation.

Honig, M. I., Copland, M. A., Rainey, L., Lorton, J. A., & Newton, M. (with Mat-son, E., Pappas, L., & Rodgers, B.). (2010). *Central office transformation for dis-trict-wide teaching and learning improvement.* Retrieved from http://depts.washington.edu/ctpmail/PDFs/S2-CentralAdmin-04-2010.pdf

House, E., & McQuillan, P. J. (1998). Three perspectives on school reform. In A. Hargreaves, A. Lieberman, M. Fullan, & D. W. Hopkins (Eds.), *International handbook of educational change: Part one* (Vol. 5, pp. 198-213). Boston, MA: Klu-wer Academic.

Huberman, M. (1989). The professional life cycle of teachers. *Teachers College Record, 91*(1), 31-57.

Knapp, M. S., Copland, M. A., Honig, M. I., Plecki, M. L., & Portin, B. S. (2010). *Learning-focused leadership and leadership support: Meaning and practice in urban systems.* Retrieved from http://depts.washington.edu/ctpmail/PDFs/LeadershipStudySynthesis-08-2010.pdf

Leithwood, K., & Jantzi, D. (2008). Linking leadership to student learning: The contributions of leader efficacy. *Educational Administration Quarterly, 44,* 496-528.

Miles, M. B., & Huberman, M. (1994). *An expanded sourcebook: Qualitative data analysis* (2nd ed.). London, England: SAGE.

No Child Left Behind Act of 2001, Pub. L. No. 107-110 (2002). Retrieved from http://www.nochildleftbehind.com/NCLB-full-text.pdf

Patton, M. Q. (1980). *Qualitative evaluation methods.* Beverly Hills, CA: SAGE.

Rorrer, A. K., Skrla, L., & Scheurich, J. J. (2008). Districts as institutional actors in educational reform. *Educational Administration Quarterly, 44,* 307-358.

Seashore Louis, K., Leithwood, K., Wahlstrom, K. L., & Anderson, S. E. (2010). *Learning from leadership: Investigating the links to improved student learning: Final report of research to the Wallace Foundation.* Retrieved from http://www.wallace foundation.org/KnowledgeCenter/KnowledgeTopics/CurrentAreasofFocus/EducationLeadership/Documents/Learning-from-Leadership-Investigating-Links-Final-Report.pdf

Seashore Louis, K., & Smith, B. (1991). Restructuring, teacher engagement and school culture: Perspectives on school reform and the improvement of teacher's work. *School Effectiveness and Improvement, 2*(1), 34-52.

Seashore Louis, K., Toole, J., & Hargreaves, A. (1999). Rethinking school improvement. In J. Murphy & K. Seashore Louis (Eds.), *Handbook of research on educational administration* (2nd ed., pp. 251–276). San Francisco, CA: Jossey-Bass.

Strauss, A., & Corbin, J. (1998). *Basics of qualitative research: Grounded theory procedures and techniques.* Thousand Oaks, CA: SAGE.

Tyack, D., & Cuban, L. (1995). *Tinkering toward utopia: A century of public school reform.* Cambridge, MA: Harvard University Press.

U.S. Department of Education. (2004). *Overview: Four pillars of NCLB.* Retrieved from http://www2.ed.gov/nclb/overview/intro/4pillars.html

Wallace Foundation. (2006). *Leadership for learning: Making the connections among state, district and school policies and practices.* Retrieved from http://www.wallacefoundation.org/SiteCollectionDocuments/WF/Knowedge%20Center/Attachments/PDF/FINALWallaceCLSPerspective.pdf

CHAPTER 3

# GROWTH AND DEVELOPMENT OF CHILDREN

## William Ruff and Sharon Gieselmann

In 2002, a new era in educational accountability reform was launched with the reauthorization of the Elementary and Secondary Education Act. This new version, the No Child Left Behind Act (NCLB), altered the politics of education (DeBray-Pelot & McGuinn, 2009) and significantly complicated the choices school and school system leaders must wrestle within fostering the growth and development of children (Travers, 2009), such as equity versus excellence and eliminating fine arts and electives versus keeping these courses for students. As the reauthorization cycle for the Elementary and Secondary Education Act begins again, it is important that we look at the perceptions superintendents and principals held about educating the whole child while implementing school improvement mandates (narrowly defined as making schoolwide gains on quantitative tests) at the dawn of the 21st century. Specifically, this legislation impacted superintendents' and principals' perceptions about how they could meet the stated purpose of education to meet federal mandates and educate the whole child. The Association for Supervision and Curriculum Development (2005) *Position Statement on the Whole Child* called for schools to utilize a comprehensive approach for student learning that not only

*Snapshots of School Leadership in the 21st Century:*
*Perils and Promises of Leading for Social Justice,*
*School Improvement, and Democratic Community,* pp. 31–54
Copyright © 2012 by Information Age Publishing
All rights of reproduction in any form reserved.

emphasizes academic skills but also recognizes students' emotional and physical health, civic mindedness, engagement in the arts, motivation, preparation for the workforce, economic self-sufficiency, and readiness for the world beyond their own borders. Hence, the predominant view of educators was that student success is more comprehensive than what high-stakes assessments are designed to measure. However, what gets measured gets the attention of teachers, school administrators, local and state education officials, parents, and community members.

## CLARIFYING THE PARADOX

John Dewey (1933) proposed that education was best served when the whole child was considered, including all aspects of the child's development. He and other progressives believed that education was more than preparation for the future; it was life itself. Further, he supported emphasizing both content areas with structured learning activities and experiences that motivated, interested, and actively engaged students. These ideas, he maintained, would provide a means of social reform and improvement of life for all Americans. Although progressive education fell out of favor in the late 1950s when a call for more efficiency and focused rigor occurred, this philosophy has re-emerged as current school administrators aspire to educate the whole child. The present accountability era, however, provides a quandary for school administrators and building leaders as they focus on children in their districts and buildings. Hershberg, Simon, and Lea-Kruger (2004), using case study research, found that this school improvement era presents the toughest challenges ever for school administrators, as current public education systems typically fail to provide leaders with adequate tools and resources to lead and manage their schools effectively. Eisner (2005) reminded administrators and teachers that children respond to educational situations not only intellectually but also socially and emotionally. Neglecting the social and emotional aspects of students' development prohibits children from fulfilling their need to live a satisfying life.

However, Zellmer, Frontier, and Pheifer (2006) surveyed school districts in Wisconsin and found that, due to NCLB, resources are often diverted away from teaching and learning and utilized for test preparation, administration, and reporting. School staff members devote countless hours to these test-related tasks, resulting in limited instructional time for students. We must realize that schools are the only universally accessible organizations where there are enough adults to provide consistent support for the growth and development of our children, and next to the family, they have the most significant influence on children's growth and development; therefore, school and school district leaders face the challenges of meeting both developmental and academic needs in the present accountability era (Comer, 1996, 2004).

School leaders can provide leadership in facilitating a child-centered environment, one that moves beyond student success defined by a test score. Lyons and Algozzine (2006) noted that the greatest impact of NCLB was in how student achievement is monitored. In looking at how NCLB measures performance, Elmore (2003) wrote,

> NCLB aggravates a trend in state accountability policies. It focuses primarily on measuring growth in school performance against fixed standards—the so-called Adequate Yearly Progress requirement—and only incidentally on building capacity of individual educators and schools to deliver high-quality instruction. (p. 6)

Standardized test results can be useful as one measure of a student's knowledge to be compared with other evidence assembled by teachers who know a particular student's strengths and weaknesses. But the meaning of a test score is always embedded in the larger context of what we know about the whole child. This is especially true for the student who "freezes" on tests, the student who reads adequately but slowly and therefore cannot finish the test in the allotted time, the student who understands concepts but has difficulty retrieving detailed facts, the student with learning disabilities, and the student who is just learning English (Johannessen, 2004). It is also essential to consider whether the family and school have provided the resources and support necessary for student learning. Many classrooms are overcrowded and poorly equipped and lack certified teachers, especially in high-poverty schools. Research has indicated that test scores largely reflect the child's family education level and home environment (Lubienski, 2003). School leaders face environmental challenges that they must overcome with students from disadvantaged backgrounds as they strive to meet state and local expectations. Moreover, an outcome of accountability has resulted in teachers and administrators focusing on the borderline students, those students who are within 10 points of a passing score, resulting in students at the lower end of the performance range lagging further behind and high-performing students declining in achievement (Ladd & Lauren, 2009; Sanders, 2003).

Superintendents' and principals' leadership deals with a variety of equity issues in 21st-century schools. For example, curricular content assessed by standardized tests has resulted in the elimination of other content areas and activities, including electives, the arts, programs for the gifted, and even elementary school recess (Amrein & Berliner, 2002; Popham, 2001). Conversely, many school administrators resist the pressure to focus on test data numbers only and continue to track students who are disciplined, are missing from school, have adequate health care, are hungry, and have parents come to school regularly, as well as other data that go beyond a narrow definition of student achievement (Theoharis, 2009). Hence, despite the increased demands of state accountability measures via standardized tests, some administrators believe the needs of the whole child remain paramount.

School leaders face limited financial resources as they try to move their schools and districts forward. Often the resources necessary to address the needs of the whole child are not available, even though the research has indicated, for example, that lower student-to-counselor ratios decrease the recurrence of student discipline problems and the number of children involved in various discipline-related incidents (Carrell & Carrell, 2006). Furthermore, within the last decade, school administrators are noticing increased stress levels of their students. For example, health-care professionals and parents already report that test-related stress is literally making many children sick. For many students, high-stakes testing does correlate with academic success, but it also provides for discomforts that include test anxiety, nausea, and inhibited concentration and recall, which lead to poor test performance (Gregor, 2005). Student stress and anxiety impact students' emotional and intellectual capacities because of the rigorous preparation and constant reminders to pass these tests (Hodge, McCormick, & Elliot, 1997). The narrow focus on one test to the exclusion of a more holistic approach to being educated is literally making us sick.

Bellamy, Fulmer, Murphy, and Muth (2007), in writing about the paradoxes in school leadership, noted a continuing tension among excellence, equity, and autonomy; these value-laden demands cannot be resolved, and yet we depend on schools and other social institutions to adjudicate these inherent conflicts.

> Unlike the problem of reaching high academic standards in spite of challenging social conditions, conflicting beliefs about what schools should emphasize are not problems that can be solved. Instead, they present enduring paradoxes that continually must be managed and balanced to provide some satisfaction to competing expectations. (Bellamy et al., 2007, p. 5)

On a daily basis, it is the local school and school district leaders who must balance these tensions, because it is at this local level that the nexus of need, expectation, and resources becomes realized. The formal political authority over the goals of schooling at all levels of the educational system expresses itself in the form of requirements levied on professional educators, incentives, and resources allocations. Policy makers have a broad and significant influence on the work of professional educators. Yet, the contextualized goals of each school and each school district are shaped by the daily decision making of teachers, principals, and superintendents as they find practical solutions to an ongoing stream of local situations. Bellamy et al. (2007) expressed this idea well:

> Principals cannot succeed by simply accepting the goals that are established either by professional associations or through the political process. Instead, the goals established through these groups provide a foundation upon which local goals must be fostered, defined, clarified and tested with the local school community—its students, families, staff, and other community members. (p. 25)

## CONCEPTUAL LENS AND METHODS

Local school leaders must make daily decisions that accomplish the mission of public education as defined by the expectations of a myriad of internal and external stakeholders. Because local superintendents and principals must determine the most practical way of negotiating the needs of their constituents in how the child is educated, pragmatism was selected as the conceptual lens used in evaluating the transcripts.

Pragmatism is the belief that theory and practice cannot be separated. Theory exists as a means toward intelligent practice, and practice is the means of informing which ideas are better than others. William James (1907), a prominent American philosopher, wrote, "Ideas (which themselves are but parts of our experience) become true just in so far as they help us to get into satisfactory relations with other parts of experience" (p. 28). Through this lens, we are able to see how superintendents and principals can hold multiple competing values while simultaneously making decisions that attempt to satisfy their personal beliefs and the conflicting expectations of which they are held accountable.

How do superintendents and principals maintain a focus on the education of the whole child when what gets measured is a narrow range of minimum student achievement standards developed by each state? Answers to this question come from the transcripts of 14 superintendent and 13 principal focus groups. The theme of growth and development of children emerged and was at odds with how administrators meet federal and state requirements. Using the constant comparative method (Glaser & Strauss, 1967), we read all transcripts twice and then coded the statements mentioning the following topics:

- the developmental needs of children,
- purposes of education,

- child-centered focus, and
- benefits and liabilities of NCLB for students.

These topics are the areas we identified in the reading of the transcripts overall. Finally, we read the transcripts a final time, specifically looking for contradictions to these grounded results around the growth and development of children. In the end, we derived three themes from the codes for both superintendents and principals: (a) structuring a focus on children, (b) challenges in facilitating a child-centered environment, and (c) issues of equity for child-centered learning environments. A fourth theme emerged from the principal data: (d) stress on children.

## SUPERINTENDENTS' PERSPECTIVES REGARDING THE GROWTH AND DEVELOPMENT OF CHILDREN

The major themes in the data from the superintendents' focus groups included the pressures related to structuring a focus on children, challenges in facilitating a child-centered environment, and issues of equity for child-centered learning environments. In this section we elaborate on these themes and subthemes.

### Structuring a Focus on Children

The focus group transcripts revealed that the structure of the school district organization must be organized around a focus on children. Specifically, superintendents described four subthemes: (a) school governance structures, (b) parent involvement and child-centered education, (c) reliance on teachers to be child centered, and (d) school improvement planning that concentrates on students.

#### School Governance Structures

The metaphor of schools as factories is not a new phenomenon and has been a popular conception of schooling for more than 3 decades. For example, Pink Floyd described rigid and monotonous schooling in their protest song, "Another Brick in the Wall" (Waters, 1979). Yet despite this recognition and decades of school reform to individualize learning, why does this perception continue to exist among school system leaders and in schools? Several superintendents provided comments suggesting that current governance structures detract from, rather than support, a concentration on student learning and growth. One superintendent indicated that the current legislation is similar to previous reform efforts that prescribed a one-size-fits-all solution, when one size does not meet all students' needs (Superintendent 76, medium-sized district, Midwest, 2005). Another district leader worried that our school governance structures fail to take into account growth of the whole child.

> There's a phrase that I use often: Not everything that's important can be measured. And not everything that can be measured is important. And school is a place for kids to grow up. It's a place for kids to learn how to work with one another and how to become better citizens. We can't measure all that stuff with numbers. (Superintendent 74, medium-sized districts, Midwest, 2005)

Superintendent leadership requires the ability to structure schools so that students have optimal performance opportunities to learn. In spite of political agendas from the community, superintendents saw their school governance role as creating a vision for their districts so that students have the best opportunity to learn from child-centered teachers, while using all available resources for teaching and learning. Superintendent 69 shared that district leaders must understand that students' needs take precedence over local political issues and the self-serving needs of those in the community and district (medium-sized districts, Southwest & West, 2006). Another district leader reiterated this idea by stating,

> In my 20+ years as superintendent, I've seen a real shift in demands by parents, communities, and special interest groups. And I think doing what's right for kids has taken on a different perspective. It's tough work when you are bombarded by all of these different groups. You have to help your boards stay on course and make decisions that are best for kids. (Superintendent 77, medium-sized districts, Midwest, 2005)

### *Parent Involvement and Child-Centered Education*

Several superintendents noted that creating an environment that facilitated parent involvement included forums that allowed parents to address their concerns and helped provide a focus on the child. Superintendent 16 believed that parents are very interested in and supportive of education. He periodically held parent coffees that provided opportunities for these stakeholders to discuss issues and successes (small districts, Southeast, 2006). However, this notion of inviting stakeholders to discuss concerns created challenges for administrators. As he further described,

> Parents think that we [superintendents] can do a lot more than we can and that we have total control of things, when we really live by policies and work for school boards. We have to answer to all of our constituents—the students, the parents, the community—so it's complicated. (Superintendent 16, small districts, Southeast, 2006)

Furthermore, superintendents believed that they must be advocates for all children and families, even those who were not currently involved or lack successful parenting skills. One superintendent stated this quite plainly:

> I find myself teaching the parents. Now, they may be misinformed, unedu-cated, illiterate—I've had all of those. But if you can work through these and make that parent understand that you're not out to get their kid, that you're really trying to come together and make a decision for what's best for that child, then sometimes you can build a relationship. (Superintendent 19, small districts, Southeast, 2006)

Some superintendents believed that when families lack parenting skills, school districts had an obligation to assist them to benefit children. For example, Superintendent 21 shared, "When a parent indicated that help was needed to guide his/her child, we [the district] were going to express interest and do what we could to help; it was our responsibility" (medium-sized & small districts, Southeast, 2006).

### Reliance on Teachers to be Child Centered

Another subtheme emerged that related to a reliance on teachers to be child centered. School superintendents placed a greater emphasis on pro-viding professional development activities for teachers that helped them meet the academic and emotional needs of all students. Superintendent 31 elaborated:

> It is getting everybody [teachers] to look outside their world of the work-sheet that they are putting on the tables and realize that for those kids, for some of them, to be even sitting in that chair that day is remarkable. I try to provide activities and things where they can see the bigger picture of what the student's world is like. (medium-sized & small districts, Southwest & West, 2005)

### School Improvement Planning That Focuses on Students

Another facet of structures that facilitated a child-centered focus was school improvement. School leaders must work with other stakeholders to ensure that every student has a chance for success. Many superintendents felt it was their responsibility to move each student forward, regardless of their family or socioeconomic background via their district school improvement plans. Superintendent 69 indicated,

> They must have that belief in all children. They [children] can achieve and will achieve. And the ultimate goal of any leader, whether it's a school board member or anyone, any leaders that we have, and their ultimate goal is to educate our children—all children. (medium-sized districts, Southwest, 2006)

## Challenges in Facilitating a Child-Centered Environment

The second major theme is challenges in facilitating a child-centered environment. Within this category are two subthemes: student advocacy and distance from the classroom.

### Student Advocacy

Many superintendents shared that maintaining a child-centered environment and meeting the needs of the whole child were challenging during this accountability era. One superintendent talked about the importance of personally knowing the students and also ensuring that the board members understood the needs of the students. This individual stated,

> We talk about students, but we don't really know the students.... We had an enormous amount of kids dropping out of school. We brought a group of those kids [dropouts] face to face with every school board member for a couple of hours ... and listened to what these kids said. What they [board members] started to realize was that the assumptions that they made about why those kids dropped out, or what those kids needs were, were just the furthest thing from true. They started to realize they [dropouts] probably worked harder than kids that are in school to make their life work. (Superintendent 69, medium-sized districts, Southwest, 2006)

Superintendent 55 shared the feelings of many administrators by talking about the competing demands of the position that limit a leader's time for advocating for all students.

> The practicing pragmatist in me says that kids are so far down on the pecking order in terms of what we are able to deliver them regarding child-centered learning because we have all these things. I guess my concern is I'd like to believe that I'm a fairly articulate curriculum person. I spend about 2% of my time on curriculum. I spend 98% of my time on everything else to fend off the very things that we're discussing here, unions, contracts. I spend more time with attorneys now than I ever dreamed of. (Superintendent 55, medium-sized districts, New England & Mid-Atlantic, 2006)

### Distance From the Classroom

Often, school superintendents believed that being far removed from what happens in the classroom day-to-day posed challenges for them as school administrators. Yet, some superintendents attempted to maintain a focus on student needs by regularly spending time in schools with principals and students. Superintendent 67 described how he spent a minimum of an hour with each principal weekly in his or her respective school setting and also spent time with students. "I said at least every other time,

I'm going to spend at least half of that hour with kids.... I've had lunch with them, I've gone into a class" (medium-sized districts, New England & Mid-Atlantic, 2005).

## Issues of Equity for Child-Centered Learning Environments

The third major theme is issues of equity for child-centered learning environments. The goal of equity is to ensure that children have equal educational opportunities. Superintendents reported that they did not push aside inclusive social justice practices to achieve school improvement goals, but instead the two unfolded and were integrated together into their daily professional practices. Among the superintendent focus groups, the discussion of educational equity centered on concerns with marginalizing low-performing children and accountability's limited attempt at providing an equitable education for all students. Superintendent 66 indicated, "You have legislators who are ignorant about what is going on for kids with handicapping conditions. They are flat-out ignorant. They don't know and, in many cases, don't want to know" (medium-sized districts, New England & Mid-Atlantic, 2005). Moreover, accountability for special education students created additional concerns for superintendents. For example, one superintendent commented,

> You bring up special education and No Child Left Behind. They're both federal laws, and they contradict. By law, in special education, you have to be 2 years behind to qualify for a learning disability. You have to be 2 years behind! No Child Left Behind—every single kid has to pass at grade level. It's unconstitutional how they're [the laws] going at each other. (Superintendent 72, small districts, Midwest, 2005)

In contrast, some superintendents believed school improvement helped districts focus on the needs of all children. For example, Superintendent 7 stated,

> No Child Left Behind, I think, has helped in a broader sense in terms of helping people recognize the challenges of different ethnic groups, different racial groups. It's given me a little more power to take a look at [students receiving] free and reduced [price] lunch in the long run. (small districts, Midwest, 2006)

## PRINCIPALS' PERSPECTIVES REGARDING THE GROWTH AND DEVELOPMENT OF CHILDREN

The major themes regarding the growth and development of children from the principal focus group data included the pressures related to structuring a focus on children, challenges in facilitating a child-centered environment, issues of equity for child-centered learning environments, and stress on children. This section elaborates on those themes and sub-themes.

## Structuring a Focus on Children

In the focus groups, principals indicated that the structure of the school must be organized around facilitating all aspects of student learning, including students' social and emotional needs. Specifically, principals described three subthemes: (a) the expanding role of public schools, (b) time constraints associated with curricular mandates, and (c) supporting learning for all students.

### Expanding Role of Public Schools

First, many administrators recognized schools assumed more responsibilities with educating the whole child in recent years. For example, elementary school Principal 48 stated, "The role [of public schools] has changed so much in the last 15–20 years. We've got to feed them breakfast and lunch; we've got to supply the counselors to give them therapy" (Southwest, 2006). Then, leaders and schools must also determine how best to support their students and families, as described by elementary school Principal 40: "Whatever the child comes to school with, is what you have to work with and sometimes that requires being a surrogate parent, helping with counseling, and holding parenting classes with the parents" (Southwest, 2006). Moreover, elementary school Principal 61 shared this example of meeting the needs of the whole child and those of their families:

> My building [faculty] has always worked very hard academically ... but the social reality of the child was totally missing.... We started a lot of movie nights, carnivals, festivals, and family-oriented programs to try and get the family involved, because they didn't have the financial means to do those things. (Midwest, 2005)

### Time Constraints Associated With Curricular Mandates

Whereas elementary school Principal 6 described school improvement as "one of the best things that has ever happened to education" (Midwest, 2004), others shared the difficulties with structuring a focus on children because of district-mandated school improvement documents, such as curriculum maps and pacing guides that provide rigid schedules for teaching state standards. Their teachers feel intense pressure to follow these guides but also to help all children meet the academic benchmarks associated with them. For instance, elementary school Principal 33 shared that one of the challenges with attempting to meet district goals was that teachers sometimes ignored students' needs. Principal 33 stated, "I'm fielding more calls from parents who are telling me that teachers will not give their kids the [instructional] time.... 'My student has a question and she doesn't want to answer it'" (West, 2006). Elementary school Principal 7 further defined the difficulties with helping every child reach measures of academic proficiency and stated, "We have to look at students as individuals. We're not a factory, they're not cookie cutters, and they are not all going to be at this same point on the same day" (Midwest, 2004). High school Principal 83 summed up the feelings of many principals by sharing, "I think educational leaders have to know what they stand for.... I believe all kids can learn; time is the barrier" (Midwest, 2006).

### Supporting Learning for all Students

Elementary school Principal 41 expressed that educating the whole child meant that schools must structure student learning around academic content, extracurricular programs, and educational experiences beyond the typical curriculum. For example, Principal 41 stated,

> Our test scores are never going to be the best in the state, but you know, I don't care, because we are going to do what is best for kids, and that means that we have before-school programs, afterschool programs, and we teach a rich curriculum. Yes, we follow our district's curriculum, but we also do a variety of other things like taking students on a 3-day science camp.... We could probably have used that classroom time a little more efficiently, but we are again educating that whole child socially, economically, and psychologically. (Southwest, 2006)

As leaders, structuring the school environment around the needs of all children was paramount in asking questions around practices that lead to school improvement, as noted by elementary school Principal 4.

> I think what school improvement has done for us is stop and make us question what we do and that we have truly evaluated what processes are in place to support these kids when they are not achieving academically and socially. (Midwest, 2005)

Further, elementary school Principal 16 described school improvement: "We are looking into the needs of all children, our English language learners (ELLs), children with disabilities, even meeting the needs of those who excel ... but, really, reflecting on our practice and doing what's best for every child in the classroom" (Southwest, 2006). In sum, principals recognized the role of public schools had changed but remained concerned with meeting the academic, social, and emotional needs of all their students, in spite of the rigid time constraints surrounding school improvement measured by state assessments established by their states and districts.

## Challenges in Facilitating a Child-Centered Environment

The second major theme is challenges in facilitating a child-centered environment. Principals shared a variety of comments regarding the challenges with facilitating a child-centered environment. They included three subthemes: (a) narrowing of the curriculum, (b) teacher development concerning the whole child, and (c) parent concerns with educating the whole child.

### Narrowing of the Curriculum

Many principals thought that school staff had become more astute with individualizing instruction for students, yet expressed concerns about the content measured on these high-stakes assessments. Although principals indicated that children had wider gaps in academic and social readiness than in the past, the pressure to prepare students for the state assessment often led to a standard, one-size-fits-all curriculum. For example, elementary school Principal 3 shared,

> We are heavily testing in math and communication arts.... We are not testing them over how to work in a global society.... Are we really testing the whole child? Are we giving them a fair advantage to show where their niche is and that they are successful? My professional opinion is no. Not every child is going to be successful in those two areas, but I know that's what we are required to do. (Midwest, 2005)

When viewing the needs of the whole child, principals mentioned the importance of analyzing data beyond that measured on standardized tests, such as improvement in student dispositions, preparation for productive citizenship, and getting along in the workplace. High school Principal 77 stated, "We are quickly becoming less focused on creating citizens, quality citizens for this county" (Midwest, 2006). Further, high school Principal 83 shared,

> We're spending about 100% of our time in demonstrating test-score proficiency on NCLB, and we're graduating a senior with about 75% of what he/ she needs to know in the real world. And that is a rough pill to swallow for an administrator. (Midwest, 2006)

### Teacher Development Concerning the Whole Child

Regarding teacher development, principals provided teacher trainings that addressed issues of educational philosophy as well as instructional techniques. Teachers have become more astute in meeting a student's academic and emotional needs than in the past because of school- and district-level study groups and in-classroom coaching. Many administrators described how they focused on helping each child make 1 year's worth of academic growth. Further, some school principals described coaching and collaboration models where educators not only met the academic needs of the students but also improved student self-esteem. Conversely, when teachers lacked a student-centered approach, principals felt they must model this philosophy even more to maintain an educational environment that focused on educating the whole child. In some ways, principals believed school improvement made it easier to motivate staff members to focus on the whole child, because they could tell staff members that they had no choice because of the mandates. As elementary school Principal 20 shared, "It's given us [administrators] some backbone" (Southeast, 2006).

### Parent Concerns With Educating the Whole Child

Another challenge for school leaders was that parents desired to learn more about their child than merely their performance on the last school or state assessment. Although the content of parent conferences typically described academic progress, parents wanted to learn about their child's social and emotional growth as well. For example, elementary school Principal 61 shared,

> I had a parent come in one time, and I stood up and applauded her. The parent looked around and she said, "Before we do anything I just want one thing. Don't anybody tell me about test scores, don't anybody tell me about proficiencies or achievements. I want to know about my kid first." We all stood up and clapped. We talked about her child and how the child interacted with people and then we went to test scores. (Midwest, 2005)

## Issues of Equity for Child-Centered Learning Environments

A third major theme is issues of equity for child-centered learning environments. Equity issues have challenged school administrators, and as elementary school Principal 46 stated, "A principal has to make sure there is equity" (Southwest, 2006). In this section, four subthemes are included: (a) contradictory viewpoints about low-performing students, (b) limited opportunities for gifted students, (c) expectations for ELLs, and (d) staff and program elimination associated with whole child development.

### Contradictory Viewpoints About Low-Performing Students

Principals noted that in previous years, some schools purposely disregarded some student groups because the school administrators feared they would not pass the state-mandated assessment, thereby lowering their building's overall score. For example, elementary school Principal 35 stated,

> They [special education students] did not have to take the test, but you have an ethical responsibility to all of your students, because as soon as you say they don't have to take the test ... then they [school staff] are not teaching those children at the level that they need to be taught. (Southwest, 2005)

Some administrators believed the needs of the lowest performing students continued to be ignored because of school improvement, which in this case is synonymous with test scores going up. School staff felt pressured to meet their district and state assessment goals and therefore favored those students who could meet proficiency levels and be promoted to the next grade level. More specifically, elementary school Principal 16 reported,

> The focus on higher order thinking pressed the teachers to work hard on what we call bubble students, those close to passing [promoted], and leaving the students at the bottom of the barrel who needed the most help or be retained. If I look at it from a social justice aspect, these students were the ones we should be looking out for, the ones who were going to be retained because of the system. (Southwest, 2005)

Furthermore, some principals expressed concerns that the developmental need of special education students were not being met because of school improvement mandates. Teachers sometimes expected special education students served in inclusion classrooms to complete grade-level work, even if their level of development or individualized educational program goals indicated they performed below grade level.

In contrast, some school principals' desires for social justice helped low-performing students receive more academic assistance than they typically had in the past, including small-group interventions. High school Principal 79 commented, "We probably tended to ignore them [low-performing students] in the past.... Now they are a main focus for us" (Midwest, 2006). Moreover, high school Principal 26 shared,

> We let too many kids slip through the cracks too early, and then we decide we're going to shut their lives down because we didn't provide the type of instruction that would have kept them from slipping through the cracks. I think it's an abomination. (Southeast, 2006)

### Limited Opportunities for High-Ability Students

School improvement mandates led to decreased expectations for high-ability or gifted students. Principals expressed concerns that the language of proficiency in the current school accountability model had placed a greater emphasis on interventions for struggling students while providing limited resources, if any, for high-ability students or those who have the potential to excel. High school Principal 77 believed schools had contradictory views of educating students; school staff stated their desires to meet the needs of all students, including the brightest, but those students were the ones often overlooked in favor of helping the average or below average students (Midwest, 2006). Furthermore, principals thought that schools provided fewer opportunities to meet the needs of advanced students, specifically those that provide additional challenges outside of the narrow academic focus today. Schools utilized resources such as after-school tutoring programs to help lower performing students, but few administrators described opportunities for helping advanced students reach higher levels of academic performance.

### Expectations for ELLS

Principals shared concerns surrounding the inequities associated with educating ELLs. Some principals believed that school improvement mandates caused schools to concentrate on preparing ELL students to complete the state assessment, rather than providing them quality opportunities to explore and learn more about American culture and the English language. School principals struggled with requiring all students, particularly those with developmental language needs, to complete the state assessment, often before they are competent in the English language. Specifically, elementary school Principal 61 commented, "I believe that every child learns at their own pace and with their own style. We give them a test in March, and it's the same format for every kid" (Midwest, 2005). This factory-type model disregarded ELL students' academic and social needs with state mandates that superseded ELL students' developmental needs.

### Staff and Program Elimination Associated With Whole Child Development

Principals shared that school improvement led to the elimination of exploratory or extracurricular courses in some school settings. Many school leaders indicated that the current school curriculum did not address the whole child, but in fact lessened the number of programs that met the needs of the whole child. For example, middle school Principal 63 described how exploratory classes such as technology, music, and art often enriched the curriculum for adolescents beyond that of basic academic subject but had been eliminated for some students because of the content on the state assessment, specifically the need to improve reading scores. To accomplish this, middle school Principal 63 explained,

We eliminated one of those exploratory programs, and therefore we punished children, kids that did not do well in reading. They are not going to have the exploratory options and opportunities.... I feel disappointed that we got rid of half of our exploratory classes.... We compromised the middle school philosophy. (Midwest, 2005)

Last, principals shared that maintaining a focus on the whole child was important in their respective buildings, but often schools terminated programs or staff members to help schools meet accountability goals. In some cases, principals recognized that schools hired additional classroom teachers or paraprofessionals to provide new schoolwide academic interventions. However, many administrators and schools felt pressured to help children perform well on the state assessment, so they eliminated school counselors; social workers; teachers of gifted education; and curricula not found on the state assessment, such as music and art, which helped educators address the needs of the whole child.

## Stress on Children

The fourth major theme is stress on children. School improvement's psychological impact on American children has received a great deal of attention and was described in the focus groups. The pressure students experienced surrounding their need to pass high-stakes assessments occurred because of ramifications that related to rigorous test preparation, grade-level promotion, and high school graduation. Elementary principals expressed trepidations about increased stress faced by their students and staff regarding performance on these tests and the resultant impact on their students' mental health. Elementary school Principal 2 shared that the teachers "want to do well on the tests, and I am beginning to see some of the stress coming on the kids. [Students] are worried about how well they will perform on the test" (Midwest, 2005).

Many principals believed, with an average of 3 weeks out of a 9-month school year consumed with testing, that schools were spending too much time assessing students. Principals at all school levels indicated that this overemphasis on testing and test preparation not only had increased students' stress levels but also had diminished their interest in learning and limited the attention given to meet students' social and emotional needs. Secondary school principals in particular described the results of constantly tested and stressed elementary and middle school students; they produced student learning gaps at the high school level along with student desires to drop out of school because of the stress associated with passing the state's graduation proficiency exam.

## SUPERINTENDENTS AND PRINCIPALS:
## COMPARISONS AND CONTRASTS

In reviewing the transcripts, superintendents and principals shared both positive and negative outcomes of school improvement that ranged from how it served as a catalyst for change to the obstacles it created for schools when addressing the social and emotional needs of students. For example, both superintendents and principals talked about the importance of meeting the academic needs of all students, including students who often were ignored in the past, such as special education students and children of poverty. However, their lens at times lacked social justice perspectives as they spoke about how low performers were now getting the attention they needed, but often at the expense of other students. Several responses from principals indicated that a new class of marginalized students has been targeted—the lowest performers and the high performers who are expected to perform well on standardized tests, even if schools fail to address their learning needs. Given the post-NCLB context of American education, establishing clear goals and developing the systems needed to efficiently obtain the goals of both a rational and pragmatic approach toward establishing excellence appear to come at the expense of equity. As excellence is established at the systems level, new sets of challenges regarding inequities present themselves. For example, superintendents and principals noted the need to provide the extra assistance for all low-performing students to increase proficiency levels. Yet when focusing on increased proficiency, new challenges in equity arise, with marginalized children scoring at either end of the bell-shaped curve.

Some superintendents and principals took a humanistic approach with school improvement and recognized that schools and districts must help their families by creating family involvement programs that address students' social and emotional needs. For example, principals on many occasions discussed the expanding role of public schools to include more things. Additionally, both leadership groups believed that school improvement helped them focus on meeting the needs of more children, but principals specifically spoke about how high-stakes accountability led to curricula dominated by test preparation and academic interventions and the elimination of programs that focus on the whole child, such as the fine arts. These decisions to eliminate programs such as the fine arts lack a pragmatic approach of teaching reading and numeracy with other subjects. Further, principals expressed concerns about students' high stress levels as schools pushed children to meet individual and school assessment targets, despite increased gaps in school readiness. In some cases, principals voiced opinions about how district mandates such as curriculum maps and pacing guides provided challenges for schools as they were forced to provide a one-size-fits-all curriculum model to students regardless of their developmental levels. Superintendents and principals described the importance of addressing parent concerns about school improvement to secure their support through forums at the district level and providing more information about each child's social and emotional progress, not just their academic performance, at the school level, seeking to find more balance. Both superintendents and principals shared how they had created teacher trainings that targeted the needs of the whole child to positively impact a student's academic, social, and emotional growth. Both groups of administrators were concerned with having child-centered teachers in the district and classroom. Last, superintendents spoke about the political and community agendas associated with school improvement from a school governance perspective.

In comparing the themes from the superintendent focus groups with the themes from the principal focus groups, superintendents viewed a more systemic and organizational approach versus an individual and more student-centered approach to student growth and development. On one hand, the majority of the discussions by superintendents pertaining to the whole child focused on structural aspects of schooling and school governance issues, such as improvement planning, "fending off" detractions from a student-centered environment, and using NCLB as a means of integrating change that better incorporates the two concepts of excellence and equity. On the other hand, principal focus groups discussed how to facilitate a child-centered environment and develop a school culture focused on the individual children. For example, the principals talked about determining how to best support both students and their families, developing faculties that can differentiate instruction, and modeling the way for a student-centered approach to teaching to flourish amid such a strong emphasis on high-stakes testing. Furthermore, examples of stress and anxiety of students in a post-NCLB era only emerged in the principals' discussions. Such a concentration of themes demonstrates how administrators viewed their own roles regarding educating the whole child, seeking to find a balance but understanding the limitations of what they might be able to accomplish. For superintendents, their roles centered on creating and sustaining the child-centered environment more around the culture of the school through supporting teachers and parents in their endeavors to provide more opportunities for meeting the needs of the whole child.

## IMPLICATIONS FOR PRACTICE, LEADERSHIP PREPARATION, AND POLICY

Jean-Marie and Normore (2008) wrote, "Critical leadership is defined as a continued analysis of what occurs in an organization by those engaged in critical reflection and re-evaluation of current practices" (p. 7). Administrators' perceptions of their implementation of school improvement mandates indicated that collectively they demonstrated critical leadership by integrating individualized caring for students with student achievement. Furthermore, amid the criticism of NCLB there has been little recognition regarding the systemic impact of such critical leadership on implementation of policy. Accountability mandates have changed educational leadership practices in many ways. Although school superintendents and principals desire to provide students with an education that focuses on their academic, social, and emotional needs, the competing demands of school improvement, defined as higher scores on state achievement tests, often create barriers for school leaders that disconnect what they know from what they do. The classroom and school environment can be a powerful tool for focusing students' attention on learning while offering them a secure and supportive learning experience.

Educational leaders in the focus groups seemed to agree on the need for excellence at the systems level—schools and districts—and equity at the individual level. Reconciling excellence and equity in practice is complex. Superintendents noted the distance between their office and the classroom. Furthermore, the tools most readily available fall under policies and procedures that fit a one-size-fits-all model versus one that looks at individual students. As a result, other stakeholders, such as parents and teachers, must be relied upon to be systemic advocates for the needs of individual children. Similarly, this was evident in the principals' statements about the increasing social role of the school, the narrowing and prioritizing of the curriculum, promoting parent involvement, and providing for teacher development.

A tension exists for educators as they attempt to balance concern for the growth and development of children with concern for their performance on a single standardized test. This quandary is not new to educators; it was seen at the beginning of the 20th century in the debates between Dewey and Elliott over the meaning of progressive education—experiential learning activities versus bureaucratic efficiency. During the day-to-day decision making required of superintendents and principals, educational leaders understand the bureaucratic demands for efficiency. Yet, they also understand on a broader level that schools must provide meaning, which unites individual learning and development at social, emotional, and intellectual levels. Weber (1947) indicated that the more calculating and bureaucratic an organization becomes, the more depersonalized and oppressive the organizational routines turn out to be, diminishing meaning in individual actions with bureaucratic efficiencies. In superintendents' and principals' decision making, they sought balance between bureaucratic needs of efficiency and the holistic needs of individual students. While immersed in this leadership task, superintendents and principals linked pragmatism and critical leadership by reflecting upon and reframing their varied beliefs regarding doing what is best for students academically, socially, and emotionally, choices they interwove with the legislative expectations to which they are held accountable.

## FUTURE TRENDS

Schools play an important role in raising healthy children by fostering not only their cognitive development but also their social and emotional development. Education initiatives that link current practice with promising new research in neurological and cognitive sciences offer real possibilities for improving teaching and learning regarding educating the whole child, especially for students with diverse learning needs. Brain research supports the notion that a positive emotional climate allows for higher levels of learning and student performance (Hardiman, 2003). Elias et al. (1997) posited that a universal school-based effort to promote students' social and emotional learning represents a promising approach for enhancing children's success in school and life. Further, Durlak, Weissberg, Dymnicki, Taylor, and Schellinger (2011) affirmed in their large-scale meta-analysis that school-based programs that promoted students' social and emotional development contributed to an 11 percentile gain in academic performance. School administrators pressured to meet the demands of the NCLB legislation and improve the academic performance of their students might welcome programs that boost achievement by 11 percentile points. Durlak et al.'s findings are noteworthy, especially for educational policy and practice, as the results add to a growing body of research indicating that social and emotional learning programming enhances students' connection to school, classroom behavior, and academic achievement (Zins, Weissberg, Wang, & Walberg, 2004). If school leaders are to empower all individuals to learn, they must understand and apply this information from neurological and cognitive science within their professional practice.

There is broad agreement among educators, policy makers, and the public that educational systems should graduate students who are proficient in core academic subjects, able to work well with others from diverse backgrounds, practice healthy behaviors, and exhibit responsible and respectful behaviors (Association for Supervision and Curriculum Development, 2007). However, affective areas of education that are the foundation for growth and learning are not included on the high-stakes assessments or used to evaluate a student's growth. Comer (2005) indicated that philosophical beliefs about educating children and lack of formal preparation in child and adolescent development contribute to why schools fail to educate the whole child. He further asserted that child development remains a limited focus because many educators differ philosophically regarding school and life performance; they believe genetics and the home environment predispose student performance, despite recent findings that intelligence is interactive and a developmental outcome of various stimuli. Therefore, implications from this research include the need to prepare aspiring school leaders to become advocates for educational equity and child development (Cambron-McCabe & McCarthy, 2005) while they are formally enrolled in university preparation programs or with continued education.

Preservice educational leaders and those practicing in the field must understand that the social and emotional life of the child and their academic proficiency are both essential components for determining student success. School improvement goals that address improving educational equity have not been reached and, rather, have narrowed the education of children to routines of learning content that matches a minimum standards test while failing to provide for their social and emotional needs (Kohn, 2005; Popham, 2001). There is significant pressure on novice educational leaders to focus on the efficiency of the school system and student proficiency as defined by state assessment goals rather than the needs of the whole child. Although superintendents and principals, those at the novice level and those who are veteran administrators, must continue to manage their districts and schools efficiently, they must now do so while incorporating child-centered practices and by modeling a whole-child focus into the daily routines of the school and district. Furthermore, school and district leaders must possess critical leadership skills that integrate both excellence and equity at the individual and systems levels and reflect a holistic view of education—a pragmatic approach of blending theory into practice. These tenets of educating the whole child are undervalued in the current political context of contemporary American education and must be inculcated into the mindset of school and district leaders via leadership preparation programs, educational policy, and practical experiences in the field.

## REFERENCES

Amrein, A. L., & Berliner, D. C. (2002). *An analysis of some unintended and negative consequences of high-stakes testing* (EPSL No. 0211-125-EPRU). Tempe: Arizona State University, Educational Policy Studies Laboratory.

Association for Supervision and Curriculum Development. (2005). ASCD's position statement on the whole child. *Educational Leadership, 63*(1), 17.

Association for Supervision and Curriculum Development. (2007). *The learning compact redefined: A call to action—A report of the commission on the whole child.* Alexandria, VA: Author.

Bellamy, G. T., Fulmer, C. L., Murphy, M. J., & Muth, R. (2007). *Principal accomplishments: How school leaders succeed.* New York, NY: Teachers College Press.

Cambron-McCabe, N., & McCarthy, M. (2005). Educating school leaders for social justice. *Educational Policy, 19*(1), 201-222.

Carrell, S., & Carrell, S. (2006). Do lower student-to-counselor ratios reduce school disciplinary problems? *Contributions to Economic Analysis & Policy, 5*(1), Article 11.

Comer, J. P. (1996). *Rallying a whole village: The Comer process for reforming education.* New Haven, CT: Yale University Press.

Comer, J. P. (2004). *Leave no child behind: Preparing today's youth for tomorrow's world.* New Haven, CT: Yale University Press.

Comer, J. P. (2005). Child and adolescent development: The critical missing focus on school reform. *Phi Delta Kappan, 86,* 757-763.

DeBray-Pelot, E., & McGuinn, P. (2009). The new politics of education: Analyzing the federal education policy landscape in the post-NCLB era. *Educational Policy, 23*(1), 15-42.

Dewey, J. (1933). *How we think: A restatement of the relation of reflective thinking to the educative process.* Boston, MA: Heath.

Durlak, J., Weissberg, R., Dymnicki, A., Taylor, R., & Schellinger, K. (2011). The impact of enhancing students' social and emotional learning: A meta-analysis of school-based universal interventions. *Child Development, 82,* 405-432.

Eisner, E. (2005). Back to whole. *Educational Leadership, 63*(1), 14-18.

Elias, M. J., Zins, J. E., Weissberg, R. P., Frey, K. S., Greenberg, M. T., Haynes, N. M., … Shriver, T. P. (1997). *Promoting social and emotional learning: Guidelines for educators.* Alexandria, VA: Association for Supervision and Curriculum Development.

Elmore, R. F. (2003). A plea for strong practice. *Educational Leadership, 61*(3), 6-10.

Glaser, B. G., & Strauss, A. L. (1967). *The discovery of grounded theory: Strategies for qualitative research.* Chicago, IL: Aldine.

Gregor, A. (2005). Examination anxiety: Live with it, control it, or make it work for you? *School Psychology International, 26,* 617-635.

Hardiman, M. (2003). *Connecting brain research with effective teaching: The brain-target teaching model.* Lanham, MD: Scarecrow Press.

Hershberg, T., Simon, V. A., & Lea-Kruger, B. L. (2004, December). The revelations of value-added. *The School Administrator, 61*(11), 10-14.

Hodge, G., McCormick, J., & Elliott, R. (1997). Examination-induced distress in a public examination at the completion of secondary schooling. *British Journal of Educational Psychology, 67,* 185-197.

James, W. (1907). *Pragmatism: A new name for some old ways of thinking.* New York, NY: Longmans, Green, & Co.

Jean-Marie, G., & Normore, A. H. (2008). A repository of hope for social justice. In A. H. Normore (Ed.), *Leadership for social justice: Promoting equity and excellence through inquiry and reflective practice* (pp. 3-35). Charlotte, NC: Information Age.

Johannessen, L. R. (2004). Helping "struggling" students achieve success. *Journal of Adolescent & Adult Literacy, 47,* 638-647.

Kohn, A. (2005). The whole child. *Educational Leadership, 63*(1), 20-24.

Ladd, H. F., & Lauren, D. L. (2009). *Status vs. growth: The distributional effects of school accountability policies* (CALDER Working Paper 21). Retrieved from http://www.urban.org/publications/1001304.html

Lubienski, S. T. (2003). Celebrating diversity and denying disparities: A critical assessment. *Educational Researcher, 32*(8), 30-38.

Lyons, J., & Algozzine, B. (2006). Perceptions of the impact of accountability on the role of principals. *Education Policy Analysis Archives, 14,* 16. Retrieved from http://epaa.asu.edu/ojs/article/view/87

Popham, W. J. (2001). *The truth about testing: An educator's call to action.* Alexandria, VA: Association for Supervision and Curriculum Development.

Sanders, W. L. (2003, April). *Beyond No Child Left Behind.* Paper presented at the meeting of the American Educational Research Association, Chicago, IL.

Theoharis, G. (2009). *The school leaders our children deserve: Seven keys to equity, social justice, and school reform.* New York, NY: Teachers College Press.

Travers, E. (2009). *Complicated choices: Struggling to meet NCLB requirements and remain faithful to a school's educational vision and practice.* Philadelphia, PA: Research For Action.

Waters, R. (1979). Another brick in the wall, Part 2 [recorded by Pink Floyd Inc]. *On The Wall* [record album]. Los Angeles, CA: Capitol Records.

Weber, M. (1947). *Theory of social and economic organization.* New York, NY: Oxford University Press.

Zellmer, M., Frontier, A., & Pheifer, D. (2006). What are NCLB's instructional costs? *Educational Leadership, 64*(3), 43-46.

Zins, J. E., Weissberg, R. P., Wang, M. C., & Walberg, H. J. (Eds.). (2004). *Building academic success on social and emotional learning: What does the research say?* New York, NY: Teachers College Press.

CHAPTER 4

# SCHOOL SUPERINTENDENTS AND PRINCIPALS MEETING THE ACADEMIC NEEDS OF ALL LEARNERS

**Elizabeth Murakami-Ramalho and Mariela A. Rodríguez**

In this chapter we examine the pressures faced by superintendents and principals in accommodating No Child Left Behind (NCLB, 2002) accountability requirements in relation to meeting the needs of all children. Changing school systems from exclusionary philosophies to more inclusive philosophies has required a paradigm shift for school and district administrators and the virtual transformation of academic environments in which these educators work to alter existing exclusionary practices. We defined these exclusionary practices as teaching to a select group of students and ignoring the needs of other students, especially students with special needs. It is a widely accepted fact that certain curricular and learning cultures favor a select group of students over others. NCLB challenged educators to address specific learning needs of all students, especially students with special needs, and in order to make school-wide improvement gains, held schools accountable to show learning gains for all subgroups, in particular students with special needs.

*Snapshots of School Leadership in the 21st Century:*
*Perils and Promises of Leading for Social Justice,*
*School Improvement, and Democratic Community,* pp. 55–73
Copyright © 2012 by Information Age Publishing
All rights of reproduction in any form reserved.

This meant structural changes in how teaching and learning occurred in many schools. To illustrate the dramatic changes required by this federal mandate, we center the chapter on the expectations of superintendents and principals to make the necessary modifications that they were forced to undertake, especially in regard to addressing accommodations for students with special needs. They grappled with the conflicting policy mandates of both fulfilling requirements of individualized education plans (IEPs) while simultaneously following through on NCLB mandates. We hope readers consider how these superintendents and principals arrived at a better understanding of what transitions occurred in placement, curriculum, and assessment practices with students, particularly those with special needs, over the first decade of NCLB implementation in the United States. We believe chapter findings have broader implications for how we think about educating all students and how we analyze reform mandates that may place leaders in untenable positions. We highlight how school leaders struggled to meet both accountability demands and specifically designed learning plans for special needs students, often finding them having to choose between one of the two options.

## PERSPECTIVE AND RATIONALE

The most dramatic change in the NCLB mandate was in its purpose. In the past, the educational philosophies in different states resulted in educational policies that were exclusionary, focusing on preparing only the students whom educators perceived as having the greatest potential to learn and succeed. Often, educators within these schools rejected a "significant number of students on the basis of race, ability, or gender" (Hardman & Dawson, 2008, p. 5), creating severe academic gaps between and among students that resulted in high dropout rates. Critics of these exclusionary practices have concentrated on how the consequences of this rigid curriculum became a self-fulfilling prophecy, predicting who would succeed and deserved support, and who would fail and had little or no support. For example, Hardman and Dawson (2008) contended that the most challenging aspects of the NCLB reform involved moving away from present practices of low expectations to policy-to-practice routines that translated into "(a) assessment and curricular materials that are accessible to every student, (b) use of research-based instruction consistent with individual need and ability, and (c) sufficient material and human resources to deliver the instruction and to assess student learning" (p. 7). However, Hardman and Dawson also cautioned that current instruments and instructional materials had to "catch up" with the policy requirements, and that the present instruments and instructional materials had not yet been proven effective to meet the needs of various students—not to mention pedagogical practices. Teaching to meet the needs of students required a dramatic rethinking of present educational practices and a thorough understanding of what was assessed. This meant changing mindsets of what leaders expected in the classroom and altering how teachers taught students with varying needs to achieve the standards.

Thus, NCLB legislation required alignment between state standards and assessment to measure Adequate Yearly Progress (AYP) of students (U.S. Department of Education, 2002) and an understanding that students would need different instructional strategies to achieve the standards. Mandates included the expectation that by 2014 every student would demonstrate proficiency. Martone and Sireci (2009) affirmed that even though

> politicians, educators, and parents debate the merits of standardized testing, the psychometric characteristics of tests are rarely the basis of concern. Rather, criticisms have focused on "opportunity to learn" issues such as failure to test students on what they were taught, and the need to narrow the curriculum because of mandated testing. (p. 1332)

Indeed, the concerns of aligning curriculum and assessment were legitimate, especially when the mission of NCLB (2002) was to "close the achievement gap with accountability, flexibility, and choice, so that no child is left behind" (§ 1). This was especially true for students with special needs. The curriculum of standards-based assessment was fast becoming, however, a standardized curriculum for many students, sidestepping the very issue of meeting the needs of individual learners.

## CONCERNS ABOUT THE AFFECTIVE ASPECTS OF SCHOOLING

Of much concern to those involved in the implementation of NCLB was the increased focus on assessment and accountability in schools at the expense of developing the affective side of teaching and learning to create opportunities to develop nurturing relationships between students and teachers. The NCLB reform indirectly compelled superintendents and principals to reduce the nurturing aspect of schooling environments by focusing school time on preparing students to meet state and national benchmarks. This decision compromised time that otherwise might have been spent on developing social skills and participating in collective student activities, if not eliminating these areas altogether, to work on basic numeracy and literacy skills, often referred to as drill and kill (Capper, Rodríguez, & McKinney, 2010; Diamond & Spillane, 2004; Frattura &

Capper, 2007; Gerstl-Pepin, 2006; Lasky & Karge, 2006; Parrish & Stodden, 2009).

Because NCLB introduced a heightened level of accountability that impacted curriculum, instruction, and assessment in schools nationwide (Roach, Niebling, & Kurz, 2008; Sunderman, Kim, & Orfield, 2005), especially in the core subject areas of reading and mathematics, teachers felt an intense pressure to concentrate their efforts on the most likely students to respond to their instruction by passing the state tests. The focus on students who were likely to pass without additional help increased the demands and expectations for student assessment around a standard set of curricular expectations that lead to students being labeled in terms of their potential to pass these state exams. This assessment of who might pass and who might fail was quickly being translated into how teachers in some schools spent time with students who were unlikely to pass state tests, even with increased help, as well as students who were very likely to pass state tests.

By definition, curriculum, instruction, and assessment represent what is taught in schools, how it is taught, and how student progress is assessed—there is not necessarily a one-size-fits-all curriculum, but a continuous alignment of these three areas. According to Roach et al. (2008), alignment defines "the extent to which curricular expectations and assessments are in agreement and work together to provide guidance for educators' efforts to facilitate students' progress toward desired academic outcomes" (p. 158). Specifically, some schools shaved instructional time from other subjects like science and social studies during the school day to allow for extended instructional time in the core subjects in which students were being tested (i.e., literacy and numeracy), at the expense of other areas (Center on Education Policy, 2008). Students who needed extra tutorials in these subjects attended before- and after-school tutorial sessions. Moreover, the difficulty for superintendents and principals in meeting the needs of all learners, while at the same time aligning the curriculum and instruction for students in the regular classroom (Sorrentino & Zirkel, 2004), was to challenge some leaders to come to grips with a number of issues. Examinations of issues included such things as (a) how to match weekly lessons and learning needs of students; (b) how to prepare students with special needs at the same pace as the general classroom students; and (c) how to serve students who required special assistance, such as nonnative speakers and students with special needs.

## SCHOOL ADMINISTRATORS AND THE NCLB–INDIVIDUALS WITH DISABILITIES ACT TENSIONS

A daunting challenge facing school leaders, as identified by Bowen and Rude (2006), included guidelines set forth by NCLB regarding alternative assessments and AYP. Most importantly, these assessment guidelines required superintendents and principals to choose between the requirements to assess students through state-mandated assessments and addressing students' skill levels as determined by their IEPs. This inconsistency resulted in either–or choices for educators, often at the expense of the child, because the number of exceptions allowed per school was limited.

Since the federal mandate's expectations for high academic success were nonexclusionary, the Individuals With Disabilities Education Act (IDEA) Amendments of 1997 and the Individuals With Disabilities Education Improvement Act (IDEIA, 2004) were reviewed by the federal government in order to strengthen guidelines for students in need of special services. IDEIA (2004) ensured that "the education of children with disabilities can be made more effective by having high expectations for these children and ensuring their access to the general education curriculum in the regular classroom, to the maximum extent possible" (§ 1400[c][5][A]). The Education for All Handicapped Children Act (1975), the precursor to IDEA, had identified six main principles, including the need to develop an IEP for all students receiving special education services, so that these students received their rightful free and appropriate public education.

IDEA required an IEP be designed for each student receiving special education or related services. The IEP must be crafted by a committee formed by a parent, a teacher, a school staff, and possibly the student. The intent of the IEP was to prescribe how the student would progress through the general curriculum. The goal of an IEP and the accountability provisions of NCLB were on a collision course. Ananda (2003) explained,

> The law's [NCLB's] accountability provisions state that irrespective of IEPs, special needs students who have been tested with some accommodations in test format and content cannot be counted as meeting the proficiency standard of the accountability system. This means that while a school may meet NCLB's assessment requirements by testing special needs students with IEP-specified accommodations, the same school may fall short of its accountability goals (i.e., making adequate yearly progress) because the use of these accommodations automatically means a student cannot be considered "proficient" for accountability purposes. (p. 4)

How best to make decisions regarding accommodations based on how to align curriculum, instruction, and assessment effectively required links between data and pedagogy to guide superintendents and principals in their expectations for teaching and learning decisions. Martone and Sireci (2009) commented,

> In a perfect world, what a student is tested on should be derived from what is expected of the student as detailed in the state or district standards, as well as from what is taught to the student by his or her teachers. (p. 1334)

Variability existed in terms of expectations and standards from district to district and state to state, with accommodations based on how best to align curriculum, instruction, and assessment within existing resources. The problem could be further exacerbated in smaller school districts with limited resources. The conditions under which superintendents and principals made decisions were therefore very resource dependent. In some school districts, this narrowed options available.

The challenge for Voices 3 superintendents and principals was in relation to following the IEP requirements and measuring student progress toward meeting annual achievement goals for this specific population of special needs students. According to NCLB regulations, up to 3% of students receiving special education services could be exempt from completing the state-mandated assessment. Thus, only 3% of the school's population could complete an alternative assessment. All the other students with IEPs must be on grade level (Mele-McCarthy, 2007). Given this strict policy, school principals, teachers, and staff felt immense pressure to focus on students with the best chance of passing the standardized tests—rather than following the academic objectives of their special needs students' IEPs. This was especially true in schools where more than 3% of students were receiving special educational services. Thus again, leaders felt they had to choose either to follow the IEP and risk not making AYP or to compromise the students' IEPs in order to make AYP, in the process doing a disservice to the student.

With the NCLB federal mandate, and because of the rewards or sanctions based on student performance, educators faced tough decisions. It was of utmost importance that school administrators not only understand the complexities of serving students in need of special education services but also interpret how these mandates affected these students (Bouck, 2009) and therefore determine how they might define student success (i.e., meeting the goals of the IEP, passing the state test, or both). It was in this context that we interviewed superintendents and principals across the country. These leaders expressed grave concerns about the difficulties of wrestling with the conflicting legislative mandates of NCLB and IDEIA.

## CODING AND ANALYZING SUPERINTENDENTS' AND PRINCIPALS' RESPONSES

Our analysis coded superintendents' and principals' transcripts for concerns regarding meeting the needs of all learners. A secondary coding analysis (Saldaña, 2009) identified frequency in patterns of these concerns among participants and subsequently resulted in our thematic groupings in which we present our findings.

As the NCLB mandate was implemented, and superintendents and principals were planning adaptations to the new law, they had to focus on four important aspects related to serving students with special needs: (a) development of mechanisms to inform the improvement of curricular practices, (b) specifics related to special education adaptations, (c) affective aspects of meeting the needs of all learners, and (d) some evidence of organizational learning and relearning to match the large-scale reform pressures to their contexts. We present superintendents' and principals' perceptions regarding such challenges they described in meeting NCLB mandates and the requirements of IDEIA.

## Development of Mechanisms to Inform the Improvement of Curricular Practices

An important aspect of NCLB accountability is how it changed the way districts and states would use data to improve curricular practices. When superintendents and principals first sorted student achievement data by subgroups such as race or ethnicity, English language learners, and special needs students, they were challenged by the uneven results in their districts and schools. Superintendents and principals discussed a perceived divide between accountability expectations at the local and national levels, concerns about political and legislative implications, and the necessity for discussions with their local school boards, in adapting new strategies to achieve federally mandated goals in their school districts. Initial reactions included concern and confusion as they reflected on the NCLB federal mandate:

> I think it's put a severe impact—it's been a severe impact on districts. In the sense, it's become more of an accountability issue. They've emphasized more in testing. And also, what they have done, I'm trying to think, no one can—you know, always No Child Left Behind, but no one can hide. There's no hiding now because of the way they test now, they've delineated minorities. They've delineated special ed[ucation]. (Superintendent 69, medium-sized districts, Southwest & West, 2006)

This superintendent described the impact of the legislation on traditional practices. Specifically, there was no hiding from the accountability issue. Superintendent 33 discussed the political issue related to the pressures felt by districts around the country:

> Accountability is heavily driven from the legislature, from the political world—it has always been around some form of accountability within the system. But, if you really get down to the brass tacks, there's a lot less focus

on [the state test] by our parents in our district than there are with the legislators who represent our district. (medium-sized districts, South & Southwest, 2005)

Superintendents and principals agreed that NCLB helped to motivate
educators to make improvements in the curriculum and instruction practices in their schools for students who had been underserved. Middle
school Principal 74, for example, introduced the issue of student diversity.
She reflected on the quality and effectiveness of the instruction that
underrepresented students were receiving:

No Child Left Behind gives you a different perspective. It helps you dig
deeper into the data.... It's forced us to look at a whole diversity issue that
we've never had before.... So I think that through No Child Left Behind I'm
facing a diversity issue for the first time, but it's all in looking at their
instructional needs and how that affects their needs. (Midwest, 2006)

Elementary school Principal 11 concurred with the value of the accountability component of NCLB by stating, "There are a lot of frustrating
things about it [NCLB], but it has made us more accountable and made
classroom teachers more accountable to their students, to focus in more
on some of their kids" (Midwest, 2004). Thus, the impact of the legislation led to some schools revisiting their educational practices in order to
help each child succeed. Principals expressed that federal legislation had
served as an impetus to challenge the status quo and to get educators
motivated to revisit the curriculum and align it to the students' needs.
Principal 33, a male elementary school principal, reflected on the benefit
of the legislation enacted to ensure that all students are meeting their academic potential:

The words "No Child Left Behind" help[ed] me to, without talking about
the law—but those words, help[ed] me to bring them [students] along and
let them know that "as a child you will not be left behind," because it's frustrating, and sometimes those kids get forgotten—not forgotten, but left
behind. (Southwest & West, 2006)

When discussing issues of curriculum instruction, female middle school
Principal 73 agreed that federal legislation encouraged them to join their
teachers and staff in discussions about ways to improve curriculum development and instructional delivery. She highlighted the important role of
an instructional leader:

The one thing it's [NCLB] done, it forced us to talk about instruction. It
forced us to look at data. We've also talked about it at our leadership team
this week that we're not a culture that is comfortable talking to the position

of principal about instruction. I can't just be a manager; I have to be an instructional leader. (Midwest, 2006)

The examination of concerns related to accountability issues resulted in more focus on discussing issues related to curriculum and instruction. Superintendents and principals expressed the need to quickly adjust their work frames to make decisions about what had to be tackled first. Female Superintendent 31 reflected on how standards might level the playing field for all students:

> Accountability is nothing to fear. We want to do the best we can for every student, and I think it has given focus, more than I've seen in 30 years of education, to people rallying around a certain set of standards and things like that, that hopefully can even the playing field. (mixed medium-sized & small districts, Southwest & West, 2005)

Superintendent 38, in a small district, attested to how data had influenced curricular decisions but made it clear that it was the leader's role to make sense of the data:

> We have 20 years of data and we have our own assessments that we have developed that reflect our curriculum in a much better curriculum match, and we use[d] that to make hopefully good instructional curricular decisions. Our staff has been really concerned. But I say, "Let me handle that, and let the board and I handle that, and you do what is right for kids. Don't get caught up in the rest of this." (Midwest, 2004)

Superintendents interviewed in this project agreed NCLB requirements added some stress to their jobs. Nonetheless, they recognized a revision of curricular practices was due to meet the needs of all students.

## Specifics Related to Special Education Adaptations

A point of contention when discussing the impact of NCLB on special education was that of reconciling the IEP with the state's testing program to measure AYP. School plans for special needs students are required and must be followed by all educators who work with students with exceptionalities. The IEP is specifically designed for each student based on his or her academic and cognitive abilities and needs. Every teacher who works with students with special needs must implement required modifications to the general curriculum to meet the special needs of these students. Superintendent 72 expressed frustrations regarding the contradiction between NCLB-mandated assessments and those determined within a student's IEP:

> You bring up special ed[ucation] and No Child Left Behind. They're both federal laws, and they contradict. Because in special ed., by law, you have to be 2 years behind to qualify for a learning disability. You have to be 2 years behind! No Child Left Behind [requires that] every single kid has to pass at grade level. It's unconstitutional.... Whatever the IEP says, it overrules No Child Left Behind. (medium-sized districts, Midwest, 2005)

Such contention between fulfilling IEP goals for students and following through on NCLB mandates dominated conversations among the superintendents and principals. This issue remains challenging for school district leaders across the country. In 2004, male Superintendent 24 remained optimistic and concluded how these contractions might be resolved:

> Okay, on one hand you have laws about special education and ... how kids need to be accommodated and so on and so forth, and then you have NCLB saying, "Yeah, well now we don't want to listen about any excuses about IEPs. Everyone's going to be 100%." ... I think there's some greater awareness of it [NCLB] and—even the title itself—who's going to disagree that no child should be left behind? I mean no one's ever thought that, I don't think— well, maybe some people have, but it's never been a part of any of my beliefs, and so—yeah I think it'll—I think we keep working at what we do and things will kind of fall into place. (small districts, Midwest, 2004)

Superintendents reiterated the responsibilities ahead and optimism in understanding large scale reform implications. Paramount to the implicit contradictions in NCLB and IDEIA was the need to keep working on what was in the interest of students and to believe that new structures and processes would emerge, as Superintendent 24 stated, by simply "working at what we do."

## Principals' Focus on Affective Aspects of Meeting the Needs of All Learners

Principals stated that they were on task in developing affective aspects of meeting the needs of all learners. These principals reported practical approaches that they engaged related to the influence of NCLB. A shift in educational philosophies from exclusionary to inclusionary practices required principals, in addressing the needs of all children, to be attentive to challenging assumptions of school personnel and parents. Some expressed their agreement with positive features of NCLB. To this end, they described how the mandate influenced their leadership at the campus level. These principals felt conflicted about how to put the needs of children first, before shifting attention to the accountability mandates. Elementary Principal 10, for example, stated, "So hitting roadblocks and bureaucracy against what's best for the child. Knowing this is a battle I can't win and I have to back off, and that was very frustrating. I lost a lot of sleep over that" (Midwest, 2004). This principal could see that standards could easily be translated into mechanization, and that was a wrenching ethical issue for her.

Elementary school principals described initial difficulties reconciling carrying out the legislative mandate with keeping the best interests of students as a priority. For example, Principal 7 stated,

> That is a big issue, weighing the legal aspects versus what's best for kids. We always have to look at what's best for that individual child and I don't think that anything is black and white, but we need to look at individual students. (Midwest, 2004)

Elementary school Principal 28 indicated the need to reflect and change practices:

> You are slowing down because you are afraid to make narrow decisions based on policies, and you forget that you are serving children and parents. And so what I have had to do as a principal is I have to focus on the children and let state accountability ratings issues aside. (Southwest & West, 2006)

In relation to students with special needs, female elementary Principal 56 added,

> I almost feel like these children are being left behind because their needs are not being met. The only thing that is important is how you score on that test. So if that's where your focus is, that's where your attention goes, that's where your resources go, when what that child needs is more than that. (Midwest, 2005)

Thus, the pressure of the accountability mandate affected the decision making of these principals to put the needs of students first. Additionally, the need to refocus teachers to serve all learners using fairness and high expectations was highlighted by male elementary Principal 33, who stated,

> You know, I think if there is positive in it, if I ever use it to my advantage, it's in talking with teachers who are dealing with special populations and changing their approach to being fair, doing what they really need to,

understanding the special education folks, bringing their attention to the IEPs, and those kind of things. (Southwest & West, 2006)

Principals interviewed expressed genuine care about the academic achievement of all students in their schools. They emphasized the value of principals who lead not only with their head but also with their heart (Rodríguez, Murakami-Ramalho, & Ruff, 2009). These principals discussed the importance of the leader setting the tone and being the steward of the mission for student success.

## Organizational Learning and Relearning

Leithwood, Harris, and Strauss (2010) found that large-scale governmental reforms can implicitly indicate schools are far from delivering quality education, when in reality what is needed is for schools to change their improvement processes and adapt to changing conditions. This requires relearning. Perhaps the first step in relearning is realizing that present behaviors need to change. Superintendent 7 explained how she had recently read about second-order change:

> Second-order change is whenever things need to change and it takes different skill levels than [are] apparently in existence, and you are moving somewhere that's not just a logical extension of the past. When you are in second-order change, it is very uncomfortable. It takes people criticizing that there's not enough communication going. We do not have the kind of resources needed. We are focusing on every student. That is a second-order change. (small districts, Midwest, 2004)

Similarly, participants in the Voices project expressed the need to develop new organizational learning strategies to meet NCLB requirements. Female Principal 18 noted,

> You have to be able to go in and—and know the curriculum and understand how students learn, and you have to be willing to push teachers in that direction. And we're going to reap the rewards at the end, and so are the students, because that's what's best for them. So, you know, I think, continuing to have these high expectations where each of the subgroups that you're working with—and not leaving anybody out, finding a place for everyone and hiring the staff to support that, to support that mission, is important. (Southwest & West, 2005)

Like the elementary school principal above, these leaders seized this opportunity to create change in their schools through instructional leadership to bring about increased academic achievement of students in need of special services. They demonstrated the value of the school leader guiding teachers toward a new mindframe in preparing students and aligning curriculum and instruction to improve student learning at their schools. Another female elementary principal recognized,

> I really do think that it brought to light the fact that we had taken our special ed[ucation] students and were giving them an alternative curriculum and watering down and overaccommodating and really not maybe expecting as much of them as we should, and I think that was a very good thing, and it made me as a leader revamp a lot of what we were already doing. You've got to address that, so I think that was a good aspect of it. So, those are, I think, the main two areas where it has changed me as a leader and having to refocus on some areas that we had been able to just get by. (Principal 20, Southeast, 2005)

Principals were encouraged to move their campuses beyond the status quo. This entailed aspects of organizational learning—and relearning. NCLB encouraged teachers and administrators to move in new directions regarding curricular alignment to meet needs of each student on campus. There was agreement about the influence that a school leader must have when enacting change and moving teachers toward a common vision.

## CONCLUSION

This chapter informs practitioners, educational professors, and policy makers about the conflicts in the implementation of federal policy and the development of individual academic student needs. We recognize that in the initial struggles to meet federal policies' accommodations, both superintendents and principals certainly increased their leadership focus on curricular alignment. Inclusionary practices, as suggested by federal policies, in fact propelled several initiatives toward tighter alignment of curriculum, instruction, and assessment and higher expectations for all students.

The disaggregation of data contributed to the identification of students' achievement of curricular goals and revealed instructional disparities that detracted from the goal of meeting the needs of all children. Attention to different subgroups and these students' performance in schools strengthened the instructional focus for superintendents and principals to grapple with how this might be accomplished. However, when the attention shifted away from human conditions to measurements, there was a risk that students could become objectified, distancing these students who were most at risk of not passing tests from being legitimate beneficiaries of the educational enterprise. Thus, there is a perceived danger that ensuring that students can pass a state-mandated test may become the focus for teachers and administrators. This concern warrants further exploration as educators across the country face choices when attempting to meet the requirements of NCLB while maintaining quality education for all students and meeting IEP goals.

Accountability perspectives, curriculum development, delivery of instruction, social development, and the education of students in special instructional programs are key issues. Superintendents benefit from continuously performing alignment analysis based on state and national expectations to ensure the intended curricula, as established by the district, state, and nation, are properly delivered by schools and their teachers. Principals, in their turn, can develop personal relationships with teachers, students, and parents in the development of curricula based on a collective and inclusive philosophy of education, modify teachers' expectations for every child, and use research results to adjust practice. In all cases, studies are still needed to analyze the effects of narrowing the curriculum to meet high-stakes testing expectations and its long-term impact.

We recognize that even though school districts and schools require more guidance in meeting the expectations of federal policies, collectively, superintendents and principals in the Voices 3 project were generally invested in creating school improvements that would positively impact students. As teachers and parents join with leaders to promote the success of their students and children, it is our hope that the intentional efforts taken by superintendents and principals to adapt curriculum and instruction will create more inclusionary practices and bear good fruits in building stronger democratic communities of practice.

## RECOMMENDATIONS

The academic needs of all learners in a large sprawling social system like the U.S. public schools, and particularly the needs of those who diverge from the majority in background, ability, or propensity, is a complex problem. Our responses to how to do this in the past often have been misguided and insufficient. Learners with special needs often have not reaped the benefits promised by our education system, especially when ignored or pushed aside. We have enumerated in this chapter, based on the experiences of superintendents and principals, the ways in which federal requirements to bring increasingly larger proportions of students, including those with special needs, to meet state standards for literacy and numeracy in exchange for federal funding resulted in dramatic consequences. First, even though NCLB requires superintendents and principals to use data to adjust their planning and decision making to bring it into line with the needs of the actual students they serve, the 3% rule is applied to all schools and districts. So, this rule imposes a cruder decision making method on superintendents and principals than it requires them to use. Second, before NCLB, we had IDEA, a complex solution to a complex problem. In place of prescriptions, IDEA required multiple forms of data and multiple kinds of input, from educators and families together, and deliberation to reach consensus on an appropriate IEP. It was often an onerous process precisely because it was a complex solution to a complex problem. It is easily apparent that it would run afoul of NCLB's simple solution. Third, superintendents and principals demonstrated in the data that those they serve need many things besides the ability to score well on a mechanical assessment of academic proficiency. Superintendents' and principals' knowledge of this is hard won, from years of studying and working with children and their families. They understand the importance of the affective aspects of teaching and leading education. NCLB's clear and simple solution is to tell them, in effect, "De-emphasize the view you have of your constituents in service of the view distant policy makers have of them." Fourth, NCLB responds to the urgency of meeting the needs of all learners by establishing a timeline and prescribing sanctions for those who fail to meet it—instead of planning and funding the vast amount of organizational learning required for some 13,000 districts and nearly 100,000 public schools to retool to meet the needs of all learners.

Nonetheless, it is clear to us from the Voices 3 transcripts that NCLB has had some salutary effects. The superintendents and principals stated their commitments to the goals. We write this just as Congress is deliberating on the reauthorization of the Elementary and Secondary Education Act and considering how to honor NCLB's strengths and mitigate its drawbacks. In support of all public policy officials striving to improve education for all children, we offer these recommendations.

First, show appreciation of the complexities of the challenges faced by special needs children. Policy makers must avoid temptations to substitute for grappling with complex situations simple, across-the-board prescriptions like the 3% rule. The motives behind NCLB are salutary, and superintendents and principals praised those motives. Policy makers at the state and federal level can continue to advocate for inclusion of these children in the success public education promises. Preparation programs and professional development efforts should never cease to emphasize the importance of providing exemplary education to special needs children and provide requisite knowledge about the current best practices to do so effectively. Concurrently, leaders of public education in schools and districts must commit to ongoing learning for the long haul.

Second, the general public could be made more aware of the most important virtues of IDEA. IDEA, over time, has proven to be a successful piece of legislation providing effective guidelines to create equity and access for individuals with disabilities (U.S. Department of Education, 1996). These guidelines stressed the importance of integration and inclusion of students in need of special services in K-12 schools in order to consider the integration and inclusion of these individuals later in colleges and society. Its position has been that the needs of special education children vary and that no one solution or one expert can meet all those needs. The cost of diagnosing, deliberating upon, and addressing the needs of the special education child is high, not because educators are frivolous in spending, but because meeting the ideal of exploiting the potential of all children and future citizens is a lofty one. Engaging the child, his or her parents, the teachers, and other specialists in the decision consumes time and energy and requires a team approach. But this process makes far more sense than an edict from above that offers a sweeping prescription for all such children. On one hand, educational leadership preparation programs and professional developers must ensure that all decision makers throughout educational systems understand how to meet children's needs as effectively and efficiently as possible. On the other hand, practitioners must embrace the knowledge and the commitment to serve them well.

Third, more alignment is needed between public educators and policy makers. School administrators and public school educators must be part of educational decisions at state and federal levels—their perspectives should not be ignored during public policy deliberations. They are the fruits of the understanding of children and communities' complex needs and carry the knowledge of the necessary alignment about how best to serve those needs. Such understanding comes only from experiences.

Fourth, we need to reconsider the virtues of simple classification systems that categorize schools as either winners or losers. Honig (2008) called into question the assumption of policy makers that classify schools as low performing to motivate everyone concerned to address the situation and to remedy it. Honig noted "the deleterious effects" (p. 636) of people being repeatedly reminded of their inadequacy—and being conditioned over time to accept those effects and learning to live with them. Such effects can hardly contribute to the educational success of all learners. She called attention to the possible virtues of terms like *novice*, which emphasizes the road one is on and the learning and development still required. Such a seemingly slight wording change may well make a profound difference in educators' attitudes and commitment.

## FINAL THOUGHTS

Although findings provided concrete examples of the internal policy inconsistencies faced by superintendents and principals—inconsistencies that required enhanced organizational learning and adaptation—we do not see these inconsistencies as resulting in either–or choices for educators but rather in decisions that recognize a more systemic perspective that engages both educators and policy makers in dialogue and learning from one another about how to reconcile conflicting mandates around some guiding principles. Thus, we view leaders' responsibilities as strategically engaging in organizational learning about how to both meet accountability mandates and fulfill expectations for accommodating students with special needs.

Differentiating instruction has challenges and requires teacher expertise to know what strategies are successful for individual students. Reorganizing schools so that communities of professional practice continue to learn together can result in greater collective efficacy and a learning-partnership culture within the community (Acker-Hocevar, Cruz-Janzen, & Wilson, 2011). At the same time, educators must play a more proactive role in engaging with policy makers to educate them in regard to some of the issues through their organizations. The role of the leader to focus on learning of all students means that the leader understands how to have differentiated instruction and differentiated strategies for students. Students who need more assistance may translate more into students who need different assistance, but not at the expense of a nurturing school environment. Never should students be dehumanized because they may fail a state exam. Education is a human enterprise.

## REFERENCES

Acker-Hocevar, M., Cruz-Janzen, M. I., & Wilson, C. L. (2011). *Leadership from the ground up: Sustainable school improvement in traditionally low performing schools.* Charlotte, NC: Information Age.

Ananda, S. (2003). *Rethinking issues of alignment under No Child Left Behind.* San Francisco, CA: WestEd.

Bouck, E. C. (2009). No Child Left Behind, the Individuals With Disabilities Education Act and functional curricula: A conflict of interest? *Education and Training in Developmental Disabilities, 44*(1), 3-13.

Bowen, S. K., & Rude, H. A. (2006). Assessment and students with disabilities: Issues and challenges with educational reform. *Rural Special Education Quarterly, 25*(3), 24-30.

Capper, C. A., Rodríguez, M. A., & McKinney, S. A. (2010). Leading beyond disability: Integrated, socially just schools and districts. In C. Marshall & M.

Oliva (Eds.), *Leadership for social justice: Making revolutions in education* (2nd ed., pp. 173-193). Boston, MA: Allyn & Bacon.

Center on Education Policy. (2008). *Instructional time in elementary schools: A closer look at changes for specific subjects.* Retrieved from http://www.cep-dc.org/displayDocument.cfm?DocumentID=309

Diamond, J. B., & Spillane, J. P. (2004). High-stakes accountability in urban elementary schools: Challenging or reproducing inequality? *Teachers College Record, 106,* 1145-1176.

Education for All Handicapped Children Act, Pub. L. No. 94-142, 20 U.S.C. 1400 et seq. (1975).

Frattura, E. M., & Capper, C. (2007). *Leading for social justice: Transforming schools for all learners.* Thousand Oaks, CA: Corwin Press.

Gerstl-Pepin, C. I. (2006). The paradox of poverty narratives: Educators struggling with children left behind. *Educational Policy, 20*(1), 143-162.

Hardman, M. L., & Dawson, S. (2008). The impact of federal public policy on curriculum and instructions for students with disabilities in the general classroom. *Preventing School Failure, 52*(2), 5-11.

Honig, M. I. (2008). District central offices as learning organizations: How sociocultural and organizational learning theories elaborate district central office administrators' participation in teaching and learning improvement efforts. *American Journal of Education, 114,* 627-664.

Individuals With Disabilities Education Act Amendments of 1997, Pub. L. No. 102-17 (1997).

Individuals With Disabilities Education Improvement Act of 2004, Pub. L. No. 108-446 (2004).

Lasky, B., & Karge, B. D. (2006). Meeting the needs of students with disabilities: Experience and confidence of principals. *NASSP Bulletin, 90*(1), 19-36.

Leithwood, K., Harris, A., & Strauss, T. (2010). *Leading school turnaround: How successful leaders transform low-performing schools.* San Francisco, CA: Jossey-Bass.

Martone, A., & Sireci, S. G. (2009). Evaluating alignment among curriculum, assessments, and instruction. *Review of Educational Research, 79,* 1332-1361.

Mele-McCarthy, J. A. (2007). Approaches to assessment: IDEA and NCLB. *Perspectives on Language and Literacy, 33*(1), 25-30.

No Child Left Behind Act of 2001, Pub. L. No. 107-110 (2002).

Parrish, P. R., & Stodden, R. A. (2009). Aligning assessment and instruction with state standards for children with significant disabilities. *Teaching Exceptional Children, 41*(4), 46-56.

Roach, A. T., Niebling, B. C., & Kurz, A. (2008). Evaluating the alignment among curriculum, instruction, and assessments: Implications and applications for research and practice. *Psychology in the Schools, 45,* 158-176.

Rodríguez, M. A., Murakami-Ramalho, E., & Ruff, W. (2009). Urban elementary principals leading with heart: Social justice agents and community builders in historically underserved contexts. *Educational Considerations, 36*(2), 8-13.

Saldaña, J. (2009). *The coding manual for qualitative researchers.* Thousand Oaks, CA: SAGE.

Sorrentino, A., & Zirkel, P. A. (2004). Is NCLB leaving special education students behind? *Principal, 83*(5), 26-29.

Sunderman, G. L., Kim, J. S., & Orfield, G. (2005). *NCLB meets school realities: Lessons from the field.* Thousand Oaks, CA: Corwin Press.

U.S. Department of Education. (1996). *Eighteenth annual report to Congress on the implementation of the Individuals With Disabilities Education Act.* Washington, DC: Government Printing Office.

U.S. Department of Education. (2002). *Elementary and secondary education: Key policy letters signed by the Education Secretary or Deputy Secretary.* Retrieved from http://www2.ed.gov/policy/elsec/guid/secletter/020724.html

CHAPTER 5

# LEADERSHIP PRACTICES AND PROCESSES THAT IMPACT PERSONNEL, PROFESSIONAL DEVELOPMENT, AND TEACHER PROFESSIONALISM AND INFLUENCE SCHOOL IMPROVEMENT

**Betty J. Alford and Julia Ballenger**

Promoting learning in schools is a primary role of superintendents and principals (Matthews & Crow, 2003). Leaders establish conditions that can support continuous improvement through their actions (Bellamy, Fulmer, Murphy, & Muth, 2007). Leithwood and Riehl (2005) identified three major clusters of leadership actions instrumental to continuous improvement and school success: (a) setting direction, (b) developing people, and (c) redesigning the organization. Donaldson (2001) concluded that leadership actions influence whether reform efforts succeed or fail and thus impact overall school improvement over time. Personnel recruitment and

*Snapshots of School Leadership in the 21st Century:*
*Perils and Promises of Leading for Social Justice,*
*School Improvement, and Democratic Community*, pp. 75–95
Copyright © 2012 by Information Age Publishing

selection, professional development opportunities, and actions leaders take to reinforce certain values within the culture of teacher professionalism represent key leadership leverage points. These leverage points are (a) set direction, (b) determine assignments of responsibilities, (c) identify needs for ongoing professional development, and (d) challenge existing values and beliefs that run counter to school improvement.

In this chapter, we analyzed the data from superintendents and principals' voices for subthemes related to the three themes of personnel, professional development, and teacher professionalism. We situated the findings within school improvement, where each area has the potential to add or detract from the leader's efforts to promote overall growth. Both superintendents and principals recognized that personnel, professional development, and creating a culture of teacher professionalism are essential components for doing what is best for students in their districts and schools but did not describe the three areas as working in concert with one another. On one hand, these three areas are under the broader umbrella of the human resource's frame; on the other hand, these three areas relate directly to how leaders influence change using the human side of the educational enterprise to make school improvement gains.

To report the findings, we read all transcriptions and employed open coding and then axial coding to identify the subthemes presented under each of the three themes. In the process, we each coded the data independently and then debriefed with one other about our schemas across subthemes. We agreed on findings across the three major themes. In addition, we maintained an audit trail of our final analyses to further ensure trustworthiness of our findings and document the decisions we made together about the most representative quotes for each subtheme.

In the next section, we introduce our conceptual framework and describe the factors that impact recruitment and retention of personnel, needs and characteristics of professional development, and values and beliefs that lead to a culture of teacher professionalism. Leaders' actions, decisions, and responses in these three areas impact school improvement efforts.

## LEADERSHIP OF HUMAN RESOURCES

The literature on recruitment and retention of personnel, professional development, and professionalism discussed within leadership of human resources provides the collective knowledge of theorists and actions of national councils in informing what superintendents and principals need to know and be able to do to improve teacher and student learning. Both superintendents and principals play key roles in recruiting, hiring, assigning, and supporting school personnel. Their actions can foster a culture of professionalism and learning that propels school improvement, or their actions can serve as inhibitors of success. School improvement is not achieved on autopilot. It is hard work achieved by like-minded, committed teams of individuals who feel a deep moral vision to assist all students in achieving high levels of learning success (Sergiovanni, 2007).

The superintendent and principal are instrumental in personnel selection and assignment. Strategic leaders look for talent and plan for succession by engaging in recruitment and follow-up (Davies & Davies, 2005). The role of the superintendents and principals in building capacity in the district and the school includes hiring and assigning quality personnel. The principal, as a leader of learning on campus, is charged with the task of leading instructional reform to foster quality teaching for a student population that current teachers may or may not have been adequately prepared to teach. An important part of a leader's follow-up is providing quality professional development to assist teachers in their ongoing growth and development. As Chrispeels (2008) suggested, "Providing professional development for administrators and teachers to develop the knowledge and skills needed for shared leadership is an important second step in the process of learning to lead together" (p. 368). The first step is a clear rationale for shared leadership.

Hassel (1999) defined professional development as the process of improving staff skills and competencies needed to produce outstanding educational results for students. Over a decade ago, Darling-Hammond (1997) acknowledged that professional development can serve as a catalyst to provide every student with competent, caring, and qualified teachers. However, too often professional development for teachers has been fragmented, of low intellectual level, and not focused on student learning (Kent, 2005).

The National Staff Development Council (2005) raised the standards for conducting professional development in focusing on the importance of results-driven, collaborative, job-embedded professional development. Research identified characteristics of effective professional development. These characteristics include learning that is (a) collaborative; (b) job embedded; (c) aligned with student needs; (d) based on data analysis; and (e) supported with rigorous content standards, assessments, and curriculum (National Staff Development Council, 2005).

Although these characteristics are essential, Kruse, Seashore Louis, and Bryk (1995) identified two major sets of conditions that also must be addressed in order to produce quality professional development. One is structural. Superintendents and principals must structure the time for teachers to meet and talk, encourage interdependent teaching roles, establish systems of open communication, and empower teachers to make decisions about what is best for all students. The other condition is what Kruse et al. referred to as the culture of the organization. The culture encompasses openness to teacher improvement, trust and respect for teachers, and supportive leadership. Newmann and Wehlage (1995) stated, "If schools want to enhance their organizational capacity to boost student learning, they should work on building a professional community characterized by shared purpose, collaborative activity, and collective responsibility among staff" (p. 37). DuFour, DuFour, Eaker, and Many (2006) identified core interrelated elements of professional learning communities: (a) focus on learning for all, (b) a collaborative culture, (c) collective inquiry into best practice, (d) an action orientation, (e) a commitment to continuous improvement, (f) and a focus on results. Fullan (2005) acknowledged the complexity of developing professional learning communities in schools and noted that transforming the culture of the schools and the systems within which they operate is central to school improvement. Professional learning communities help to develop a new culture that supports ongoing improvement.

In a culture of professionalism, all educators assume the responsibility for improving the quality of teaching and learning for every student through positive actions. Superintendents, principals, and faculty might, for example, analyze students' performance data and consider obstacles to educational attainment that the schools themselves may be perpetuating (Nieto, 1999). For systemic changes to occur in school practices, policies, and processes to promote equity and excellence in schools, leadership at all levels is needed (Scheurich & Skrla, 2003). In order to achieve school improvement, promoting values of equity and social justice is important (Scheurich, Skrla, & Johnson, 2000) as well as an inherent belief among school participants that change can occur (Dantley, 2005).

## FINDINGS: SUPERINTENDENTS' VOICES

Emergent themes from the data included decisions of hiring, dismissing, or reassigning key personnel; provision of time for professional development; and recognition of the importance of professional development to school improvement. In addition, shifts to increased teacher professionalism emerged from the data as a theme.

### Personnel Decisions

In considering what matters in leadership for school improvement, personnel was a key factor expressed. Superintendent 23 stressed, "Personnel, they're the ones on the front line. As administrators, that's the place … where we can really have the most direct impact on students" (small-sized districts, Midwest, 2004). Making needed changes in personnel is complex. Superintendent 33 further described, "I spent my extra pool of money to find a highly qualified math teacher, but I was then unable to have that extra classroom aide that might more directly meet the needs of the students" (mixed medium & small-sized districts, Southwest & West, 2005). In this age of accountability, administrators must conduct an analysis of needs and make wise decisions in order to allocate limited resources in the best manner possible. Challenges include hiring and dismissal decisions.

### Hiring Decisions

A challenge is ensuring that the best principals and teachers are in place. Superintendent 31 described, "Placing the best teachers to teach the students really impacts student accountability. When you have the right people in place, you've done a lot for students and student accountability. That's been real hard" (mixed medium & small-sized districts, Southwest & West, 2005). Superintendent 33 added, "As Jim Collins points out in his book, *Good to Great*, you have to make sure the right people are on the bus first, and then you've got to have them in the right seats. That is a difficult personnel decision" (mixed medium & small-sized districts, Southwest & West, 2005).

Superintendents stressed the importance of alignment between the values and beliefs of the district and of persons who are employed. The superintendent is a primary communicator of the vision of the district. Superintendent 33 stressed, "If you have a long-term vision, and you base your decisions on that vision and do not waiver, your students will improve" (small-sized districts, Southwest & West, 2004). Superintendent 66 emphasized,

> When I interview, I do a monologue. I tell people that there are three things I want to cover. One is our values and beliefs, and if their values and beliefs don't match, then they shouldn't accept an offer, even if it's given. (medium-sized districts, New England & Mid-Atlantic, 2005)

### Dismissal of Personnel

Superintendent 33 elaborated on the difficulties in dismissing an incompetent teacher:

> Every piece of research shows that if you want to talk about student achievement and help students perform, it's all about the person that stands in front of the class. However, if you don't have the right person and you try to dismiss them, you deal with all the negative publicity and all the negative things. (mixed medium & small-sized districts, Southwest & West, 2005)

The superintendents acknowledged that in decisions to dismiss personnel they accepted the final responsibility for the decision. Superintendents expressed that these decisions were not best made by committee. Superintendents also shared that board members' personal agendas had to be recognized and avoided in decision making. Superintendent 2 pointed out,

> I've had to counsel out a couple of teachers and even ask for a resignation. It was a tough thing to do, but it was the right thing to do. It was a difficult decision, but in the big picture, it was the right decision to make. (small-sized districts, Midwest, 2004)

Superintendent 4 described the process of attaining documentation and dismissing a teacher who was also a friend. Superintendent 4 stated,

> It was difficult personally, but I think as long as you believe that what you are doing is right, and you use the old benchmark of what is good for students and really mean it, I think it makes things line up pretty easily in terms of what has to happen. (small-sized districts, Midwest, 2004)

### Reassignment of Personnel

Sometimes, seeking to promote learning meant reassignment of teachers rather than dismissal. Superintendent 58 explained, "We moved a middle school teacher to high school and made a couple of changes in personnel to get the math program in place" (medium-sized districts, Midwest, 2005).

## Professional Development

Another key factor in school improvement shared by the superintendents was professional development. Superintendent 58 made an often-heard comment: "We now spend a lot of money on professional development and focus on what we want to accomplish" (medium-sized districts, Midwest). He further stated, "We are finding ways to pool our resources so that we can be effective and make a substantial shift in math education." Superintendent 65 explained:

> As superintendent, you are responsible for all the principals and all the people. It doesn't just happen. It really requires nurturing and then setting goals with them and holding people accountable. This has been primarily with the administrators, but also recognizing teacher leaders and recognizing what their roles can be in influencing and improving student learning in the respective school is important. (medium-sized districts, New England & Middle Atlantic, 2005)

### Challenges in Professional Development

Some superintendents also struggled with the need to provide time for professional development when it took time away from instruction. Superintendent 64 reinforced a point made by many: "To me, the biggest resource we have is the teacher time with students every day and then to be able to make that [instructional time] the most productive" (medium-sized districts, New England & Mid-Atlantic, 2005). Superintendent 16 added, "We do offer staff development. I just don't think you should take time away from instruction" (medium-sized districts, Southeast, 2006).

### The Importance of Professional Development

The balance between the need for instructional time and the need for professional development was not voiced as a conflict for many additional superintendents. The following comment captures the views shared by many superintendents. Superintendent 58 noted,

> We are going to invest in people. That is our business. We now spend a lot of money on professional development. We will send them wherever we have to, whatever it costs to get what they need to be successful. (medium-sized districts, Midwest)

The responsibility for ongoing learning to achieve school improvement is a key feature of teacher professionalism as teachers and administrators broaden their roles to foster enhanced student learning.

## Teacher Professionalism

Teacher professionalism in this age of accountability includes an increased emphasis on collaborative planning rather than teaching in isolation. When school principals involve teachers in collaborative planning as they lead school improvement efforts, teacher professionalism is strengthened.

### Shifts in Responsibilities

Promoting teacher professionalism resulted in shifts in responsibilities for teachers as well as for central office administrators. For teachers, additional responsibilities have been added in seeking to promote learning. Superintendent 16 articulated, "We've started a lot of new programs like Saturday School and an after-school extended summer school and remediation through high school" (medium-sized districts, Southeast, 2005). Superintendent 57 described this shift in responsibility: "We had to change the mindset of central office as a place to go for garbage bags to a place to get guidance about curriculum" (medium-sized districts, Midwest, 2005).

### Fostering a Professional Learning Community

Engaging teachers as professionals as part of a team to promote learning was cited by many superintendents as a vital part of the district improvement process. Superintendent 31 stated, "When I first got to the district, it was just seeking to move from an underperforming label. What we did was to set up a professional learning community. Within a year, we moved from low performing" (mixed small & medium-sized districts, Southwest & West, 2005). The emphasis on trying to build a professional learning community involves collaborative planning with teachers as professionals.

### Fostering Collaborative Decision Making for Teacher Professionalism

Superintendents expressed that viewing teachers as a true part of the professional team involved engaging them in decision making, data analysis, planning, and evaluation; yet, at times the decisions were not collaborative. While there was strong consensus that teachers as professionals need to be part of decision making, superintendents were quick to add that not all decisions are collaborative. Superintendent 2 described his decision to lock down schools for safety versus a curriculum decision:

> I made the news on three different channels because I locked down every one of our schools because we had a real threat of someone's going to shoot somebody. It was not a decision we made as a group. I didn't bring all my principals in. On the basis of the information, I made the decision. (medium-sized districts, Southwest & West, 2006)

In contrast, this same superintendent described the district's decision to implement Reading First across the district as a consensus decision (Superintendent 2, medium-sized districts, Southwest & West, 2006). Superintendent 3 expressed the view that was shared by many: "If you want their support, you have to involve the staff in decision making" (small-sized districts, Southwest & West, 2004).

### Promoting Shared Values

The two primary guiding values evident across all the interviews were "What's in the best interest of the students?" and "The function of schools is to promote learning." Repeatedly, superintendents expressed a focus on seeking to do what is best for students. Superintendent 35 emphasized this point by saying, "I'm betting that all four of us [in this focus group] work as hard as we can to promote our district where we live because we think this is what's best for students" (small-sized districts, Midwest, 2004). However, as this superintendent further pointed out, "I think the most difficult part of that is that it comes down to leadership making sure that 120–150 other employees are on the same page and have the same belief, and that is what leadership is about." Making decisions based on this principle does not always lead to an easy decision. Superintendent 77 shared,

> In my 20+ years as a superintendent, I've seen a real shift in demands by parents, community, and special interest groups, and I think doing what's right for students has taken a whole different perspective. It's tough work when you are bombarded by all these different groups and people making demands, and you have to help your board to stay on course and make decisions that are best for students, and educating them can be tougher every day. (medium-sized districts, Midwest, 2005)

The first guiding principle conveyed repeatedly by superintendents of "what's best for students" was reinforced by a second guiding principle heard repeatedly, that is, that the school's primary function is to promote learning. This involves choices and trying to meet individual differences. Superintendent 3 explained:

> I would think every decision that I make, I try to weigh and balance how it impacts students in the learning process. For example, when we employ individuals, do I employ the best possible person for the children? Am I doing the best thing for the children, or do I employ someone who is not as well qualified or experienced? Have I provided the best learning environment for students in our system? Am I using the resources that are allocated in a manner that will enhance learning and enhance teacher morale? (medium-sized districts, Southeast, 2005)

The superintendents' voices reverberated with the importance of providing leadership that makes a positive difference. Making wise decisions regarding personnel, providing quality professional development, and engaging teachers as professionals were cited as actions that mattered greatly in achieving school improvement. Likewise, leaders were aware of the complexity of these tasks.

## FINDINGS: PRINCIPALS' VOICES

The roles of principals in leading school improvement are challenging. These roles entail decisions about personnel and professional development to lead schools to places where all students are learning at high levels. Emergent themes in making wise decisions regarding hiring, dismissal, or reassignment of personnel; fostering quality professional development; and strengthening teacher professionalism characterized vital roles of principals in the school improvement process.


## Personnel Decisions

Personnel decisions impact student performance. Principal 27 related, "Those students who need the best teachers are usually the ones who have the poorest teachers. We need leaders with the strength to look at the total school to realize what is needed and to do something about it" (high schools, Southeast, 2005). These decisions involve hiring, dismissal, and reassignment of personnel.

### Hiring Decisions
Hiring the best people for the school can be difficult, as Principal 15 expressed:

> I think it's most important to have the right people within the school. It appears this would be an easy task with so many applicants, but it's such a difficult task to really have the kind of staff you want for a school. (elementary schools, Southwest & West, 2005)

Principal 5 further explained, "Some of the decisions you make in hiring or what you do in your school may not be the most popular, but they might be the best for the students" (elementary schools, Midwest, 2005).

### Dismissal of Personnel
Sometimes what is needed is dismissal of personnel, and the decision is always hard. In issues of dismissal of teachers, principals explained that the decisions are not collaborative ones. For example, Principal 4 stated,

> We had a teacher, very well known in the district, but we did not renew her contract, and it was in the best interest of students. There was a lot of repercussion because we couldn't reveal the reasons, but we've got to do what's best for our students. (elementary schools, Midwest, 2005)

Principal 2 stated an often-repeated view, "There are some situations like a personnel issue where you would like people to know the whole story, but you can't. It makes it tough sometimes and hard to deal with" (elementary schools, Midwest, 2005). Sometimes, rather than dismissal of personnel, reassignment is needed.

### Reassignment of Personnel
The benefits of reassignment of personnel may not be immediately realized. As Principal 17 reported,

Sometimes, you see that someone needs to move to a different grade level, but they don't. I've moved people to different grade levels with the individuals kicking and screaming, and then he or she would later tell me, "I'm glad you moved me." (elementary schools, Southwest & West, 2005)

Making decisions based on the guiding principle of what's best for students does not mean that the decisions will always be popular.

Principals' voices were clear that personnel decisions are highly important in the school improvement process. The work is not easy, but principals are in a key position to influence change. Principal 60 expressed poignantly, "I got into administration to affect more change and to contribute more" (elementary schools, urban, Midwest, 2005).

## Professional Development

Quality professional development is a key factor in achieving change in schools. Although principals repeatedly acknowledged the importance of hiring the right individuals for specific jobs, principals clearly described professional development as instrumental in school improvement efforts. These principals participated with their teachers in professional learning communities.

### The Importance of Professional Development

Principals' use of book studies as a form of professional development not only resulted in building the capacity of teachers to improve instruction but also enabled teachers to focus on student learning. Elementary school Principal 4 modeled ideas learned from two books, as he explained, "I read *Professional Learning Communities* and *Whatever it Takes,* and I modeled that with my staff. Within 2 years, we got state recognition as a distinguished school.... It does work, but everybody has to be on the same page" (Midwest, 2005). Professional development occurred in dialogue and courageous conversations:

> Systemically, all of our staff meetings went from gripe sessions to an issue that dealt with students. They became children-centered meetings.... We discussed what we're going to do with an extended-day program. Staff meetings became brainstorming meetings around issues and solutions on how to best to meet the needs of the students. (Principal 85, high schools, Midwest, 2006)

### Challenges in Professional Development

There have been challenges associated with professional development. Not all share the goal of working together for school improvement. Principal 2 explained:

We want that [collaborative time to analyze data and plan lessons in response] to drive their instruction to study the standards and benchmarks, and still some people will tell you what you are hoping to hear, I guess, within your team meetings. But then, once they've walked through the door and you go into the classrooms to see how things are going, you see that they are not quite buying into the things that you have going on at your school. That has been a big disappointment for me. (elementary schools, Midwest, 2005)

There is also a balance on time in the classroom versus time in professional development. Principal 6 shared a common frustration:

I have a real frustration when teachers are pulled from the classroom to do school improvement or to do curriculum. I think there is a balance there. There is only so much time you have in a day, and time on task is really critical in the classroom. (Midwest, 2004)

The need to have teachers present in classrooms instructing students versus the need to have them participate in professional development was a challenge identified by principals. Professional development matters, but it must be targeted and sustained over time. There may still be some resistance to change, but positive results are achieved from targeted professional development, and teacher professionalism is strengthened.

## Teacher Professionalism

Teacher professionalism in this age of accountability includes an increased emphasis on collaborative planning rather than teaching in isolation. Teacher professionalism has been strengthened in many instances as school principals involved all teachers in decision making, data analysis, and collaborative planning as they led school improvement processes. Teacher professionalism includes shifts in responsibilities, fostering a professional learning community, fostering collaborative decision making, and promoting shared values.

### Shifts in Responsibilities

Teachers have sometimes been resistant to changes in professional responsibilities as schools seek to become professional learning communities. Principal 19 described a common problem by stating, "Our teachers are having such a hard time with change. I think a key to all of this is communication, just communicating and having those crucial conversations" (elementary schools, Southwest & West, 2005). Some principals voiced that it can be disheartening when teacher professionalism is not reflected by all faculty members. Principal 16 shared, "I think it is disappointing that some teachers are not buying into what we're trying to do. We have collaborative time set for teachers to look at data and develop lesson plans, but not all buy in" (elementary schools, Southwest & West, 2005). However, as principals also pointed out, even with some disappointments, collaborative decision making has been positive and is necessary in this age of accountability.

### Fostering a Professional Learning Community

In the professional development communities described by principals, teachers worked together for the improvement of instruction. Data analysis and problem solving were key practices as teachers engaged as professionals in school improvement processes. Principal 5 shared another representative comment, "Disaggregating data is such an eyeopener. The teacher can no longer just shut the door. Teachers must work together" (elementary schools, Midwest, 2005). By working together, teachers served as leaders in improvement processes and strengthened the collaborative culture of the school. Collaborative decision making was a vital process in these efforts.

### Fostering Collaborative Decision Making

Principals are providing multiple opportunities for faculty input, as Principal 1 pointed out: "We have a lot of opportunities for shared decision making" (elementary schools, Midwest, 2005). Principals' voices reinforced that part of working together as true professionals in the school is engaging in inquiry and collaborative planning.

Principals in this study recognized the value of engaging all teachers as professionals in the process of collaborative planning. Principal 55 expressed a commonly stated view, "I think teachers want ownership and involvement or to be part of the educational process" (elementary schools, urban, Midwest, 2005).

### Promoting Shared Values

Principals repeatedly referred to "what's best for students" as well as "promoting learning" as beliefs that guide their actions. Furthermore, the principals viewed their roles as ensuring that the faculty also shared these guiding beliefs as professionals. Principal 17 emphasized, "I think part of doing what is best for students is aligning your staff in having the same vision and philosophy" (elementary schools, Southwest & West, 2005). While acknowledging that people, not programs, are ultimately responsible for promoting learning, principals also pointed out that they are constantly seeking resources that may be useful for the school in fulfilling the school's mission. The most consistent theme across all the principals interviewed for this study was the view in decision making that "it's all about the student." In making consensus decisions, principals emphasized that the guiding principle in decision making was, "What's best for students?" Doing what is best for students and being truly democratic means looking out for the interests of each individual. Principal 80 explained, "We try not to answer a building-level question without answering with, 'How does this decision affect students, and is it best for students?'" (high schools, West, 2006).

Principal 5 reinforced the challenge of putting students first. He explained,

> My challenge has been to get teachers to buy into that it's really not about them. It is about the children and to actually operate and to teach and to live with that thought process. A lot of the decisions that are made are: "How am I going to make my day easier? If I can do it this way, this will save me about 15 minutes." However, if you give that little extra effort, if you go that extra step, then the whole class will benefit. The children will actually benefit. That has been an interesting challenge for me. (high schools, Southeast, 2005)

All decisions based on what is best for students are not clear cut, as Principal 86 emphasized:

> Those of us who are really student centered, we live in that gray daily. We understand the gray. We see the gray, and we're very willing to make decisions within the gray. If we truly see that this student has a better chance of learning from this situation if this is our course of action, then we make the decision. (high schools, West, 2006)

It is also easier to espouse the belief in what's best for students as a guiding belief than to follow through and ensure that our actions model this belief. Principal 35 expressed this challenge by asking, "Is it best for students? We ask this question all the time, but sometimes we do what's best for ourselves as adults" (elementary schools, Southwest & West, 2006).

The second guiding belief that was frequently expressed was the belief that everyone should work to promote learning. Principals' focus on learning helped in modeling this guiding belief, as Principal 4 elaborated:

> I always had aspirations to be an administrator, so I was closely watching my principal and looking at his behavior, and his mantra was, "It is not about bricks and mortar, but it's about teaching and learning." If it was not about teaching and learning, it just did not fly in his building. So, that, to me, had

the greatest impact and has helped mold me as an administrator today. (high schools, Southeast, 2005)

These guiding principles of what's best for students and an emphasis on promoting learning, in summary, are not always easy to attain as principals work with personnel matters, professional development issues, and teachers as professionals. Nonetheless, principals affirmed the importance of their work. Principal 61 stressed, "It's frustrating sometimes, but knowing that I affect 360 students in my building is a great privilege" (elementary, schools, Midwest, 2005).

The role of the principal is complex in working with personnel, professional development, and teacher professionalism. The principals' voices in this study reinforced that the principal must seek resources not readily available, strengthen teacher morale amid accountability pressures, and maintain a common focus while also encouraging creativity. Principals stressed individual needs must be met even while collective needs are addressed. As Principal 84 stressed, "The first thing is that even at the high school level you need to look at the individual needs, and what's good for the masses isn't always good for the individual" (high schools, West, 2006). Principals emphasized that all educators must consider the needs of each child as they promote learning for all.

## COMPARISON: SIMILARITIES AND DIFFERENCES

In comparing similarities and differences in the major themes emerging from the data analysis relative to the areas of personnel, professional development, and professionalism of teachers, the complexity of superintendents' and principals' roles in fostering those components of school improvement emerged. The importance of key beliefs in guiding actions, the roles and issues in fostering collaborative decision making, and a recognition of what matters in leadership for school improvement also emerged as primary areas of comparison of similarities and differences.

### Complexity of the Roles of Superintendents and Principals

Both superintendents and principals recognized the complexity of their roles. An understanding of how to lead school improvement is crucial for the success of both superintendents and principals. The differences lay more in their spheres of primary influence. Superintendents primarily influenced the central office staff, principals, and teachers, whereas the principals had the greatest influence on the teachers and the actions of the campus personnel. Because of this influence, hiring, assignment of personnel, and professional development were very important to both superintendents and principals. Superintendents were cognizant that the building principal plays a tremendous role in the culture of the school. Both superintendents and principals were vitally aware of the crucial role of teachers in promoting learning. Leithwood and Riehl (2005) suggested that the principal is second only to the teacher in school influences on student learning, and the principal is the primary determiner of school culture.

Both superintendents and principals play vital roles in school improvement, and their effectiveness influences school results. Duffy (2003) emphasized that the superintendent's communication of a clear vision for the district is essential for school effectiveness since a superintendent can block the efforts of principals. The superintendent is also a primary voice to the school board and the community stakeholders who can work to either accomplish or to dismantle a school improvement effort. Just as the superintendent is instrumental in supporting and paving the way for successful implementation of new ideas, the principal is key to supporting and paving the way for teachers and also serves as a buffer for teachers. For example, principals may request a change, but the superintendent must support this change for the improvement to occur. Teachers may express a need for professional development, for example, and the principal can be instrumental in providing the resources to make this possible. However, even with professional development, achieving change is not easy.

In the age of accountability both superintendents' and principals' roles are multifaceted and varied. Their duties are diverse, such as maintaining safety; supporting student achievement; working toward equity and excellence; engaging faculty in planning and learning together and serving as a colearner; and hiring, assigning, evaluating, and possibly reassigning or dismissing personnel. The intricacy of both superintendents' and principals' roles was clearly evident in the data from this study. Both superintendents and principals recognized that they played primary roles in decision making and communication of the district and school vision for student learning, but they also recognized that they faced decisions about multifaceted issues without clear-cut solutions. The importance of basing actions on guiding beliefs rather than a rule book was voiced by both superintendents and principals.

## The Importance of Key Beliefs in Guiding Actions

Overwhelmingly, the most often expressed principle upon which to base decisions and actions that was voiced by both superintendents and principals was what's best for students. This belief served as the foundation for the planning and implementation. Both superintendents and principals were clear that students must achieve to high levels in order to be successful and that they held responsibility for ensuring that learning occurs. They cited doing what's best for students in describing decisions regarding personnel selection and professional development. They also expressed that an essential component of professionalism was the acceptance of this guiding belief.

The second primary guiding belief voiced by both superintendents and principals was that the essential function of the school is the improvement of learning. Building the capacity of the faculty was expressed as crucial in this task. Both superintendents and principals believed in the importance of promoting student learning as the basis of all personnel decisions. Personnel decisions and decisions about professional development were all centered around the need to promote student learning. However, even with this guiding belief, the need to have teachers in the classroom and the need for professional development were competing priorities.

Superintendents were largely directly responsible in considering the professional development of principals, whereas principals were primarily responsible for professional development for campus personnel. Instituting book studies was an emergent and growing form of professional development for principals and for teachers. Also, the promotion of collaborative planning in professional learning communities was discussed. Principals believed teacher engagement in designing and promoting school improvement resulted in greater teacher buy-in.

## The Roles and Issues in Fostering Collaborative Decision Making

Both superintendents and principals expressed that collaborative decision making is a way of strengthening commitment to common goals. However, both superintendents and principals reinforced that in decisions to dismiss an employee, the decision rested with the administrator, and often confidential information could not legally be shared that would help others to understand the decision. The absence of information often caused controversy for both superintendents and principals with an unpleasant backlash against the decision. In these instances, both superintendents and principals returned to the two guiding principles that influenced their decisions in order to maintain their resolve and weather any controversies that resulted.

Both superintendents and principals expressed concerns that personal agendas sometimes influenced decision making of stakeholders. Superintendents referred to board members and community member's personal agendas, whereas principals referred to the personal agendas of teachers. When the motive for actions was not whether the decision was best for students, principals found that their role changed from a collaborator to an enforcer of what is best for students rather than what is convenient for teachers. In collaborative decision making, principals voiced the need to keep decisions focused on the guiding principles of "What's best for students?" and "Is this promoting learning?" Principals viewed engaging faculty in professional learning communities, collaborative decision making, and ongoing improvement processes as vitally important. While the superintendent focused on systemwide improvements, the principal primarily focused on campus-based reforms.

## What Matters in Leadership for School Improvement

Both superintendents and principals consistently voiced recognition of what matters in leadership regarding personnel, professional development, and teacher professionalism. Superintendents and principals agreed professional development was essential in leadership for school improvement. However, principals consistently shared more specific examples of benefits of professional development than the superintendents. Both principals and superintendents struggled with the need to provide time for professional development while also keeping teachers in the classrooms instructing the maximum time possible.

## IMPLICATIONS FOR PRACTICE

Implications for practice included the following. Leadership involves steadfastness in daring to make a difference, finding a way when there is no way, and seeing firsthand that which is under consideration, as well as reflection and action (Duffy, 2003). Voices 3 superintendents and principals would agree. They viewed personnel decisions and provision of professional development as vital to the leader's success in accomplishing goals. They believed in strengthening a professional learning community wherein teacher professionalism is a vital component. They also believed in professional development inclusive of data analysis, collaborative planning, and focused learning activities.

Administrator leadership programs should assist both superintendents and principals in recognizing the values of fostering teacher leadership and in strengthening teacher professionalism in schools. Administrator preparation programs also must engage educational administration candidates in dialogue about issues of equity and excellence; about gray areas in decision making; about the importance of basing decisions on guiding principles; and about the importance of sound decision making in hiring, assignment, and dismissal. In short, administrator preparation programs must prepare school superintendents and principals for the complexity of their multiple roles as school leaders while igniting their passion to make a positive difference in promoting leaders who will serve as leaders of school improvement; advocates of social justice; and democratic, collaborative leaders. The voices of superintendents and principals support the importance of personnel decisions, professional development, and teacher leadership in meeting the goals of school improvement in an environment where democratic practices and an emphasis on equity and excellence prevailed. They also suggest that the work is difficult, although the intrinsic rewards are many.

## CONCLUSIONS AND RECOMMENDATIONS

Superintendents' and principals' efficacy matters in fostering personnel selection, professional development, and teacher professionalism for school improvement. In principal and superintendent preparation programs, an emphasis matters on developing the will to make a positive difference through leadership and enhancing the knowledge and skills to do so. The voices of these superintendents and principals reflect ways that these processes develop when a clear focus on the mission of school improvement is maintained. Leaders must believe that they can impact change and understand effective ways to do so (Leithwood & Riehl, 2005). In this age of accountability, we have learned the benefits of collaborative planning, the importance of considering equity and excellence as goals, the value of data analysis, and the strengths realized through quality teachers and leadership. Their voices also reflect the enormity of the responsibilities and the commitment required to fulfill multifaceted roles in an age of accountability. Their voices provide directions for areas of emphasis in school leadership programs and inspiration for ongoing improvement of preparation and professional development processes.

The superintendents and principals understood the benefits of collaborative planning, the importance of considering both equity and excellence as goals, and the strengths realized through quality professional development. They described teacher professionalism through shared decision making and developing professional learning communities. Superintendents and principals recognized that the greatest resource in a school is a quality teaching faculty. These administrators acknowledged that difficult decisions had to be made related to firing incompetent teachers. To maintain a quality faculty, a system must be in place to ensure that teachers have the pedagogical skills, academic knowledge, and genuine care for all students' success. We recommend that principals implement proactive actions to ensure quality faculty by ensuring that each teacher has the appropriate assignment, necessary resources, and necessary support to best meet student needs.

The superintendents and principals voiced the importance of fostering teacher professionalism through collaborative planning and quality professional development. Thus, professional preparation for superintendents and principals must equip future administrators with the knowledge, will, and skills essential in fostering a democratic school environment wherein the voices of all are heard and the needs of all are met. Doing so can help to ensure that personnel contribute to strong collaborative efforts that, indeed, promote learning for all students.

## REFERENCES

Bellamy, G. T., Fulmer, C. L., Murphy, M. J., & Muth, R. (2007). *Principal accomplishments: How school leaders succeed.* New York, NY: Teachers College Press.

Chrispeels, J. H. (Ed.). (2008). *Learning to lead together: The promise and challenge of sharing leadership.* Thousand Oaks, CA: SAGE.

Dantley, M. E. (2005). Moral leadership: Shifting the management paradigm. In F. English (Ed.), *The SAGE handbook of educational leadership: Advances in theory, research and practice* (pp. 34-46). Thousand Oaks, CA: SAGE.

Darling-Hammond, L. (1997). *Doing what matters most: Investing in quality teaching.* New York, NY: National Commission on Teaching and America's Future.

Davies, B., & Davies, B. J. (2005). Strategic leadership. In B. Davies (Ed.), *The essentials of school leadership* (pp. 10-30). Thousand Oaks, CA: SAGE.

Donaldson, G. A., Jr. (2001). *Cultivating leadership in schools: Connecting people, purpose, and practice.* New York, NY: Teachers College Press.

Duffy, F. (2003). *Courage, passion, and vision: A guide to leading systemic school improvement.* Lanham, MD: Scarecrow.

DuFour, R., DuFour, R., Eaker, R., & Many, T. (2006). *Learning by doing: A handbook for professional learning communities at work.* Bloomington, IN: Solution Tree.

Fullan, M. (2005). *The new meaning of educational change* (4th ed.). New York, NY: Teachers College Press.

Hassel, E. (1999). *Professional development: Learning from the best.* Oak Brook, IL: North Central Regional Educational Laboratory.

Kent, A. (2005). Improving teacher quality through professional development. *Education, 124,* 427-435.

Kruse, S., Seashore Louis, K., & Bryk, A. (1995). *Building professional learning in schools.* Madison, WI: Center on Organization and Restructuring of Schools.

Leithwood, K. A., & Riehl, C. (2005). What do we already know about educational leadership? In W. A. Firestone & C. Riehl (Eds.), *A new agenda for research in educational leadership* (pp. 12-27). New York, NY: Teachers College Press.

Matthews, L. J., & Crow, G. M. (2003). *Being and becoming a principal: Role concep-tions for contemporary principals and assistant principals.* Boston, MA: Pearson Education.

National Staff Development Council. (2005). *Standards of practice for professional development.* Oxford, OH: Author.

Newmann, F. M., & Wehlage, G. (1995). *Successful school restructuring: A report to the public and educators.* Alexandria, VA: Association for Supervision and Curricu-lum Development.

Nieto, S. (1999). *The light in their eyes.* New York, NY: Teachers College.

Scheurich, J. J., & Skrla, L. (2003). *Leadership for equity and excellence: Creating high achieving classrooms, schools, and districts.* Thousand Oaks, CA: Corwin Press.

Scheurich, J. J., Skrla, L., & Johnson, J. F. (2000). Think carefully about equity and accountability. *Phi Delta Kappan, 82,* 293-299.

Sergiovanni, T. I. (2007). *Rethinking leadership: A collection of articles* (2nd ed.). Thousand Oaks, CA: Corwin Press.

CHAPTER 6

# ASSESSMENT

**Sally Hipp and Jacquelyn Melin**

State assessments are the means used to determine whether schools have been successful in teaching students the knowledge, reasoning, and skills defined in each state's content and achievement standards. The goal of the No Child Left Behind Act of 2001 (NCLB, 2002) is to have all students in the United States reach the level of "proficient" on state assessments in reading and mathematics by 2014. Since the 2005–2006 school year, every state that accepts federal funding is required to assess annually students in reading and mathematics in Grades 3–8, plus once in high school. States must publicize assessment results for each school, or they may lose federal funding. As Adequate Yearly Progress (AYP) on state assessments has such important consequences, we discuss how the NCLB testing environment affects what superintendents and principals reported. We analyzed qualitative data obtained through Voices From the Field: Phase 3 (Voices 3) interview transcripts using methods frequently cited by qualitative researchers (Bogdan & Biklen, 1992). Transcripts were read twice and coded. The codes were then collapsed into larger themes and subthemes described by the participants. The chapter focuses on the themes and subthemes that address the following questions:

1.  How are the politics of NCLB connected to assessment practices?

*Snapshots of School Leadership in the 21st Century:*
*Perils and Promises of Leading for Social Justice,*
*School Improvement, and Democratic Community*, pp. 97–119
Copyright © 2012 by Information Age Publishing
All rights of reproduction in any form reserved.

2.  How does the emphasis on assessment required by NCLB affect teaching and learning?
3.  Is the assessment required by NCLB an equitable way to assess the progress of students who differ in race, socioeconomic status, culture, special needs, and limited English proficiency?
4.  How do these assessments relate to school improvement?

Although all four of these questions are addressed, superintendents and principals expressed most of their concerns about assessment primarily on how assessment related to teaching and learning. Therefore, Question 2 is addressed in greater detail.

## A HISTORICAL PERSPECTIVE ON ASSESSMENT

Public education in the United States is regarded by many as one of our finest national accomplishments. We founded our public education system on cornerstones of democracy and an educated and informed citizenry (Popham, 2001). Specifically, consistent with the principles of democracy, the public school system offers our children a path to success—presumably available to all students. However, in recent history, there have been periods of widespread discontent with public education. One such period was in 1957, with the launching of Sputnik. Until that time, most citizens assumed students were learning what they needed to learn and teachers were teaching what was expected to be taught. The launch of Sputnik brought U.S. citizenry to the realization that American students might be behind Soviet students in science and mathematics.

Because widespread concern often brings about legislative responses, in 1958 the National Defense Education Act passed and refocused education on science and mathematics. This marked the beginning of a new wave of federal involvement in schools and set the stage for the creation of the U.S. Department of Education in the late 1970s.

The United States allocated substantial funds in 1965 with the passage of the Elementary and Secondary Education Act. Before then, relatively few federal dollars flowed from Washington, DC, to local school districts. NCLB (2002) reauthorized the Elementary and Secondary Education Act and required states to administer annual tests to assess overall student performance. The current emphasis on using tests to evaluate school systems, schools, and students can be traced back to this initial act of Congress in 1965 (Nichols & Berliner, 2007). Prior to the passage of NCLB, many states had adopted minimum competency tests to ensure all students leaving school would have the ability to read and do basic mathematics. However, there is a big difference between these minimum competency tests and the high-stakes tests of the NCLB era. Although students could be denied a diploma for not passing the tests prior to NCLB, there was little consequence for teachers or schools for lagging student achievement (Nichols & Berliner, 2007).

During the 1970s and early 1980s, discontent with the public schools continued to grow. This discontent fueled the idea that our public schools were not as good as schools in other nations. By the late 1980s, most states established some type of state-mandated testing program (Popham, 2001). Some of the testing programs included norm-referenced tests. These types of tests allowed for a comparison of one student's skills to another student in his or her age group. Examples of these tests include the Iowa Test of Basic Skills, the Metropolitan Achievement Tests, and the Stanford Achievement Test Series. These tests are still in use today in many U.S. public schools. Additionally, most states established criterion-referenced tests that measured how well a student learned a specific body of knowledge and the corresponding skills associated with applying that knowledge.

When newspapers began to publish test scores for different schools, the public viewed these scores as a ranking of instructional quality in a given school with comparisons across schools. Attention given in the 1990s to achievement tests and scores helped fuel a preoccupation with assessments as a proxy for evaluating school effectiveness and improvement. School boards demanded their school administrators improve student test scores. Superintendents' and principals' evaluations hinged on student test scores and improvements on standardized achievement tests. This set the stage for the most comprehensive change to date in American education legislation.

In 2002, President George Bush signed NCLB into law. This law has become more consequential than any other federal initiative in the history of U.S. schools (Abernathy, 2007). The first goal of NCLB was to close the achievement gap between minority and nonminority students and between educationally disadvantaged children and their more educationally advantaged peers (Harris & Harrington, 2006). The second goal was to create and implement an assessment regime with significant consequences that held schools and school systems accountable for improvements with all subgroups (Peterson & West, 2003).

## LITERATURE REVIEW

### How the Politics of NCLB Connect to Assessment Practices

Politicians have long been interested in how well our schools are doing. The agreement to form the U.S. Department of Education in 1979 suggests education is a national interest. In 2010, the U.S. Department of Education administered a budget of $69.9 billion in discretionary appropriations (U.S. Department of Education, 2011). This is an immense change in the investment of taxpayers' monies from no department devoted solely to education (prior to 1979) to now.

How are our schools doing? This question seems so simple and the answers seem so complex. To know how our schools are doing requires we know how well children in our schools are learning. This also requires we know what our children are learning. Standardization of curricula and outcomes makes comparisons easier among children, among schools, among districts, and even among states. Comparisons, however, are difficult to make when each state is responsible for writing its own standards and assessments. Wallis and Steptoe (2007) found levels of proficiency on high-stakes assessments vary from state to state, with wide differences reported in quality of content standards and assessments.

The politics around NCLB first surfaced when the law passed Congress in 2002. NCLB consisted of what Hill (2007) would call "conservative ideas—testing, accountability, and incentives—wrapped in liberal clothing—a big federal program that seeks, as its primary objective, the equalization not only of educational opportunity but also of educational outcomes" (p. 272). A left–right coalition successfully guided NCLB through Congress. Now, NCLB faces both conservative and liberal opponents.

## How the Emphasis on Assessment Required by NCLB Affects Teaching and Learning

One of the themes emerging from the literature about assessment written between 2000 and 2006 was the emphasis placed on annual state assessments. Standards-based tests and students' abilities to pass them are at the foundation of the NCLB legislation. Numerous studies have investigated the effects of state-mandated assessment programs. Most of these studies have addressed the effects on teaching and learning; strategies used to deliver instruction; test preparation; and the psychological effects of these tests on students and teachers regarding pressure, morale, and motivation. Some negative consequences to state-mandated assessments surfaced in the literature and included (a) overemphasizing a single, annual test; (b) narrowing the curriculum; (c) teaching to the test; (d) cheating by administrators and teachers; and (e) declining staff morale (Nichols & Berliner, 2005).

### Overemphasizing a Single, Annual Test

School leaders have many concerns about putting so much emphasis on a single, annual test. One test cannot tell much about a student, and a year's education is too complex to reduce learning to that single test focused on only one aspect of a truly educated child (Goldberg, 2005). A comprehensive survey conducted by the nonpartisan research group Public Agenda in 2003 of leadership under NCLB implied that superintendents and principals are very focused on raising academic standards and increasing accountability. Sixty-four percent of the superintendents and 73% of the principals said, however, that NCLB relies too heavily on testing (Farkas, Johnson, & Duffett, 2003). Superintendents and principals responses implied that testing alone was not the answer to school improvement.

Moreover, school leaders have expressed concern over multiple-choice and short, constructed-response items dominating large-scale, high-stakes tests that only go so far in measuring complex thinking skills. Posner (2004) stated, "The kinds of problems that can appear on a standardized test are, of course, quite limited in form and complexity, as the student is allocated only a minute or two to complete each one" (p. 750). Darling-Hammond (2002) and Popham (2001) expressed similar concerns about the disproportionate time spent on high-stakes tests in schools. They feared tests overemphasize lower order thinking skills and put pressure on teachers to focus on fragmented skills, taking time away from more authentic learning.

### Narrowing the Curriculum

The intense demand to prepare students for high-stakes tests causes administrators and teachers to devote a great deal of classroom time and resources to the test, especially in the areas of reading and mathematics. Nontested subject areas, including history, art, music, physical education, and foreign languages, are not receiving equal attention, diminishing teaching social and higher level thinking skills (King & Zucker, 2005).

In a national survey called Quality Counts 2001 (before NCLB was enacted), 66% of the 1,019 K-12 public school teachers who responded said they were concentrating on tested information to the detriment of other important areas of the curriculum and they felt their teaching had become too focused on state tests (Kober, 2002). Another survey conducted in 2003 by the National Board on Educational Testing and Public Policy found that 79% of teachers in states with annual state tests reported that instruction in the tested subjects had increased either "a great deal" or "moderately" (Pedulla et al., 2003). Educational experts, teachers, and parents pointed out that, although other curricular areas are not tested under NCLB, they are still important to the development of children and young adults (see Chapter 2 for more a more complete discussion of this).

## Teaching to the Test

The pressure of state assessment and accountability systems spurred administrators and teachers to engage in various kinds of activities referred to as "teaching to the test." Although unethical test preparation must never be tolerated, studies indicated that teachers and administrators did not always understand the difference between ethical and unethical test preparation actions (Hoffman, Assaf, & Paris, 2001; Stecher, Chun, Barron, & Ross, 2000).

In a nationwide survey by *Education Week*, supported by the Pew Charitable Trust, 79% of the teachers responding said they spent "a great deal" or "somewhat" of their time preparing their students with test-taking skills, even though they were not happy with this practice ("Quality Counts," 2001). Although some of these practices are useful if used sparingly, too often they are used in unacceptable doses. This happens when test-taking skills "take up too much time, become the main focus of teaching and are near-clones of the real test questions" (Kober, 2002, p. 6). Data from various studies showed that teachers spent a considerable amount of time teaching to the test. Hoffman et al. (2001) surveyed Texas reading teachers and supervisors about how often certain kinds of test preparation were being used in their schools. Some of the practices rated "often" or "always" included (a) teaching test-taking skills, (b) having students practice with tests from previous years, (c) teaching or reviewing topics that will be on the test, and (d) using commercial test preparation materials. These activities peaked in the weeks prior to the state test and were used more frequently in schools with lower test scores.

A New Jersey study of 376 elementary and secondary teachers found teachers reported they teach to the test (Centolanza, 2004). Teachers acknowledged that the practice was discouraging because they soon realized they often neglected individual students. They had little time to teach creatively, and they bored themselves and their students by doing repetitive practice problems as they prepared for the test (Centolanza, 2004).

The literature suggested high-stakes tests encourage teachers to use many test preparation strategies. Although using test preparation strategies may result in improved test scores on the state tests, this improvement may not represent an actual improvement in the knowledge and skills of the students. In fact, preparation activities such as coaching and gearing instruction toward the test may yield invalid test results.

## Cheating by Administrators and Teachers

Campbell's law was named for the social scientist and researcher Donald Campbell in 1975. Campbell's law stipulates that "the more any quantitative social indicator is used for social decision making, the more subject it will be to corruption pressures and the more apt it will be to distort and corrupt the social processes it was intended to monitor" (Campbell, as cited in Nichols & Berliner, 2007, p. 27). Nichols and Berliner (2007) pointed out that Campbell's law can be applied to the pressures put upon administrators and teachers. "If you use high-stakes tests to assess students, teachers, or schools, the corruption and distortions that inevitably appear compromise the construct validity of the test" (Nichols & Berliner, 2007, p. 4).

Not only are school districts judged by their test scores, but funding also is adjusted based on scores. This high-stakes assessment environment has led to widespread cheating. The *Los Angeles Times* reported that more than 200 teachers were investigated for helping students with the state exam (Haysaki, 2004). From 1994 to 2003, Wesley Elementary School in Houston won accolades for teaching low-income students reading and defying the odds on state test scores with high scores with a high-poverty and high-minority population. These remarkable scores caught the attention of the nation. However, after an investigation of the school's practices, students fell from the top 10% in the state of Texas to the bottom 10% in just 1 year; the teachers admitted that cheating was standard procedure (Nichols & Berliner, 2007).

### Declining Staff Morale

As additional pressure is put on teachers to increase students' test performance and instruction becomes merely test preparation, teachers felt that the skills they brought to their craft were being minimized. Studies also have indicated that high-stakes tests have increased stress and decreased morale among teachers.

A survey conducted by the National Board on Educational Testing and Public Policy (Pedulla et al., 2003) asked questions regarding teachers' attitudes and opinions about state-mandated tests. Survey topics included questions about (a) how the state test affected classroom instruction and assessment; (b) feelings of pressure associated with improving student performance; (c) test preparation; (d) teacher and student motivation and morale; and (e) school, teacher, and student accountability. Survey results revealed teachers in schools with high-stakes assessment programs reported feeling pressured from either their district superintendent or building principal. Almost half of all teachers responding indicated morale was low in their school. In a Texas survey, 85% of responding teachers agreed with the statement, "Some of the best teachers are leaving the field because of the TAAS (Texas Assessment of Academic Skills)" (Abrams, Pedulla, & Madaus, 2003, p. 20).

In another study, conducted by RAND Education in school districts from California, Pennsylvania, and Georgia (Hamilton et al., 2007), survey questions asked about AYP pressure and staff morale. Findings noted three quarters of superintendents and about half of principals and teachers in all three states reported staff morale had changed for the worse due to the imposed accountability systems, compared to only 10–20% of respondents who thought morale had changed for the better. Superintendents responded principals may feel accountability pressures more strongly than teachers. An interesting result across all three states showed teachers in schools that made AYP were just as likely as teachers in schools that did not make it to report a negative influence on morale.

## Assessment Under NCLB as a Means to Equity

NCLB outlined a charge for educators to meet the growing needs of students in this era of accountability. Leaders' tasks included creating more equitable educational opportunities for all students. The NCLB legislation stressed states and schools would be held accountable for the academic achievement of all students, particularly those who fell into the following subgroups: English language learners, special education students, economically disadvantaged students, and students from the major racial and ethnic-minority groups (Tillman, 2006). The testing requirements of NCLB sought to eliminate the achievement gap between subgroups and the general student population.

As part of NCLB legislation, results from state reading and mathematics tests must be disaggregated by major subgroups (Popham, 2005). If any of the groups failed to make AYP 2 years in a row, the school was placed on an improvement track, and students in those groups could transfer to another school in the district. If the school continued to fail to make AYP, possible additional corrective actions could include (a) replacing school staff relevant to the failure, (b) instituting a new curriculum, (c) significantly decreasing management authority in the school, (d) appointing outside experts to advise the school, (e) extending the school year or school day, or (f) restructuring the internal organization of the school (Popham, 2005).

Test scores are the vehicle whereby schools show they have made AYP; that is, "that the student population as a whole, as well as each identified subgroup of students, must meet the same proficiency goal" (Ryan, 2004, p. 940). Proponents of standards-based tests argued this requirement was necessary because high expectations must be set for all students to address the needs of those student groups who have been segregated by low expectations.

## How These Assessments Relate to School Improvement

Combining academic standards, standardized assessments, and accountability for student outcomes designed to improve students' academic achievement has become known as standards-based accountability. Studies have indicated that standards-based assessment can influence both what is taught and how it is taught. States have used results of these tests to persuade teachers to make desired changes in curricula and instruction.

Hamilton et al. (2007) investigated how superintendents, principals, and teachers responded to the standards-based accountability systems states adopted since the implementation of NCLB. A portion of the study addressed how superintendents, principals, and teachers from each state focused on improving student achievement as a result of pressure to make AYP. Superintendents from the three states reported that they focused on using student achievement data from state tests for the following reasons: (a) to develop a district improvement plan to inform instruction, (b) to obtain principal and teacher research-based professional development, (c) to make changes to district and instructional materials, and (d) to help individual schools develop school improvement plans (Hamilton et al., 2007). Principals in the Hamilton et al. study also reported using the data for similar purposes and added they used the data to identify students who needed additional instructional support. Principals in all three states often took immediate action by providing teachers with pacing schedules, sample lessons, and classroom feedback related to the implementation of state standards and assessments. Principals reported teachers in their schools reviewed state test results and used them to tailor instruction (Hamilton et al., 2007).

Since the success or failure of school improvement hinges on what occurs in the classroom, it is not surprising that most principals in the RAND study reported they increased professional development for their teachers. Most professional development efforts emphasized the alignment of curricula and instruction with state standards and tests. Some districts also assigned instructional coaches to teachers and principals as another form of professional development.

Researchers from the Center on Education Policy (2006) found that schools used test data for school improvement to inform decisions; aligned curricula, assessment, and instruction; and provided support for low-achieving students. More specifically, to use data effectively, many schools created common benchmark assessments, developed comprehensive student information systems, modified instruction for students based on data, and facilitated teacher conversations about underperforming subgroups of students (Zavadsky, 2006).

## VOICES 3 PERSPECTIVES OF SUPERINTENDENTS AND PRINCIPALS

The superintendents and principals expressed concern about assessment and the consequences of state-mandated tests on their students and their districts. In the following section we provide examples of these concerns and benefits seen by the participants. Findings reflected how assessment connects with politics, teaching and learning, subgroups, and school improvement.

## How the Politics of NCLB Connect to Assessment Practices

Superintendents in this study bemoaned the fact that politicians are trying to answer questions that they felt educators should be answering. The superintendents wondered whether one of the purposes of annual state testing is to make public schools look bad so as to pave the way for massive school reform.

> I don't think there's anyone in this room that is against higher standards, and I think that's what No Child Left Behind attempted to promote across the board. In practicality, I've always viewed it as a political answer to an educational issue. It's highly political, and every time we attack an educational problem with a political response we never solve the educational problem. (Superintendent 50, New England & Mid-Atlantic, 2006)

The distrust and frustrations of some of the superintendents came out very clearly. "I think it [NCLB] is set up to make public schools fail. I think that's the goal of it" (Superintendent 4, small-sized districts, Midwest, 2004). Another superintendent felt that the goals of NCLB were impossible to attain.

> My biggest disappointment with accountability testing set up the way it is in [this state] it's an impossible goal. When you put something out there that's impossible and tell people to reach it, there's a frustration that's being reached and experienced all the time. I mean, our teachers are very focused on getting the best scores out there. (Superintendent 6, small-sized districts, Midwest, 2004)

A different superintendent wondered about the sustainability of this reform. "It is just another political platform. What will change with the next political group?" (Superintendent 50, mostly small-sized districts, Southwest & West, 2006).

What one state may call "proficient" may not be "proficient" in another state. Feeling comparisons across states were unfair, some superintendents called for a national test rather than 50 different state tests to measure student achievement. "This law is a disaster because everyone has a different set of tests. So they really should go to a national test. If they want to play this game, go to a national test and a national curriculum" (Superintendent 51, medium-sized districts, New England & Mid-Atlantic, 2005).

Sometimes administrators thought legislators on federal or state levels did not know what they were requiring of students. Principal 10 put it this way:

> For me it's a lofty ideal that these people sitting over in Washington, DC, come into a classroom, come into a building and see the children that go home and have no one at home, have no food at home. The least of their worries is whether they're going to pass that [state] test come February. (elementary school, Midwest, 2004)

Principal 51 stated, "I think No Child Left Behind is a very biased initiative by the radical right to punish public schools. I don't think there is any question" (elementary school, Southwest & West, 2006).

## How the Emphasis on Assessment Required by NCLB Affects Teaching and Learning

Superintendents and principals in the Voices 3 study were concerned about many of the same issues regarding assessment that appeared in the literature between 2000 and 2006. Superintendents in the Voices 3 study were especially troubled with the narrowing of the curriculum that emphasized testing in only language arts and mathematics. Superintendents were afraid the focus on language arts and mathematics would force them to do away with curricular offerings that made their district unique. They feared the rest of their curriculum (e.g., social studies, music, and the arts) would suffer from excessive emphasis on language arts and mathematics. Superintendent 55 stated, "If you buy into the notion that the educational journey for our kids entails more than—certainly entails mathematics and reading but it entails more than that. There's more to a child's educational journey than those two content areas" (Midwest).

A superintendent from another region of the United States bemoaned how certain curricula areas get neglected with the overemphasis on language arts and mathematics:

> I think that as a leader, one of the things that it's done, at least in my district and my community, is it makes me really bring home the message that ELA [English language arts] and math are not the only things that we want these children to be proficient in. And I have to keep that in the forefront that we have a wonderful arts program and a music program that are just as important in developing children into productive democratic citizens, as being as proficient in English and math. And that message tends to get lost with NCLB. (Superintendent 54, New England & Mid-Atlantic, 2006)

Superintendents in Voices 3 also spoke of their concerns about the pressures associated with standards-based testing. Superintendent 35 revealed just how high stakes the testing is:

> When it really comes down to funding, it really comes down to us continuing to exist—we will teach to the test. If we learn this test, we will be a good district. Well, what have we done there? There is nothing educationally sound about that at all. (small-sized districts, Midwest, 2004)

Voices 3 principals expressed the most distress about putting so much emphasis on a single, annual, multiple-choice test. They felt multiple measures are needed to address the depth and breadth of student learning and to better respond to students' individual differences. Elementary school Principal 61 communicated,

> I have a lot of problems with NCLB. I believe that we don't want to leave any children behind. But, I also believe every child learns at their own pace and their own style and that we've done so much with brain theory in our building and learning strategies, and then we give them a test in March and it's the same format for every kid, even if there's a different learning style or different technique of learning. So I struggle with that constantly. I just think there are a lot of different ways to do this, and we're just throwing them all into one way of assessing them, and it just battles with everything I know about styles of learning, brain theory, etc. (Midwest, 2006)

Middle school Principal 62 was uneasy about the conflict between the middle school student-centered, developmentally appropriate philosophy and annual standards-based, objective tests that are based on one right answer instead of an authentic assessment philosophy that engages students.

> It is not only one test, it is one objective test, and we are all middle school administrators saying that we all know that authentic assessment is what is really fun and creative and really gets the kids engaged in our curricular areas, and here we are giving our students authentic assessment, and come March, we throw them (a), (b), (c), (d) objective tests, and "one of these is the right answer and do the best you possibly can." It goes against our total philosophy. (Principal 62, Midwest, 2005)

High school Principal 83 echoed similar thoughts:

> Because we're being driven by standardized test scores. Standardized test scores don't always ask kids to think. Standardized test scores, quite often, ask kids to remember. And so, at the same time we're trying to prepare them for a global economy where they've gotta be thinkers—complex thinkers; they've got to go out and solve problems—the same time we've got to pre-

pare them for these very standardized test[s] that quite often are remember and memorize. That's where I think there is a disjunction with No Child Left Behind is that it's standards-test driven. Now, I'd like to see the test use more of those thinking skills. But, I just don't see that happening to the extent I wish it did. (Midwest, 2006)

Principal 79 indicated concern about teaching to the test:

You can't change today and stay in tune with the [state] assessments; you can't. We focus—you walk into our building and ask any staff member what's the most important thing I do: "I am getting my students ready for the [state] assessments in reading and math." They're going to say that. I know they're going to say that. Because we drum that into them and that's just what's happening. I think it's wrong. (high schools, Midwest, 2005).

Concern about teacher morale was another issue emphasized by Voices 3 principals:

I think the NCLB has hurt the morale of teachers who are strong teachers. Because I've got teachers who stay late. I've got teachers who work hard. We work the scene. We've met on Saturdays. We've met on Sundays trying to develop things. Now, what has happened is it leads to extremes, and so the teachers who are all working hard and had all the pride, they are beaten down. (Principal 56, elementary schools, Midwest, 2005)

Middle school Principal 66 realized that teachers were being stretched to the limit:

To put labels on a school and say you are not making [adequate] yearly progress is very demoralizing to many, many teachers who go in every day and give 100% and love those kids and try so hard, and the one snapshot in time when they take the [state] tests and in those results, all the hard work and effort don't shine through; it is incredibly demoralizing for the whole profession. (Midwest, 2005)

Elementary Principal 56 bemoaned,

I had a teacher say to me the other day, "Teaching for me used to be an art and now it's a science, and I'm not sure that I was born to be a science teacher." It's a data-driven business! (Midwest, 2005)

## Assessment Under NCLB as a Means to Equity

For many superintendents and principals in this study, finding new and innovative ways to meet the needs of marginalized students was a challenge. Superintendents and principals addressed three areas on the effects of accountability on special subgroup populations: (a) positive effects of accountability on special populations, (b) specific ways in which certain groups are disadvantaged, and (c) ways in which schools and districts are meeting the needs of special populations.

### Positive Effects of Accountability on Special Populations

Many school leaders felt that an increased focus on the subgroups was a positive move forward. Students in the subgroups had been neglected far too long. Principals and superintendents wanted to see improved academic achievement in traditionally underperforming students. Superintendent 51 stated that NCLB "makes you care.... [Poor and minority kids] before could just be left behind because people didn't have to focus on them. And now you do" (medium district, New England & Mid-Atlantic, 2006). "This has made us look at individual students and look at individual subgroups in the demographics of schools, and I think that's a positive thing" (Superintendent 29, small-sized districts, Midwest, 2004). Superintendent 7 noted, "No Child Left Behind, I think, has helped in a broader sense in terms of helping people recognize the challenges of different ethnic groups, different racial groups" (small-sized districts, Midwest, 2006). Middle school Principal 66 concluded,

> In many aspects, I see it as a very good thing; we can't ignore the subgroups. We can't say that if we are doing OK overall, that is fine. We can't ignore the African American subgroups or the special education population or any other minority populations. It is always good to look at how kids are achieving and what can we do better. (Midwest, 2005)

### Specific Ways in Which Certain Groups Are Disadvantaged

School leaders especially were concerned when they had a high concentration of subgroups in their student population. The following quote is from a Native American board member who was part of one of the Voices 3 focus groups:

> We look at the Navajo country. They have no electricity and no running water. They travel miles to get to the schools. A lot of times they travel—what? Three or 4 hours after school at night to get home. When they get home, they do their work by candlelight or whatever.... So when we're looking at Indian students, probably we'll find ways that we need to get some more afterschool or whatever to tutor students so that we can excel. So those are some of the things that when we look at testing, how do we have a level playing field that's level for all of us? (Board Member 2, medium-sized districts, Southwest & West, 2005)

When students come from economically stressed homes, their school lives and their ability to concentrate on the school work are negatively affected. Principal 14 spoke to those problems in her district:

The difference is between the "haves" and the "have nots." It's a national problem, not just in [this district]. You have the opportunity to plan and do things differently when you are working with people who have the ability and the opportunity to plan. When you're working with the masses of people who are surviving, who are in survival mode, then your activities and responsibilities are a little bit different. (elementary schools, Midwest, 2004)

## Ways in Which Schools and Districts Are Meeting the Needs of Special Populations

For some of the Voices 3 school leaders, the challenges tended to outweigh any opportunities presented by NCLB for seriously addressing gaps in achievement found in the subgroups. NCLB has demanded significant resources to carry out its requirements. It also shifted societal issues and burdens to the schools.

I think we struggle, too, with English language learners with No Child Left Behind and the requirements about where they need to be proficient in their proficiency, because I don't think they have taken into consideration the amount of time it takes to learn a second language and to be proficient. We are barely making them proficient in their native language and then we have to transition them, and there is not enough time. I don't think that was taken into consideration, and I feel that this is a real struggle we have in this district.... I know I do at our school. (Principal 18, elementary schools, Southwest & West, 2005)

Superintendents, especially, felt that their district was put at a disadvantage when it had a large population of subgroups due to the expense associated with meeting the needs of those groups. (NCLB has been called an "unfunded mandate" because what is required to address the needs of students is not followed by funding to ensure that it happens.) Superintendent 21 conveyed this:

We started an ESL [English as a Second Language] program and we started training people, even before the kids arrived, on how to deal with that when they were showing up in the following semester. So I think No Child Left Behind, for those administrators who recognize that this is something that we have to live with, my greatest problem with No Child Left Behind is that I just don't think—they don't have any idea how expensive it really [is] to actually accomplish the goals that they want us to. I don't think they have any clue about that. I'm not sure they even care, but I'll say that while they're in Washington trying to figure out what's best for out here, eventually it's going to trickle down to them that they cannot do this without financially supporting the school district where we're trying to do this. (small-sized districts, Southwest & West, 2005)

## How These Assessments Relate to School Improvement

Voices 3 focus group principals indicated that they appreciate the more stringent focus that has resulted from more accountability. Elementary school Principal 18 said,

> I can say I like the accountability piece of it, because it seems like it's really aligned districts within themselves and aligned districts within their states. I don't think we have had that piece before.... I'm happy for that. (Southwest & West, 2005)

Middle school and high school principals from Voices 3 believed that the data obtained from high-stakes tests have focused staff to have a school improvement plan. In turn, this has helped them to examine their practices, identify weak areas, and focus on improving curricula and instruction.

> I think we have a real school improvement plan now. Before that, a school improvement plan used to be just ... my predecessor before me would go down and just change the date and change the little demographics, and you had to give it to the school board and you did it. Now we actually have goals within our school improvement plan that reflect the data; we do data retreats and all that now. My teachers don't dismiss the data. They feel good about understanding it. (Principal 69, middle school, Midwest, 2005)

High school Principal 75 echoed these sentiments:

> Well, from a high school that has multiple subgroups, it's had incredible impact not just on me, but I think on the entire school in forcing us to be more strategic than we even had been. I think the question is, how did it impact me? I thought that as a leader I was pretty well attuned to data-driven decision making, and we disaggregated and we had the data and were making decisions, I thought, based upon information we had. NCLB forced me to be more knowledgeable and certainly more strategic as I looked within groups and then within the standard of the question itself and what supportive or missing information was there, and we asked even harder questions than we'd asked before. (Midwest, 2005)

At this point in time, superintendents saw the huge job of professional development that would be needed for their teachers. In addition to professional development, teachers need support so they are able to transfer what they learn to their classroom practice. Teachers need to align their teaching to the state standards and, ultimately, to the material that covered on the state assessments. A superintendent explained,

All the professional development in the world isn't going to change what happens in the classroom until we get into the classroom and help teachers change, and that transfer of learning for them with the transfer of learning for students is vital and doesn't always happen. (medium-sized districts, Southwest & West, 2004)

## IMPLICATIONS

### Political Implications

Several of the superintendents and principals in the Voices 3 focus groups communicated mistrust of the way students, teachers, and schools were being evaluated. The NCLB law assumed that shaming schools by publishing test scores and then following up with sanctions would improve education (Ravitch, 2010). Although the law passed with a coalition of both the right and the left, Kohn (2004a) noted,

> Senator James Jeffords, who chaired the Senate committee that oversees education from 1997 to 2001, has described the law as a maneuver "that will let the private sector take over education, that is something the Republicans have wanted for years." (p. 84)

Some feared that the most outspoken supporters of NCLB have had absolutely no interest in improving schools that cannot meet the standards set by NCLB (Bowman, 2001; Kohn, 2004b). Public education, in that view, was not something to be made better, but something one needs to do away with.

And how could public education be done away with? Under current law, if students are in a school that does not make AYP 2 years in a row, they can transfer to another public school. Proponents of the voucher system would like it if a student could take their tax monies in the form of a voucher and transfer to a private school. In fact, Kronholz (2003) wrote an article in *The Wall Street Journal* that began as follows: "Teachers, parents and principals may have their doubts about NCLB, but business loves it" (p. B-1). In contrast, George W. Bush, in his 2000 presidential campaign, spoke about the "soft bigotry of low expectations" (Bush, 2004, para. 68). He asserted having low expectations for different groups of children is undemocratic and inherently unfair, thus affirming his support of high standards for all children.

### Standards-Based Assessment and School Improvement Implications

Comments from superintendents participating in Voices 3 and a review of the literature on assessment practices between 2000 and 2006 indicated that the NCLB focus on a single, annual test has several negative consequences. Ravitch (2010) supported these assertions, stating, "Higher test scores on standardized tests are not synonymous with good education" (p. 167). Ravitch also stated, "The problem with using tests to make important decisions about people's lives is that standardized tests are not precise instruments" (p. 152). Stiggins (2004) contended,

> For decades ... we have believed that the path to school improvement is paved with more and better standardized tests. The mistake we have made at all levels is to believe that once-a-year standardized assessments alone can provide sufficient information and motivation to increase student learning. (p. 23)

In *Assessment Manifesto: A Call for the Development of Balanced Assessment Systems*, Stiggins (2008) pointed out that schools can no longer be places were some students succeed at learning while others fail. Instead, they must become places where all students master state or national, preestablished, academic achievement standards. Because of this change, with the focus being on standards, assessment practices must also change. Some changes in assessment practices are already taking place. For NCLB accountability purposes, most states have shifted from using norm-referenced tests, where students are merely ranked, to using criterion-referenced tests that focus on the standards and help to answer the key question, "Who has and has not met standards?" (Stiggins, 2008, p. 2).

Since it is a matter of law that schools must administer annual assessments, Stiggins (2008) and others stated that this type of summative assessment is necessary for accountability purposes. However, most assessment experts agree that annual, standardized, multiple-choice tests are not sufficient to provide all the assessment information schools need to improve. Schools must begin to look at productive assessment systems that balance classroom-level assessments, program-level assessments, and institutional accountability and policy-level assessments (Stiggins, 2008).

Research has demonstrated the skilled use of feedback to students (formative assessment) may be the single most powerful means of improving learning outcomes available to teachers (Black & Wiliam, 1998). Classroom-level, formative assessments must be used to continuously provide information to teachers and students regarding where each student is "now" in the learning process and what each student needs next to be successful.

Program-level assessments include interim, benchmark, short-cycle, or common assessments administered every few weeks to "identify aspects of instructional programs that are being effective as well as those in need of improvement" (Stiggins, 2008, p. 5). Results of these types of assessments should assist grade-level teachers (at the elementary level) and department-level teachers (at the secondary level) in knowing where to focus their improvement efforts and how to quickly make those improvements. When analyzing the results of program-level assessments, teachers must work together so that rich discussions can be facilitated regarding the standards, the assessments themselves, and the instructional strategies being used. Both classroom-level and program-level assessments can help teachers and school administrators determine which students need additional help or different methods of instruction.

Another area of balance that must be considered is a balance between types of assessments being used. Instead of relying solely on multiple-choice types of assessments, there also should be a focus on task-performance assessments. This form of assessment requires students to perform by developing a product or task rather than selecting answers as on a traditional paper-and-pencil test. Expert raters, such as teachers or other trained staff, judge the quality of the students' work based on an agreed-upon set of criteria. This type of assessment is a more authentic indicator of students' knowledge and skills, as it requires students to actually apply what they are learning and leads to greater levels of understanding. Ravitch (2010) supported the use of performance-based assessments and stated,

> To lift the quality of education, we must encourage schools to use measures of educational accomplishments that are appropriate to the subjects studied, such as research papers in history, essays and stories in literature, research projects in science, demonstrations of mathematical competence, videotaped or recorded conversations in a foreign language, performances in the arts, and other exhibitions of learning. (p. 238)

The National Council of Teachers of Mathematics supported the need for balance. The council was asked, "What is the role of large-scale testing in making significant, high-stakes decisions about schools, students, and instruction?" The National Council of Teachers of Mathematics (2011) responded with the following position statement:

> The National Council of Teachers of Mathematics recognizes the importance of measuring the learning of students and the effectiveness of instruction. Large-scale tests can and should be among several measures that are used to make significant decisions about students and instruction. However, such critical decisions about students and instruction must involve more than the results of any single test. We strongly support a balance of day-to-day classroom assessments, which help teachers improve instruction, and external tests that track progress and provide for national comparisons. (para. 1)

To develop effective, balanced assessment systems, teachers and administrators must be provided with quality training regarding sound assessment practices. Besides making sure that practicing teachers receive professional development training, preservice preparation programs should include worthwhile assessment courses so that future teachers are ready to fulfill the types of classroom assessment responsibilities described above. Leadership programs for superintendents and principals must also include opportunities for future or practicing leaders to become skilled at understanding how sound classroom-level, program-level, and institutional- or policy-level assessment systems can help to assure academic success for all students. These training opportunities should be in place before moving forward in school improvement endeavors regarding current curricula, assessment, and instruction practices.

### Subgroups Implications

Participants in the Voices 3 focus groups said that data from assessments showed them the achievement gaps between the haves and the have nots. The problem is that those who are not succeeding under the assessment systems put in place by the state to answer the demands of NCLB need help if they are to succeed. Where is this help coming from? There are schools in need of additional resources.

Voices 3 superintendents and principals described some of the conditions in which the students from their districts live. When all we do is require that students of poverty perform at the same level, we are holding children responsible for failures that are far beyond their control and the control of the schools they attend. Money matters. The best informed and most affluent parents enroll their children in schools where there are small classes, ample resources, well-educated teachers, and beautiful facilities.

## CONCLUSION

The education policies we are following today are unlikely to improve our schools (Ravitch, 2010). Students need an education that has a greater focus on authentic teaching and learning than how to choose the right answer on a multiple-choice test. They need to be prepared to be responsible, productive citizens who can make good choices for themselves, their families, and our society. There is no shortcut to good education. The most durable way to improve our schools is to improve curricula, assessment practices, and instruction—and improve the conditions in which teachers work and children learn.

## REFERENCES

Abernathy, S. F. (2007). *No Child Left Behind and the public schools.* Ann Arbor, MI: University of Michigan Press.

Abrams, L. M., Pedulla, J. J., & Madaus, G. F. (2003). Views from the classroom: Teachers' opinions of statewide testing programs. *Theory Into Practice, 42*(1), 18-29.

Black, P., & Wiliam, D. (1998). Inside the black box: Raising standards through classroom assessment. *Phi Delta Kappan, 80,* 139-149.

Bogdan, R. C., & Biklen, S. K. (1992). *Qualitative research for education: An introduction to theories and methods* (2nd ed.). Boston, MA: Allyn & Bacon.

Bowman, J. C. (2001). *A lesson plan for the nation.* Retrieved from http://news.heartland.org/policy-documents/lesson-plan-nation

Bush, G. W. (2004). *Speeches from the 2004 Republican National Convention.* Retrieved from http://www.presidentialrhetoric.com/campaign/rncspeeches/bush.html

Center on Education Policy. (2006). *From the capital to the classroom: Year 4 of the No Child Left Behind Act.* Washington, DC: Author.

Centolanza, L. R. (2004). New Jersey teachers believe testing compromises sound practices. *ERS Spectrum, 22*(4), 10-14

Darling-Hammond, L. (2002). What's at stake in high-stakes testing? *Brown University, Child & Adolescent Behavior Letter, 18*(1), 1-3.

Farkas, S., Johnson, J., & Duffett, A. (2003). *Rolling up their sleeves: Superintendents and principals talk about what's needed to fix public education.* New York, NY: Public Agenda.

Goldberg, M. (2005). Test mess 2: Are we doing better a year later? *Phi Delta Kappan, 86,* 389-395.

Hamilton, L. S., Stecher, B. M., Marsh, J. A., McCombs, J. S., Robyn, A., Russell, J. L., … Barney, H. (2007). *Standards-based accountability under No Child Left Behind: Experiences of teachers and administrators in three states.* Santa Monica, CA: RAND.

Harris, D., & Harrington, C. (2006). Accountability, standards, and the growing achievement gap: Lessons from the past half-century. *American Journal of Education, 111*(2), 209-238.

Haysaki, E. (2004, September). It's back to school for 2,600 displaced students. *Los Angeles Times.*

Hill, P. (2007). NCLB school choice and children in poverty. In A. Gamoran (Ed.), *Standards-based reform and the poverty gap: Lessons for No Child Left Behind* (pp. 229-252). Washington, DC: Brookings Institution Press.

Hoffman, J. V., Assaf, L. C., & Paris, S. G. (2001). High-stakes testing in reading: Today in Texas, tomorrow? *The Reading Teacher, 54,* 482-492.

King, K. V., & Zucker, S. (2005). *Curriculum narrowing.* San Antonio, TX: Pearson.

Kober, N. (2002, June). Teaching to the test: The good, the bad, and who's responsible. *Test Talk for Leaders, 1*. Retrieved from http://www.cep-dc.org/displayDocument.cfm?DocumentID=256

Kohn, A. (2004a). NCLB and the effort to privatize public education. In D. Meier & G. Wood (Eds.), *Many children left behind: How the No Child Left Behind Act is damaging our children and our schools* (pp. 79-100). Boston, MA: Beacon Press

Kohn, A. (2004b). Test today, privatize tomorrow. *Education Digest, 70*(1), 14-22.

Kronholz, J. (2003, December 24). Education companies see dollars in Bush school-boost law. *Wall Street Journal*, p. B-1.

National Council of Teachers of Mathematics. (2011). *High-stakes tests: A position of the National Council of Teachers of Mathematics.* Retrieved from http://www.nctm.org/about/content.aspx?id=6356

National Defense Education Act of 1958, Pub. L. No. 85-864 (1958).

Nichols, S., & Berliner, D. (2005). The inevitable corruption of indicators and educators through high-stakes testing. Tempe, AZ: Education Policy Research Unit. Retrieved from http://nepc.colorado.edu/files/EPSL-0503-101-EPRU.pdf

Nichols, S., & Berliner, D. (2007). *Collateral damage: How high-stakes testing corrupts America's schools.* Cambridge, MA: Harvard Education Press.

No Child Left Behind Act of 2001, Pub. L. No. 107-110 (2002).

Pedulla, J., Abrams, L., Madaus, G., Russell, M., Ramos, M., & Miao, J. (2003). *Perceived effects of state-mandated testing programs on teaching and learning: Findings from a national survey of teachers.* Chestnut Hill, MA: Center for the Study of Testing, Evaluation, and Educational Policy.

Peterson P., & West, M. (2003). *No Child Left Behind: The politics and practice of school accountability.* Washington DC: Brookings Institution.

Popham, W. J. (2001). *The truth about testing.* Alexandria, VA: Association of Supervision and Curriculum Development.

Popham, W. J. (2005). *America's failing schools.* New York, NY: Routledge.

Posner, D. (2004). What's wrong with teaching to the test? *Phi Delta Kappan, 85*, 749-751.

Quality Counts 2001. (2001, January 11). A better balance: Standards, tests, and the tools to succeed. *Education Week*.

Ravitch, D. (2010). *The death and life of the great American school system: How testing and choice and undermining education.* New York, NY: Basic Books.

Ryan, J. E. (2004). The perverse incentives of the No Child Left Behind Act. *NYU Law Review, 79*, 932-989.

Stecher, B. M., Chun, T., Barron, S., & Ross, K. (2000). *The effects of the Washington state education reform on schools and classrooms* (CSE Technical Report 525). Los Angeles, CA: National Center for Research on Evaluation, Standards, and Student Testing.

Stiggins, R. (2004). New assessment beliefs for a new school mission. *Phi Delta Kappan, 86*, 22-27.

Stiggins, R. (2008). *Assessment manifesto: A call for the development of balanced assessment systems.* Portland, OR: Assessment Training Institute.

Tillman, L. C. (2006). Accountability, high stakes testing and No Child Left Behind. In F. Brown & R. C. Hunter (Eds.), *No Child Left Behind and other federal programs for urban school districts* (pp. 189-200). San Diego, CA: Elsevier.

Wallis, C., & Steptoe, S. (2007, May 24). How to fix No Child Left Behind. *Time, 169*(23), 34-41.

U.S. Department of Education. (2011). *Overview: Budget Office.* Retrieved from http://www2.ed.gov/about/overview/budget/index.html.

Zavadsky, H. (2006). How NCLB drives success in urban schools. *Educational Leadership, 64*(3), 69-73.

# CHAPTER 7

# DECISION-MAKING PROCESSES, GIVING VOICE, LISTENING, AND INVOLVEMENT

**by Debra Touchton, Rosemarye Taylor, and Michele Acker-Hocevar**

This chapter explores decision-making processes, giving voice, listening, and involvement within the actual perceptions of superintendents and principals who describe what giving voice, listening, and involvement meant to them in relation to their daily practices (theories-in-use; Argyris & Schön, 1978; Yukl, 2010). We situate superintendent and principal practices and rational decision-making models within a functionalist paradigm. We openly acknowledge that because functionalism is the prevailing paradigm for educational leaders' work today (Burrell & Morgan, 1988), it is impossible to ignore; yet at the same time, it has inherent limitations that must be reconciled with building more democratic decision-making communities. To accomplish this, leaders must challenge existing systems of control over decision-making processes and enact a system that promotes more involvement and shared decision making. Leaders who are thoughtful about decision-making involvement choose to articulate

*Snapshots of School Leadership in the 21st Century:*
*Perils and Promises of Leading for Social Justice,*
*School Improvement, and Democratic Community,* pp. 121–145
Copyright © 2012 by Information Age Publishing

and clarify shared decision-making models and processes. Enacting democracy within current normative assumptions of leadership control over decision-making behavior is at odds with moving toward more inclusive practices. We offer explicit models for decision-making processes for leaders to cultivate organizational cultures of shared decision making and where different perspectives can be heard to create an environment for dialogue around shared values (Sidorkin, 1999). We acknowledge inherent contradictions leaders face in promoting more democratic decision-making communities that challenge top-down mandates and hierarchical practices. Contradictions between individual and organizational expectations require leaders to be educated in new roles as collaborators and facilitators versus managers and enforcers of status quo practices.

## LITERATURE REVIEW

### Tensions Between Individual Behavior and Organizational Expectations

Drawing on the work of Getzels and Guba (1957), Argyris and Schön (1978), and Burrell and Morgan (1988) helps us unravel some of the tensions that exist as leaders build intentional democratic communities of practice. Getzels and Guba discussed disconnects between idiographic (individual) and nomothetic (organizational) dimensions of leadership behavior. These individual and organizational binaries arise when tensions occur between espoused leadership theories and theories-in-use (Argyris & Schön, 1978). For example, leaders may state that they believe in democratic decision making yet practice autocratic decision making. Burrell and Morgan explained these tensions between individual behavior and organizational expectations within a four-quadrant organizational framework that illustrates the assumptions of each of the paradigms: (a) functionalist, (b) interpretive, (c) radical humanist, and (d) radical structuralist. This framework depicts how tensions arise naturally between individuals and organizations, since no one quadrant alone can address the complex arena of human interactions, especially when factoring in the two axes on which the quadrants are organized: radical change versus maintaining the status quo, and objective versus subjective realities. Because the functionalist paradigm is both focused on maintaining the status quo, or the existing hierarchy, and also assumes that there is an objective reality, it bumps up against the interpretive and radical approaches of organizational change to challenge one best way of operation. Functionalism is the dominant ideology for educational organizations today, and leaders are expected to perform roles from within this paradigm, such as maintaining the hierarchy at all costs (Hurley, 2009). When democratic leadership behaviors and organizational expectations are in direct opposition, leaders are on a collision course, unless there is a middle ground to begin the process of organizational change.

## Finding the Middle Ground

Leaders who want to build more democratic decision-making communities in a standardized, high-stakes accountability era, where quick fixes and mandated programs leave little room (Nichols & Berliner, 2007) for dialogue and debate (Toms, 2002), may find themselves in a moral quandary about how to accomplish this (Shapiro & Stefkovich, 2005). Because hierarchy is such a strong and dominant ideological perspective within a functionalist paradigm and leaders are held accountable for decisions within their school districts and schools, pressures can be intense on leaders to conform to decision-making processes that are efficient, exert control over others, expedite the process, and yield measurable outcomes.

Furthermore, many educational decisions made by state and federal policy makers leave little room now for legitimate involvement of others, including superintendents and principals (Nichols & Berliner, 2007). Questions abound about how educators realistically might negotiate these contradictions within the prevailing paradigmatic assumptions, where authentic listening and giving voice acquiesce to pseudo-democratic practices (Acker-Hocevar & Schoorman, 2006; Schoorman & Acker-Hocevar, 2010). How do you raise consciousness of leaders at all levels to sidestep many of the inherent contradictions of building democratic decision-making communities within their organizations, given present assumptions about how schools and districts are organized for decision making? Leaders will still have to meet external mandates while developing the capacity of their school districts and schools to adopt more democratic decision-making behaviors.

To support more democratic practices, leaders must deliberately choose how to negotiate between individual beliefs and organizational expectations within their school districts and schools. How leaders think about this might provide us with some clues about what leaders do to grapple with the limitations of a functionalist approach to school organization. In other words, we can determine when a leader knows, as March and Sevon (1988) stated, "Decisions are often made in situations that are quite distant from the situations implicit in the ideas of rational choice. Neither the precise decisions, the alternatives, the objectives nor the causal structures are clear" (p. 432). Leaders are expected to demonstrate leadership behaviors that enforce decisions that may not fit their present context or values that they or their community hold. Nevertheless, we can conclude from scholars who critiqued the perils of bureaucratic dysfunction within the functionalist paradigm (Fox, 1975; Gouldner, 1970) that mindless conformity to rules, policies, and mandates will not achieve high-performing organizations. What Getzels and Guba (1957), Argyris and Schön (1978), and Burrell and Morgan (1988) pointed out, in different ways, is individual and espoused values and beliefs may conflict with what is observed in practice. That is, the leader's individual and espoused values and beliefs are at odds with organizational norms. Leaders may be required to mediate between their desires for extended deliberation and pressure from above to move quickly to implement decisions, decisions that may ignore the input and involvement of others and be the antithesis of democratic decision making. The middle ground is for leaders to articulate a clear decision-making process as a starting place that seeks to involve others in the process and explores new possibilities for advocacy as well as democracy (Senge, 1990).

## Rational Decision-Making Models That Impact Leadership Behavior

Rational decision-making models (Vroom & Jago, 1988; Vroom & Yetton, 1973; Yukl, 2010) are useful for leaders to apply as a first step in creating more democratic decision-making communities. The models provide a thoughtful way for leaders to examine current practices and initiate an explicit means for involving others. What is missing from these models is how leaders' beliefs and values might impact their use. Leaders should therefore incorporate a stated philosophy of inclusion, giving voice, listening, and involvement that underpins these models.

Vroom and Yetton's (1973) normative-rational model distinguishes between individual and group decision making. This model describes how leader behavior is determined by the decision quality (the extent to which the decision is effective—high or low) and stakeholder acceptance (extent to which decisions are accepted by stakeholders who must implement the decision). The model assists the leader in determining when to involve stakeholders in the decision-making process and to what extent, but it does not assist the leader with understanding how the leader's own values may influence which stakeholders are included (Theoharis, 2009). Thus, although the model is a starting place, it has limitations that must be acknowledged and addressed.

In further determining decision quality and stakeholders' acceptance, the model provides the leader with five decision-making leadership behaviors for stakeholder involvement—two are autocratic, two are consultative in nature, and one addresses group decision making (participatory decision making). The leader determines which decision-making behavior to employ based on the situation, the information possessed by the leader, and the stakeholders' expertise and perspectives.

In any given situation, as defined in the Vroom and Yetton (1973) model, decision-making effectiveness depends on the amount of relevant information the leader and the stakeholders possess, the amount of disagreement among stakeholders regarding the desired alternative, the extent to which the problem is structured, whether the stakeholders will cooperate if allowed to participate, or whether stakeholders will be receptive to an autocratic decision (Green, 2009). For example, the autocratic approach would not be used by the leader when stakeholders have important, relevant information lacked by the leader, if the quality of the decision is important (high quality), if the leader lacks the information and expertise needed to address the problem, if the problem is ill defined, or if interaction with stakeholders with information and expertise is required. On one hand, the leader would be best served to choose the participative decision-making approach when the decision acceptance is critical and unlikely to result from an autocratic decision and the decision quality is not in question (Green, 2009). On the other hand, a leader may have to make an autocratic decision that is in the best interest of students but that is not acceptable to some educators or the community.

Vroom and Yetton (1973) theorized that decision quality and stakeholder acceptance are intervening variables that work collectively to affect group performance and that aspects of the situation moderate the relationship between leaders' decision-making behaviors and the intervening variables of quality and acceptance (Green, 2009). Whereas the Vroom-Yetton model uses only two outcome criteria in reaching the decision, decision quality and decision acceptance, the Vroom-Jago revision model takes into account time constraints, geographical dispersion of stakeholders, and the amount of stakeholders' development (Green, 2009). The Vroom-Jago model (Vroom & Jago, 1988) identifies factors critical to the leader in determining the most appropriate decision-making approach or behavior (autocratic, consultative, or group/participatory): (a) If time is of the essence, then group/participatory decision making may not be appropriate, and (b) if stakeholders have the skills and attributes necessary to participate in the decision-making process, then under certain circumstances they should be invited to participate, thereby enhancing decision quality and acceptance. Rational models help us understand decision-making processes within the current organizational paradigm and provide a place for leaders to employ more group participation versus autocratic decision-making processes. These models can assist the leaders in exploring how to institutionalize more democratic involvement and where to begin with the processes and expectations for participation.

## METHOD

Using participant language and experiences reported by the superintendents and principals as the starting point, we followed the steps outlined in Lincoln and Guba (1985) and Miles and Huberman (1994) and came together numerous times via conference calls to discuss insights based on the analysis of the transcripts, which led to discussions about the functionalist governance structures in place at the time of the focus groups. After an initial conference call, individually, we read through the superintendent and principal focus group transcripts and identified themes. Once each author identified her own themes, we discussed the individual theme commonalities and differences. Ultimately, two themes were identified: (a) leadership decision making and (b) factors that affect decision making. These two themes resulted as we continuously revisited the transcripts and refined the coding schema in relation to the chapter's focus of "decision-making processes, giving voice, listening, and involvement," which the editors initially had identified. We did not address the politics of decision making but chose to focus on how leadership decision making and factors that influence decision making affect building democratic decision-making communities. We recognized, however, that how leaders make decisions and the factors influencing decision making are subject to the politics of local education communities and to state and national policies. We also recognized that emotional issues surround decisions that are often part of a larger narrative that we do not address in this chapter.

The first theme, leadership decision making, is composed of three threads: (a) giving voice to stakeholders, (b) tensions that arise when involving stakeholders in shared decision making, and (c) stakeholders feeling valued and empowered when principals and superintendents give voice through listening and involving stakeholders. It is important to note that for the purpose of this chapter, we define *stakeholders* as everyone involved in the business of schools and education: parents, community, students, teachers, administrators, unions, and school boards. The second theme, factors that affect decision making, is composed of context (size of school district, school level, demographics, region of the country), relationships with school boards and superintendents, communication mechanisms in place, accountability for decisions, and time commitment. We present findings through stories and quotes organized around the chapter's focus of "decision-making processes, giving voice, listening, and involvement."

## FINDINGS

### Superintendents' Perspectives: Leadership Decision Making

In analyzing the transcripts of superintendents from small and medium-sized school districts, we found that the leaders' viewpoints, values, and beliefs colored their interpretations of giving voice, listening, and involving stakeholders (community, teachers, principals, staff, and school boards). Superintendents shared frustration with listening and working with the school boards and unions who did not always seem to have students as the focus of their decisions. Superintendent 69 shared a story about when he resigned his position because the school board was not equitable, basing their decisions on race and politics, not on sound educational practice. "That disappoints me. And it sickens me so much that I resigned from a position because of that kind of thing…. You don't want a job like that. So those are kind of the tough decisions you make as a superintendent" (medium-sized districts, Southwest & West, 2006). Several superintendents described other personal conflicts.

> I think what always grounds me and what grounds my work is what's best for students. There are times when people's voices don't match with what I think are best for students, and that's something that I won't compromise on. So, even if I hear from you that you want me to do something that I morally or ethically cannot support because I don't believe it is best for kids, I won't go there. (medium-sized districts, Southwest & West)

Another superintendent described conflict in doing what is best for students in this manner:

> One of the biggest roadblocks in doing when you're trying to do what's best for kids is the roadblock that gets thrown in your face all the time, because we can't do this and we can't do that because of our contracts. It is so frustrating as superintendents because you have to play all your cards. And you continually have union issues coming up that change the way you do things. And it's very frustrating, because when union people come to talk to you, they're not coming to talk to about what's best for kids; they're coming to talk to you about what's best for teachers. (Superintendent 70, medium-sized districts, Midwest, 2005)

Aligning one's beliefs and values with giving voice, listening, and involving stakeholders created tensions for the superintendents. Giving voice especially caused tensions for the superintendents, but they agreed that providing stakeholders a means for their voices to be heard was important to the process of democratic decision making. They believed that giving voice communicated to the stakeholders that their input was valued. A superintendent from a medium-sized school district explained the tensions faced when working with his staff and cabinet to give voice and listen to community stakeholders.

> One of the interesting things I've been finding out, we had a lot of turnover in the last few years. We had a lot [of] people just getting just—just want to retire, and so we've seen a lot of people from different districts, and we are a high-poverty, high-needs district, and when you bring a voice in from the community, a lot of those staff say, "Well, what do they know? I have my doctorate; I have my PhD." And so I'm kind of mediating the resistance to listen to the voice of the staff below me that are just saying, "What do they know? They don't have teeth, they dress bad, their breath stinks," or whatever. But you know—so you say, "Oh, let's talk about this." So, that's been a real phenomenon for me in the last couple of years, trying to get everybody in the organization to listen to that voice as well. I think the data pieces are very important, but we had a group of people that—our town is real small, and the rumors can run around real fast, and so you all know about that, so we've created what we call the forum to dispel rumors because we had bond issues and things to deal with. But when we got in there, it wasn't only the school district they were upset with; it was the city, the police department; it was all of these issues, and so when we [were] done they gave us a set of recommendations and they came to the board meeting. Well when I took it to the cabinet and said, "Well how are we going to respond to these?" There was resistance in the cabinet. They would say, "Who do they think they are? You've given them too much power with their voice." I had a—I'm still working on that. They really don't want to listen to the recommendations, and this is a large citizen's group that's come forward. (medium-sized districts, Southwest & West)

The majority of the superintendents voiced the opinion that they would rather not be autocratic in their decision making, believing that involving stakeholders, giving them a voice, and listening to them are essential when building democratic communities; however, they all agreed that the final decision rests with the superintendent. Superintendents expressed the belief that those who have a stake in the decision are most likely to want to be involved in the decision making, whether or not they have the information or expertise to participate in the process. Superintendent 35 from a small school district agreed that it was important to accept and listen to stakeholders, but school district leaders walk a fine line when doing this: "There are times that they may be way off base and we know that it isn't the best for education and we obviously don't implement it, but we do listen" (Midwest, 2004).

Several superintendents differentiated having voice from having a vote in the decision-making process.

I think as long as you give people a voice, most reasonable people will recognize they don't need a vote as long as they have a voice. But when they don't have a voice, that's when they slam their hand [down] and say, "No thanks. Well then, I want a vote." (Superintendent 74, small districts, Midwest)

Superintendent 68 described how he perceived voice and vote:

I think their voice is important, but the decision doesn't reside there. The decision resides with me. And so, voice is important, but it's not the decision—you know, this is not a democratic decision. We're not going to vote on it. (medium-sized districts, Southwest, 2006)

## Superintendents' Perspectives: Factors That Affect Decision Making

The superintendents involved in this study overwhelmingly agreed that they must know the community. When speaking of experiences involving their communities in decision making, Superintendent 14 commented,

You really have to know your community and the real power brokers.... Especially in small districts, people want to know everything that happens.... You go to a restaurant, you go to put gas in your car, and you get immediate feedback on the last decision you made. (small districts, Southeast, 2006)

Repeatedly, the superintendents shared experiences such as this one, pointing out that involving stakeholders and giving them a voice in decision making is what they strive to do. Superintendent 12 from a small school district spoke of how stakeholders in rural school districts not only want a voice but also expect to have a voice and an audience with the superintendent at all times.

You have a lot of voices coming at you every single day, probably 180 degrees difference in regard to what someone wants or doesn't want and everybody wants to be listened to. The challenge for rural superintendents is to make sure that access and listening is available. (Southeast, 2006)

The superintendents indicated that they always work to balance what they believe is best for students in the school district with what others believe to be the best thing to do. No matter the size of the district, superintendents spoke of making decisions in what was best for the students in their districts. Superintendent 29 spoke of involving parents in a school district decision:

> There was a group of citizens for better schools, and it taught me right off the bat that parents really want their school to be productive for children. There isn't a parent out there that wants to send their child to a bad school. The issue is that we involved those parents to sit down with us as a staff, and we had a steering committee, input meetings; we had coffees; and we spent the summer before that school opened literally happy, identifying all the different issues, and planning some strategies and goals to see how we could turn that school around. I still consider it the most rewarding experience I've ever had in education. (medium-sized districts, Southeast, 2005)

Superintendent 28 from a small-sized school district shared an experience that describes how involving the community and practicing democratic decision-making strategies resulted in positive outcomes for the community. The school district had to make some plans to house students for the coming year. The options were to reconstruct the school building or to close the school. The superintendent established several groups—the business community, teachers, and parent groups—to obtain input from the stakeholders. Based on the information yielded by listening to these groups, the decision was made to relocate the classrooms and move forward on school reconstruction. The superintendent shared that volunteers from the community stepped up because, as she surmised, it was their decision and they were a part of the decision making. Others made unexpected monetary contributions to help the relocation, again, because they were involved in the decision-making process of rebuilding the school. Superintendent 28 stated,

> That was probably one of the most successful projects because there was very little finger pointing, or complaining or frowning after. I think that was a success story. A lot of people came together and formed a consensus and we implemented many of the recommendations. (Southeast, 2005)

Many of the superintendents, mostly from medium-sized school districts, told stories of experiences with teacher unions and working on giving voice, listening, and involving them in decision making.

> I've been working with, my association [union]. We historically have a great relationship with our association, but the last couple of years, they've wanted a voice, but they kind of wanted to pick the areas where they wanted a voice. I said, "No, if you want a voice, you're going to have a voice in all of this." ... This year, we're struggling with salaries.... Well, they wanted to say, "We want more money and less people, but you decide how to." And I said, "No, no, no, that's not how this works. Then the board and I are just the bad

guys, picking out who's not going to have a job next year." ... You know, they don't want to get into that, because a lot of these people, they've [taught] with [us] for a lot of years. Well, either we're going to have voice or we can't—think and choose. (medium-sized districts, Southwest & West)

An interesting difference between the small and medium-sized school districts was that superintendents in the medium-sized school districts spoke much more about the importance of having communication mechanisms in place for giving voice and listening to their stakeholders. Superintendents from small school districts seemed to be much more connected to their stakeholders in that the flow of communication was person to person. Superintendents from medium-sized school districts discussed the importance of establishing a variety of communication channels for stakeholders to gather information that would lead to decisions that were in the best interest of students. Superintendent 61 shared how to use information gathered through different channels: "We need to take all that information, but then we need to run it through our filter and make sure we make those decisions, and not always necessarily in tune with the input that you've gotten" (medium-sized districts, Midwest).

Several of the superintendents spoke of using social networking (e-mail and Listservs) to give voice and listen to their stakeholders. Female Superintendent 62 from a medium-sized, Midwest school district shared a communication between herself and a school board member relating to incorporating social networks to better connect with the community: "I think that just that nature of involvement, in the process of decision making in our publics is just increasing the opportunities for our leadership to be aware and to be connected."

All of the superintendents described involving, listening to, and giving voice to stakeholders as extremely important yet complex when building and sustaining democratic communities. It is essential in developing relationships with stakeholders and crucial in building a school district's capacity for participative decision making. One of the most problematic issues for superintendents who participated in the focus groups was educating the community to understand that the decision-making process is time consuming and requires the individual or group to be responsive and accountable for the decision implementation. Superintendents grapple with how best to explain to stakeholders that the decision making is a process, not a one-time event, and if they want to be involved in the process, they must not only commit the time but also be willing to be accountable for the decision and its implementation. Many of the superintendents shared that their stakeholders agree to participate in the process, yet what the participants want to do is show up, tell the superintendent what they want, get their way, and leave.

Superintendents in small and medium-sized school districts alike expressed frustration with stakeholders not making the connection that responsibility and accountability come with having a voice in decision making. Superintendent 28 expressed it this way: "Having a voice in a decision being made is different than making a decision. Having a voice means having responsibility for a decision" (medium-sized districts, Southeast, 2005). When stakeholders make the connection, however, between participating in decision making and with being accountable and responsible, they often reconsider. "'If we go this route, are you willing to accept the accountability that goes with it?' And some people will, and some people want nothing to do with that, and this changes the dynamics as well" (medium-sized districts, Southwest & West, 2006). Superintendent 53 said it this way: "The key to all shared decision making is authority; without responsibility and accountability, [it] does not work" (medium-sized districts, New England & Mid-Atlantic, 2006).

A predicament the superintendents described, no matter the district size, was ensuring stakeholders had the necessary information and commensurate expertise to participate in the decision-making process. Superintendents cannot just involve diverse groups in the decision making, but have the responsibility of providing the group the necessary information so those involved in the decision making can make decisions in the best interest of educating students. Essential factors, knowledge, and information must be included in the decision-making equation of time commitment, accountability, and responsibility for stakeholders to effectively and successfully participate in shared decision making. Superintendent 51 stated,

> It has to be informed people come to the table in whatever they're deciding. So if they're informed and knowledgeable in that area, and also there's a sense of shared accountability, it can be enormously valuable. It's when people want to share in decisions that they haven't got a clue about and don't have any accountability attached to it, then it gives shared decision making a bad name. But when it's done in an intelligent and thoughtful manner, it is very worthwhile. (medium-sized districts, New England & Mid-Atlantic, 2006)

## Principals' Perspectives: Leadership Decision Making

Principals expressed commitment to making decisions that were best for students and reported giving voice predominately to faculty, followed by students and parents. For issues affecting the majority, they described probing all constituents, much like the example provided by Principal 65.

We were at a place where we had the ideas, but we were struggling with how we were going to recognize that the only way we were going to implement [them] was to create more time and to restructure to kind of give us more of that time. So we took on a pretty big project with a group of teachers really restructuring our schedule, our school day, took away time from our lunch periods, but it allowed us to add quite a few things into our program, more consistent advisory program, elective program, more comprehensive health program, allowed us to enhance and expand our instrument and music program. But it came by lengthening our school day. We had to start earlier, and so that meant a lot of people had to come on board, the teachers certainly had to come on board with it, the school board and the community had to support it, and it was a fairly exhaustive process—to present it, to get feedback, make some refinements, and ultimately take it to the school board so they can pass the programs. (middle schools, Midwest, 2006)

Much of the tension for principals related to alignment between district office expectations and what was best for students. Principal 23 referred to an example of following district office expectations and then experiencing fallout with teachers:

I get in trouble. No, there are things that I know the way it is presented to me from the central office, you know, I can pretty much read if I am going to have a choice here or not. We changed reading programs and you know, the money was there—"Y'all did it—I thought everyone was going to do it." We were told, you know, that the whole system was going to use this reading program for K-1 and I just told the teachers, "You don't have any choice." I'm usually the rebel, but I was the one that bought into it, and now the teachers have struggled with it. (elementary schools, Southeast, 2005)

Another tension identified was when there was little opportunity for principals to be stakeholders in school district decision making and they wanted to provide input. "In our district there is almost an absence of principal dialogue in decision making" (Principal 51, elementary schools, Southeast, 2006).

Although they perceived allowing input as "a double-edged sword" (Principal 80, high schools, Midwest, 2005), principals stated that by having a voice, stakeholders feel more valued and empowered. This adds a motivational component to rational decision making but also means that people expect to be heard. The feelings of empowerment also can lead to innovative practices. Elementary school Principal 23 (Southeast, 2005) said "People need to have a voice in decision making in order to feel valued … feeling worthy." Principal 63 (middle schools, Midwest, 2005) and Principal 73 (middle schools, Midwest, 2006) said that by being empowered themselves, they saw the value and therefore empowered the teachers.

I have a terrific superintendent, he empowers us as building administrators to do things.... I find it tremendously freeing to know that I have the freedom to make mistakes and to try some things.... I look at the staff and treat them the same way.

High school principals described ethical, courageous leadership and gave examples of making decisions they believed that faculty would not have made, such as allowing student credit recovery and taking liberty with rules and guidelines to support student success.

One of the things that I frankly really enjoy as the high school principal is that I can break the rules. And what I mean by that is that if I have a unique situation, and I think it's in the best interest of their kids and their learning, I break the rules. (Principal 83, high schools, Midwest, 2006)

Female Principal 84 expressed ethical, courageous leadership this way:

There needs to be courageous leaders who are willing to step out of the beaten path and take those hits and say, "This is what I believe needs to happen for the good of all the children here." And be able to accept that there's gonna be criticisms and conflict and at the end of the day be able to go home. (high schools, Midwest, 2006)

She went on to share a specific example:

We had a student who was special ed. [education], was in our most at-risk program as a special ed. I mean for dropout. Indeed did drop out as a freshman, came back, went to Pathways, which is our alternative program. Was kicked out of there, called this summer and said, "I think I have it together, I really want to give this a try." And in the old days, a different personality would have said, "Too bad." Ya know? But we said, "Bring your mother in, we'll set up a time, let's see what our options are." So what we did is we said, "You're kinda on a probationary status; you're gonna have a reduced time. You'll be here the first 3 hours of the day; we handpicked your teachers because we believe that they'll be—you'll be best served by them. You sign a contract that says, "By this date you would have shown that your tardiness, any substance abuse, any disrespect, certainly will be at a minimum." We know he is not gonna change his colors completely. And he knows, and he did this very well, that if he need[s] to explode, he can come down and explode in our office. He can scream and holler at the top of his lungs when my door is closed. But if he does it in the general population, there's a consequence, and then we will revisit it at that designated time. There's nothing in the handbook about that; there's nothing in the school policy about that. There's "it's what we needed to do to give that kid this last chance to try to be successful."

Middle school Principal 71 pointed out that for successful shared decision making, school leaders, school district leaders, and participants need to be well informed on the target issue's content and on the decision-making process. Principal 60 stated, "People need to have an understanding of consensus if they're going to have shared decision making" (elementary schools, Midwest, 2005). Principal 66 stated, "Shared decision-making process is not easy. A leader who employs this process needs to be very skilled" (middle schools, Midwest, 2005).

## Principals' Perspectives:
## Factors That Affect Decision Making

After passage of the No Child Left Behind Act in 2002, principals used more data to inform decision making. "Disaggregating data is an eye opener. Focusing on students is everyone's job" (Principal 24, elementary school, Southeast, 2005). Principal 21 followed with, "It's given us some backbone" (elementary schools, Southeast, 2005).

Another identified factor was school district size. The advantage of being a small school district was that it was easy for the superintendent to involve principals if he or she so chose, but being small did not ensure involvement. One elementary principal in a small, southwestern school district indicated that the superintendent made all the financial decisions, including those related to Title I and other external funding sources.

> Our district does a half million dollars [from casinos] and the principals not having any input as to how that money is used. Of course, the other challenge is dealing with a new superintendent *every* 6 months and building that trust and that relationship.... We want to have just as much input into what's happening at the district level as the teachers want to have at the school level. (Principal 39, elementary schools, Southwest, 2005)

In contrast, elementary school Principal 49 suggested that being in an even smaller district "allows us to really work close to the central office" (Southwest, 2006). Principal 70 shared that his superintendent's office is on the other side of his school building:

> When we do come up with a situation where a decision needs to be made quickly ... we can pull together the team really quickly, or maybe I'm given the latitude to make the decision.... I think that our [small] size has drawbacks in certain areas but there are times where our setting is really at an advantage. (middle schools, Midwest, 2006)

The type of decision to be made is an important consideration in selecting a decision-making strategy, such as shared decision making. Shared decision making was identified as a choice for large issues, such as school change, to obtain buy-in. "Actually revamping, and you try to get people on board and moving" (Principal 20, elementary schools, Southeast, 2005).

Elementary principals gave examples of implementing task forces to address short-term issues such as a schoolwide discipline plan (Principal 16, Southwest &West, 2005), developing a calendar (Principal 55, Midwest, 2005), or curriculum-related issues (Principal 60, Midwest, 2005). An example of shared decision making involving both faculty and students for a short-term issue given by Principal 79 was to determine the best way to prepare the students for state assessments.

> Probably the thing that strikes me the most right now is that a couple of years, we got into the [state] assessments and the NCLB [No Child Left Behind Act]; we put together a committee—staff and myself, and students to decide how can we best serve kids in and work on getting them prepared for the tests. It makes me mad now that I think about it, about getting prepared for tests. But anyway, it was interesting to watch our staff and kids talk about what they thought they wanted, what the staff thought they should do, and what the kids felt like needed to be done to them, and they finally came to a pretty good compromise on how we help kids get on with it. (high schools, Midwest, 2005)

High school principals mentioned having specific organized committees that regularly met, such as faculty forums. On one hand, Principal 76 had a mechanism to get input from students (high school, Midwest, 2005) when he had lunch with different groups of students to discuss issues and develop communication. On the other hand, he believed that communicating with parents in the normal process of being a principal was adequate.

Once the decision-making mechanism was determined, principals expressed that communicating the approach was a valuable step in maintaining trust. Principal 83 expressed it this way:

> There has to be a communication on what is the method of decision that is going to be used.... We may use a consensus model; we may use a voting model, depending on the issue. But, whenever we got one to make, we make—I share the method of decision right off the [bat]. So, that there's no question about how we're gonna make the decision. (high schools, Midwest, 2006)

Communication mechanisms were infrequently mentioned, but Principal 41 suggested the need "to have established avenues for the communication, and the better that people understand the system that we are working within, all parties, then that will help us to make appropriate decisions that are efficient" (elementary schools, Southwest & West, 2005).

Principals agreed that accountability was a factor that influenced their decision making. Principal 44 summed it up this way: "It has to be a decision you can live with, because you're the one who is going to take the heat, right?" (elementary schools, Southwest & West, 2005). Elementary school Principal 60 verbalized, "But we can't get so hung up in this shared decision-making process that we forget that somebody's got to make the final decision, and then somebody's got to carry the water, you know?" (Midwest, 2005). Another principal corroborated, "As an administrator, we are the ones who are held responsible and accountable for the success of our buildings" (Principal 69, middle schools, Midwest, 2006).

Principals suggested that those who provide input should be accountable for doing what is best for students. Principal 75 provided an example of shared decision making accountability with his administrative team:

> The biggest disappointment that I've had over the years has been with my team, the administrative team, in that, there's—I have four academy principals, and I had to meet both with the groups and individually, and we try to work to make sure that we operate as a school, and so as we collectively discuss issues and we come to consensus decisions and then we leave that room. It's my expectation that we're all going to take ownership of that, and most of the times, we do, but the few times where somebody says, "Well, Principal 75 said such and such" is very disappointing to me, because that's a cowardly way out of accountability, and it's as if I made the decision and they really didn't agree with it, and that invariably is going to circle back and hit both of us blind side, and that's probably my most disappointing experience with sharing decisions with others. (high schools, Midwest, 2005)

Time was a factor identified by principals who played various roles in the use of shared decision making. "What we found ... the teachers really don't have the time, and so, if you plan meetings for them to get their input, there are a lot of times when they will say, 'Just do it'" (Principal 20, elementary schools, Southeast, 2005). Principal 21 suggested that it was a conscious decision whether or not to take teachers out of class and away from students, their primary responsibility, for shared decision making, "but you don't have a teacher in the classroom doing what they really need to be doing, teaching the children" (elementary schools, Southeast, 2005). Principal 60 shared an example of the school district curriculum director using shared decision making to adopt a curriculum that took too much time: "Finally came a time when our curriculum director just had to say, 'Hey, this is the decision that's made and it's done.' ... We had everybody in the world on it, and it took a complete year" (elementary schools, Midwest, 2005). Such extreme experiences with extended time requirements that still did not have positive outcomes are indicative of the lack of expertise and skill that principals have in preparing for, facilitating, and arriving at a shared decision that can be implemented well.

## Superintendents and Principals: Comparisons and Contrasts

Superintendents and principals agreed that giving voice, listening, and involving stakeholders were important and necessary to making decisions that were in the best interest of students, both at the school district and school levels. Both groups recognized that stakeholders wanted to be involved in the decision-making process, but not necessarily responsible or accountable for the decision outcomes. Building democratic decision-making communities was preferred by both superintendents and principals over autocratic decision making; however, both groups believed it was complex and time consuming. These two factors, complexity and time, along with the lack of stakeholder understanding of accountability and responsibility for decisions, made consistent and appropriate implementation of participative decision making problematic. In other words, complexity and time are factors that leaders must address with their stakeholders to build the capacity over a phased development for more democratic decision-making processes to take hold. Educating the community on complex issues takes time.

Superintendents and principals alike discussed the difficulty of working with stakeholders in that they want to be heard but are not always willing to be accountable or responsible for the decision. Superintendents expressed the perspective that stakeholders often were more concerned with having a voice or desiring to achieve their personal agenda without putting in the work and time required for shared decision making. In other words, stakeholders were there to talk but not to listen to others' perspectives. This often occurs because many stakeholders lack understanding of the complexity of education and participate less from a democratic perspective and more from a political perspective of getting heard and influencing outcomes for self-interest.

Democratic decision making is a time-intensive process. Principals reported that teachers do not want to give up their time to participate in decision making because they are well aware of the time involvement from past experiences, and they may not see the investment as yielding the outcomes desired. It was also clear that teachers may feel that in the past they have invested much time in a decision-making process, made recommendations, and had none of the recommendations implemented. The disconnect between decision-making involvement and actual decision implementation is particularly disconcerting for professionals, like teachers, in schools.

Both superintendents and principals acknowledged the value of giving voice and the importance of building relationships with stakeholders, yet both groups described how giving voice often caused tensions with stakeholders. Superintendents reported more tensions from school boards and unions, whereas principals discussed tensions that arose between the school and the school district office. Superintendents and principals identified tensions that resulted from trying to comply with the state and federal accountability mandates and also meet the needs of the students and community, when the greater public may not realize that there was no choice in implementing certain policies.

It seems that school district size and school size matter in the ease or difficulty educational leaders reported in giving voice, listening, and involving stakeholders in shared decision making. On one hand, superintendents from small school districts, along with principals from smaller schools, described communication as informal with stakeholders. Superintendents from medium-sized districts, on the other hand, discussed the importance of using a variety of communication mechanisms, such as social networks, to gather information from stakeholders.

The superintendents and principals in this study agreed that shared decision making is a messy, complex process and that at best, as leaders, they must seek ways to understand multiple perspectives when looking at a problem. Considering whom to involve, how to develop and educate stakeholders, how to anticipate each group's contributions, and who is accountable for the decision framed the complexity of shared decision making.

## IMPLICATIONS FOR PRACTICE, LEADERSHIP PREPARATION AND RESEARCH, AND POLICY

### Practice

Superintendents and principals believed they were accountable for the decisions made at the school district and school levels, respectively. They expressed that, under the right conditions, building democratic decision-making communities was good for developing broader perspectives. It is troubling to us that, even with the agreement that giving voice was appropriate, neither group clearly identified decision-making processes, structures, or procedures expected or used on a routine basis to accomplish this. Lack of success in building more democratic decision-making communities, many leaders noted, was related to time requirements for the process. The absence of clear expectations for the processes, structures, and procedures suggested superintendents may want to begin the process of determining the decision-making system to be used by leaders within a given district and its schools for giving voice, listening, and involving stakeholders both formally and informally, but it appeared the superintendents in this study had not done so. Without a clear set of expectations and a system in place to promote more democratic decision making, autocratic decisions may continue as the norm, and shared decision making may be more of the exception to decision-making practices. When superintendents model shared decision-making processes, other school district and school-based leaders will likely follow with similar practices.

Statements of the roles and responsibilities of all parties, and an ethical framework for decision making that school leaders, teachers, students, and community constituents agree to as part of a decision-making system, should be fleshed out. Roles and responsibilities include accountability and purposeful deliberate inclusion of all constituents, especially those who historically have been unheard and underserved. Communication by the superintendent of the expected roles, responsibilities, structures, and processes is not only important for successful implementation of a system that guides decision making but also critical to its success in becoming normative practice. Opportunities for professional development on educational issues and the decision-making processes will further develop trust among all stakeholders as well as deepen knowledge and the skills necessary to facilitate shared decision making. Trust develops with open and authentic communication related to issues and transparency on how the issues might be resolved.

## Leadership Preparation and Research

Although decision-making models, like those included in the literature review, are generally in textbooks used in courses on leadership, organizational theory, and the principalship, students may compartmentalize learning and leave these courses without specific processes and structures to build democratic communities for shared decision making. Leadership preparation programs must include strategies to modify governance structures that define and enact explicit roles and relationships that support inclusive practices of giving voice, listening, and involvement. Leadership programs also must examine the rational decision-making processes for what is not included, such as how to increase advocacy and promote democracy (Senge, 1990).

The continued emphasis on accountability for student learning, accompanied by budget shortfalls, market competition, and community coalition involvement, places a greater emphasis on the need for educational leadership graduate students to understand their own values and beliefs and their unique work contexts. Therefore, important components of leadership preparation programs are consideration of theoretical knowledge, skill development in decision-making processes, participant involvement, role designation, and clarity around values that support explicit decision-making models for developing shared-decision-making governance structures. How to build more democratic decision-making communities, with transparent and varied communication structures, is a valuable component to an educational leadership curriculum. Although these areas are necessary, they are not in and of themselves sufficient to ensure that social justice principles are also considered. Preparation programs can assist students in enhancing their leadership behaviors through grappling with their values, beliefs, and organizational expectations.

The changing political environment, funding mechanisms, increasing federal oversight in education, and diverse community contexts invite research on contemporary decision-making models, structures, practices, and the inclusion of voices typically not heard. While the superintendents and principals attributed lack of shared decision making to time constraints, they did not share strategies for greater effectiveness in their decision-making processes; in reality, they might have needed skill in facilitating and leading collaborative decision making within short time-frames. Leaders should study their practices and those within their organization to assess whether what they espouse is what they practice, whether their stated beliefs align with organizational expectations, and whether existing governance structures engender building more democratic decision-making communities or promote maintaining the hierarchy (Hurley, 2009) at the sacrifice of socially just actions.

## Policy

The federal and state levels of oversight have stripped away much decision-making authority from local educators who expect their voices to be heard in more than a one-way conversation resulting in less democratic decision making at the grassroots level. Policy makers at the local, state, and federal levels should fund research on effective decision-making processes and governance structures that result in quality learning for all students. At the state level, sensitivity to local contexts and to every constituent should inform decision-making policy. State education leaders should balance gaining favor and funding with consulting and listening to school district leaders to develop policies and make policy decisions in sync with involving others around a shared agreement of what is in the best interest of all students and their learning that may call into question a one-size-fits-all approach. From a local policy perspective, superintendents and principals should develop guidelines for decision making within a school district that value various stakeholders' roles and voices, particularly those groups that have not traditionally been included in the discussion.

## CONCLUSIONS

We argue, based on this chapter's findings, that it is difficult for leaders to enact democratic decision making within current structures and practices. Leaders described times when their individual values and the values of the organization were at odds and when they had to make choices that exposed them to professional risks; the leaders called this exercising courageous leadership. Clearly, decision making, though seen as a rational process under functionalism, cannot be divorced from the leaders' values and beliefs. This is where principles of social justice enter decision-making processes. Doing what is best for students, a stated value of these leaders, needs to be underscored in relation to how one listens to and involves the disenfranchised and the traditionally excluded. Findings suggested when superintendents and principals gave voice, listened to, and involved stakeholders in the decision-making process, they often encountered several problematic areas: Stakeholders often lacked the information and expertise for participating in decision making; when using shared decision making, the leader may not get the decision expected; and stakeholders often may want to be involved in the decision making but not held responsible or accountable for the decision-making outcomes. The day-to-day decisions about personnel, policy, and fiscal matters can be overwhelming within the prevailing functionalist paradigm of educational leaders' work. Mired in bureaucratic mindsets, educational leaders may be inclined to place policies over people, limit democratic processes, and focus on rules over relationships, thus compromising democratic ideals for the expedient or short-term solution of meeting compliance requirements and not rocking the boat. Enacting democratic governance structures within current normative assumptions of leadership control over decision making is at odds with moving toward more inclusive practices. Leaders must face these inherent contradictions to promote more democratic decision-making communities that challenge top-down mandates and hierarchical practices.

Neither superintendents nor principals seemed to have specific, identified, regularly employed processes for decision making when giving voice to stakeholders or explicit governance structures to challenge existing norms of autocratic and hierarchical organizational behavior. We acknowledge that decision making is complex, but we also believe that without a clear process in place to guide the development of democratic decision making over time, the decision-making process is arbitrary and left to the one in charge. We do not believe that the leader alone should decide which processes to use. Rather, we encourage school-district and school-based leaders to engage in an open dialogue about decision-making behaviors that give voice and involve stakeholders in how to develop processes, structures, and strategies.

The Vroom-Yetton model and the Vroom-Jago revision model have stood the test of time as many studies have been conducted and weaknesses have been identified (Green, 2009). These models place the focus of decision making on specific aspects of leader behaviors, address intervening variables, and identify factors about the situation that allow the relationship between leader behavior and outcomes to be moderated (Green, 2009). The models do not, however, take into consideration who will be held accountable for carrying out the work and who should be involved and responsible in the most intimate ways within the decision-making process. Educational leaders must be able to evaluate individual stakeholders' knowledge and expertise, and they must know how to allocate the resources needed to provide appropriate knowledge and information capital to members of the community to build capacity for shared decision making. If decision-making processes are not properly addressed by leaders, educators and community members may become disenfranchised with decision making, and superintendents and principals may lose credibility within their educational and local communities—or even worse, become critics of public education.

Present and future leaders must first and foremost know what they stand for and be aware of their beliefs and values in order to practice ethical decision making. Giving voice, listening, and involving stakeholders implies that leaders espouse and practice democratic principles in their actions and choices and promote more democratic governance structures. How do leaders put forth their values and beliefs within rational decision-making perspectives? What needs to be challenged and changed? How might superintendents' and principals' leadership behaviors within the assumptions of functionalism be reconciled with building more democratic decision-making communities that promote inclusion through a social justice framework? We suggest that leaders question one-best-way and one-size-fits-all mindsets, bring theories-in-use into greater congruence with espoused theories, and develop a unifying philosophy of shared governance with ethical principles (Argyris & Schön, 1978; Burrell & Morgan, 1988; Getzels & Guba, 1957; Yukl, 2010). Leaders must reconcile the tension between their beliefs, values, and behaviors and the organizational expectations within functionalist assumptions to positively effect changes. Superintendents and principals must explore decision-making models and make them more explicit; identify stated and unstated values of inclusion and exclusion; deconstruct democratic and antidemocratic practices within their organization; and have the courage to undertake changes from within the system to support more voice, listening, and involvement.

## REFERENCES

Acker-Hocevar, M., & Schoorman, D. (2006, October). *Building democratic faculty governance as critical decision making: The politics of listening and giving voice.* Paper presented at the meeting of the University Council for Educational Administration, San Antonio, TX.

Argyris, C., & Schön, D. (1978). *Organizational learning: A theory of action perspective.* Reading, PA: Addison Wesley.

Burrell, G., & Morgan, G. (1988). *Sociological paradigms and organizational analysis: Elements of the sociology of corporate life.* Portsmouth, NH: Heinemann.

Fox, A. (1975). *Man mismanagement.* London, England: Hutchinson.

Getzels, J. W., & Guba, G. (1957). Social behavior and the administrative process. *The School Review, 65,* 423-441.

Gouldner, A. (1970). *The coming crisis of western sociology.* New York, NY: Basic Books.

Green, R. L. (2009). *Practicing the art of leadership: A problem-based approach to implementing the ISLLC standards* (3rd ed.). Boston, MA: Pearson.

Hurley, C. J. (2009). *The six virtues of the educated person: Helping kids to learn, schools to succeed.* New York, NY: Rowman & Littlefield.

Lincoln, Y. S., & Guba, E. G. (1985). *Naturalistic inquiry.* Beverly Hills, CA: SAGE.

March, J. G., & Sevon, G. (1988). Gossip, information, and decision making. In J. G. March (Ed.), *Decision and organizations* (pp. 430-442). Oxford, England: Blackwell.

Miles, M. B., & Huberman, A. M. (1994). *Qualitative data analysis* (2nd ed.). Thousand Oaks, CA: SAGE.

Nichols, S. L., & Berliner, D. C. (2007). *Collateral damage: How high-stakes testing corrupts America's schools.* Cambridge, MA: Harvard Education Press.

Schoorman, D., & Acker-Hocevar, M. (2010). Faculty governance within a social justice framework: Struggles and possibilities for democratic decision making in higher education. *Equity & Excellence in Education, 43,* 310-325.

Senge, P. (1990). *The fifth discipline: The art and practice of the learning organization.* New York, NY: Currency.

Shapiro, J. P., & Stefkovich, J. A. (2005). *Ethical leadership and decision making in education: Applying theoretical perspectives to a complex dilemma* (2nd ed.). Mahwah, NJ: Erlbaum.

Sidorkin, A. (1999). *Beyond discourse: Education, the self, and dialogue.* Albany, NY: SUNY Press.

Theoharis, G. (2009). *The school leaders our children deserve: Seven keys to equity, social justice and school reform.* New York, NY: Teachers College Press.

Toms, M. (2002). *A time for choices: Deep dialogues for deep democracy.* Gabriola Island, British Columbia, Canada: New Society.

Vroom, V. H., & Jago, A. G. (1988). *The new leadership: Managing participation in organizations.* Upper Saddle River, NJ: Prentice Hall.

Vroom, V. H., & Yetton, P. W. (1973). *Leadership and decision making.* Pittsburgh, PA: University of Pittsburgh Press.

Yukl, G. A. (2010). *Leadership in organizations* (7th ed.). Upper Saddle River, NJ: Pearson Prentice Hall.

CHAPTER 8

# SCHOOL AND DISTRICT RELATIONSHIPS

**Thomas A. Kersten and Julia Ballenger**

Unlike many businesses that are product focused, schools are people-centered organizations. Little is accomplished successfully in schools and districts without the involvement and support of those who have some stake in the organization. How well people work together toward achieving common goals is inextricably linked to individual school and school district success and predicated on the strength of the relationships constructed within schools, between schools and school districts, and with the various publics served.

This emphasis on people is clearly reflected in school district priorities. Traditionally, school boards allocate at least 60% of their resources to employee salaries and benefits (Kersten, 2010). This level of expenditure speaks volumes about the importance placed on people in public education. The human resource investment, not only significant in terms of capital outlay, is also critical to school success and the quality of relationships built and sustained over time. This chapter explores the relationship dimension of school leadership from the perspectives of superintendents and principals. School leaders have long recognized the importance of relationships. Theorists such as Fullan (2004) and

*Snapshots of School Leadership in the 21st Century:*
*Perils and Promises of Leading for Social Justice,*
*School Improvement, and Democratic Community*, pp. 147–167
Copyright © 2012 by Information Age Publishing

Leithwood, Seashore Louis, Anderson, and Wahlstrom (2004) highlighted the importance of a school leader's ability to work effectively with a broad spectrum of individuals. Others such as Marzano, Waters, and McNulty (2005) identified relationship building as one of the key responsibilities of principals and demonstrated how positive relationships link to increased student achievement.

Years ago superintendents and principals could succeed merely by being good managers who interacted reasonably well with others. Today, this is insufficient. Standards-based reform for large-scale improvement of instructional practice and student performance often results in increased accountability for superintendents and principals (Elmore, 2000). Superintendents and principals are held much more accountable by local and state constituents than they used to be for improving student performance, even though they are dependant on others for their success. School leaders alone cannot improve schools or increase student achievement. Thus, some of the leadership functions and activities must be distributed among multiple leaders who can assume many different roles in the organization according to their areas of expertise. A few of those leaders include teacher leaders, school board members, assistant principals, and central office administrators (Spillane, Halverson, & Diamond, 2001). Just as important, administrators must support each other and maintain productive relationships to work together to address shared problems.

Additionally, as a consequence of broad-based involvement needed to achieve organizational goals, an important element of school leaders' success rests on their ability to build and sustain relationships with a wide array of multiple leaders and stakeholders. Central to this effort is creating the organizational culture in which people work well together to contribute to the school's success. However, this can be a huge challenge for school leaders, especially at a time when everyone with an investment in the local school district's success is encouraged to provide their personal perspectives. What may work well for one school may not work well for another. Mandates from the school district may exclude principal input or may serve one special interest group at the expense of another. Such a dynamic, interactive, and complex environment reinforces the link between schools and districts on the one hand and the public on the other. In addition, it ultimately impacts student success. In this chapter, we employ a relationship perspective on leadership to explore the (a) importance of building positive relationships, (b) types of relationships needed to foster goal attainment, and (c) approaches and barriers to building effective school relationships.

## RELATIONSHIP PERSPECTIVE

Green (2010) identified four dimensions of leadership. Dimension 3, Building Bridges Through Relationships, provides the lens to increase our understanding of how superintendents and principals in the Voices 3 Project described the bridges they built to goal attainment through their relationships. Green (2010) defined relationships as "a connection between people, enabling them to engage in some sort of exchange" (p. 133). The next area examines the theories that help us understand different relationships.

### Importance of Relationships

Green (2010) referred to several theorists whose work informs the importance of relationship building among educational leaders and their constituents. He began with John Stacy Adams's equity theory, which posits that individuals expect a fair balance between what their inputs are in relations to their outputs. Adams' equity theory calls for a fair balance to be struck between an employee's inputs (i.e., hard work, skill level, tolerance, and enthusiasm) and an employee's outputs (e.g., salary, benefits, and intangibles such as recognition). According to the theory, finding this fair balance serves to ensure a strong and productive relationship is achieved with the employee, with the overall result being contented, motivated employees.

Moreover, Green (2010) cited the work of French and Raven (1959) that categorized four sources of powers in social influence theory. Of these four sources of power, referent power is highly associated with building and sustaining relationships. According to French and Raven, referent power is the power from another person liking you or wanting to be like you. It is the power of charisma or referent power. Some leaders influence their faculty through their charismatic behavior.

Referent power stems from social attractiveness and credibility (Cooper & Croyle, 1984). Social attractiveness indicates the desire of a person to be like another (Goodyear & Robyak, 1981). Credibility suggests trustworthiness and expertness, similar to French and Raven's (1959) expert power. Trustworthiness, a perception that leaders will use their knowledge and skill for the good of the organization, differs from expertness. Expertise is the perception that leaders possess the appropriate knowledge and skill to solve problems (Martin, 1978). Thus, social influence theory may impact leaders' ability to build and sustain positive relationships in schools and districts.

## Types of Relationships

Various types of relationships exist among leaders and their constituents, both internally and externally. Internally, in schools, three important types of relationships must be developed: (a) principal–teacher relationships, (b) teacher–teacher relationships, and (c) teacher–student relationships. A critical element of effective leadership is the relationship that exists among school leaders and teachers. To enhance the academic achievement of all students, school leaders and teachers must work collaboratively. Another set of relationships that is important for school effectiveness is teacher–teacher relationships. School leaders must be proactive and assist teachers in building trust and establishing collegial relationships with each other. Finally, the relationship between teachers and students is a must. Students learn best from teachers with whom they are able to develop good interpersonal relationships (Green, 2010). In addition to building positive relationships with teachers and students in schools, educational leaders must build positive relationships with the external publics and establish relationships with central office administrators, staff, parents, business, and political entities in the community in order to achieve their vision and goals (Green, 2010).

Relationships are important in creating the conditions for successful change. If relationships improve, schools get better. Conversely, if relationships get worse, ground is lost. Thus, leaders must build relationships with diverse people and groups, especially with constituents who think differently. For this reason, relationship building is essential to bringing about school improvement to accomplish the goals of the organization (Fullan, 2004).

Establishing relationships with central office administrators and the superintendent to obtain resources and support needed to move the school forward is important. In Green's (2010) research with school districts, several major disconnects between school leaders and central office administrators were identified. These major disconnects were a lack of "(a) visits to schools by central office administrators, (b) lack of autonomy of school leaders, (c) understanding of everyday school practices, and (d) a lack of input sought from school leaders by central office administrators" (Green, 2010, p. 139).

## Approaches and Barriers to Building Relationships

Superintendents and principals who enjoy positive relationships with internal and external constituents do not acquire these relationships accidentally. From a review of the writings of Covey (1989), Gladwell (2000),

Maxwell (2003), and Green (2010), we found five major approaches essential to building relationships: (a) establishing trust, (b) encouraging commitment, (c) fostering collaboration, (d) ensuring effective communication, and (e) reaching closure on organizational issues. Conversely, barriers to building effective relationships among internal and external constituents are these: (a) lack of effective systems for communication; (b) conflict among diverse constituents who hold different opinions based on values of quality, choice, efficiency, and excellence; (c) competition that divides constituents into groups of us versus them; and (d) lack of commitment on the part of constituents to goal attainment. Quality relationships contribute to leadership effectiveness (Collins, 2001; Green, 2005; Maxwell, 2003). Building bridges through relationships enables superintendents and principals to develop credibility. With credibility, leaders have greater possibility for organizational success.

## DATA ANALYSIS

We employed a thematic analysis of the data by individually coding and classifying the superintendent and principal interviews to identify salient themes. In the analysis, we identified the common categories from the transcripts. Next, we typed a list of the categories from both of our analyses. From this list, we combined categories through the constant comparison method. We then collapsed and refined categories and then discussed relationships and patterns until we reached consensus on the emergent themes (Gall, Gall, & Borg, 2005). The importance of building and maintaining positive relationships with stakeholders emerged as a central theme. This central theme includes two subthemes: (a) the link between relationship building, school culture, and organizational success and (b) the recognition of the stumbling blocks leaders encounter as they attempt to build positive school cultures and achieve organizational effectiveness.

## SUPERINTENDENTS' VOICES

Although superintendents place great value on stakeholder relationships, they understand how difficult it is to build and maintain these relationships. As they lead their school districts, they often must hurdle any number of stumbling blocks in their quest to build positive school district cultures and achieve organizational effectiveness. Superintendents from various parts of the country identified very similar challenges they regularly face.

## Relationship Building, School Culture, and Organizational Success

As superintendents discussed the importance of relationship building, they shared their beliefs and priorities. Superintendent 70 summarized this well by stating, "We set the tone. The building principal is so important for the building. We're so important for the communities that we live in. If our behavior is not positive, we don't have the right attitude" (small-sized districts, Midwest, 2005).

If relationships are one key to organizational success, this raises a question: How do superintendents describe their essential role in relationship building? They spoke of collaboration in the development of professional relationships. They noted the value of cultivating relationships with administrators, teachers, school board members, parents, and the community if they and the school district are to be effective. Superintendent 29 articulated this point:

> I'm an advocate that decisions are made when you involve the individuals in the process. It builds the ownership, understanding, support, and it's through that dialogue that you create teamwork for the purpose of serving children and serving them well. (medium-sized districts, Southeast, 2005)

As superintendents discussed improving schools and increasing student achievement, inevitably they focused on the importance of collaboration in broad-based decision making. From their perspectives, school district improvements cannot be achieved without the active participation and support of stakeholders. "I don't think we operate in a vacuum. We work for our communities and teachers" (Superintendent 14, mostly small-sized districts, Southeast, 2006).

Superintendents elaborated on this theme by discussing the importance of creating an inclusive and participatory work environment. Superintendents noted the absolute value of building collaboration between teachers and administrators. They discussed how difficult it is to make any meaningful improvements without working with the faculty. As Superintendent 70 said,

> The collaboration between administration and teachers is probably one of the greatest things I've ever seen that helped bridge the gap between administration and the teaching ranks was asking what you think, rather than telling you what to think, and part of the process is being able to work with teachers. We need to work with teachers rather than against them. That whole process came through in the 1980s. (medium-sized districts, Midwest, 2005)

This in turn influences the organizational culture. Another critical piece of both relationship building and collaboration is listening. Superintendent 35 stressed, "When someone has a stake in something, they definitely want to have their voice or opinion listened to or accepted, and then decisions based on that" (small-sized districts, Midwest, 2005).

A common belief among superintendents was that administrators accomplish a great deal more when they bring teachers into the decision-making process. They recognize that teachers want to be heard, not ignored or patronized. District leaders know that although they can order someone to meet basic expectations, this does not ensure their personal investment. According to Superintendent 41, "If you want the support, you have to involve them in the decision making" (small-sized districts, Southwest & West, 2004). Just asking for their opinions and not really listening means little. Superintendent 14 advised, "You must treat [people] with respect and dignity" (small-sized districts, Southeast, 2006).

## Relationship Challenges

Although superintendents recognize the need to focus on relationships, individuals and groups with whom they must interact sometimes do not recognize the importance relationship building with administrators plays in school and student success. Some individuals and groups tend to be more interested in what they want rather than what the superintendent considers best for the organization or students. However, because superintendents lead publicly supported organizations, they must interact with a broad spectrum of stakeholders. They are not in a position to select to whom they will listen or whom they can ignore—although some individuals and groups may exert much more influence with the superintendent than others. As a result of their public positions, superintendents often navigate in less than tranquil waters, interacting with stakeholders who have narrow perspectives or personal agendas.

Superintendents from all regions of the United States who participated in focus group sessions spoke freely about the importance of relationship building to their personal and school district successes. They indicated that district leaders who have good relationships with teachers and other key stakeholders can positively affect school improvement and student achievement. Specifically, they discussed the importance of involving stakeholders in the decision making if they hope to improve schools. As Superintendent 4 stated, "If everybody believes that they have a voice and embraces that, I think you stand a better chance of getting things done and changes made ... within your organization" (mostly small-sized districts, Midwest, 2006).

Relationship building is not limited to district employers. Superintendents recognized how important it is to cultivate productive relationships with school board members and parents. However, they also pointed out that these relationships are often fraught with challenges and recognized how essential it is to find ways to work effectively with both of these groups. Superintendent 24 put the issues in perspective:

> The most important thing is to keep the wheel of successful education in balance. The principals have their role. I have my role. The board members do, too. And when any one of the spokes starts to get loose or out of balance, then it causes the ride to get bumpy.... So it's working hard to keep the wheel in balance. (small-sized districts, Midwest, 2004)

District leaders were clearly concerned about the "squeaky wheel" quality of relationships with board members and parents that can complicate district leadership. Superintendent 4 said,

> You have to address those squeaky wheels because so many times they're negative in nature, and that negativity breeds negativity and will start pulling other things down, even if it is like giving into five board members because there are open windows on the bus overnight. (small-sized districts, Midwest, 2006).

Superintendents spoke about strategies they used to build working relationships with parents and board members. The superintendents discussed their attempts to build relationships through multiple means of communication, such as one-to-one contacts, committees and advisory boards, open forums, personal visibility, and similar approaches, to meet the multiple demands of communicating with different constituent groups. They also highlighted changes they have observed in parent expectations over recent years. "In my 20+ years as a superintendent, I've seen a real shift in demands by parents and communities and special interest groups" (Superintendent 77, mid-sized districts, Midwest, 2005).

Unfortunately, these approaches were sometimes unsuccessful. Superintendents reported that parents and board members frequently had personal agendas and were skeptical about district leadership. These personal agendas complicated relationship building. Superintendents may not always know what parents and board members really want, as noted by one superintendent: "It's very difficult for me personally to distinguish between when people just want to be heard and when they really want an answer" (medium-sized districts, Southwest & West, 2004). This struggle to win the confidence and support of those not employed by the school district is a constant challenge for superintendents.

Superintendents noted that parents' personal agendas often focus on their children's needs. They discussed how some parents have an inherent distrust of administrators, including the superintendent.

> If you can make a parent understand that you're not out to get their kid, [but that] you're really trying to come together to make a decision for what's best for their child, then sometimes you can build a relationship. (Superintendent 19, mostly small-sized districts, Southwest & West, 2005)

A common barrier most superintendents faced was interacting with individuals who have answers for everything. As Superintendent 30 stated, "The hardest thing [to deal with] as the administrator, of course, is ... people who think they know but don't know at all" (medium-sized districts, Southeast, 2005). Some are parents who refuse to see the big picture. They can be disruptive or even confrontational.

> I find myself feeling like I need to be teaching the parent. Because 9 out of 10, when I have a parent come through my door, I don't care how bizarre they are, how off the wall they are.... they don't have a clue. (Superintendent 19, small-sized districts, 2005)

That is, they bring a narrow perspective to the table.

At other times, barriers are created by groups, such as unions and special interest organizations, rather than individuals. The groups, too, can create roadblocks to success. Yet, superintendents, as they did with individuals, find themselves interacting with each, sometimes without success. These groups tend to be noncollaborative. As a result, they are a source of frustration for superintendents. At times, they even interfere with district decision making. "You get bombarded by these different groups. And you have to keep your boards on course and make decisions that are best for kids.... Educating can be tougher every day" (Superintendent 77, medium-sized districts, Midwest, 2005).

Superintendents identified teacher unions as a primary stumbling block. Because unions focus on teacher interests over student and districts needs, superintendents find themselves continuously maneuvering around union-created obstacles. "It is very frustrating because when union people come to talk to you, they're not coming to talk to you about what's best for kids. They're coming to talk with you about what's best for teachers" (Superintendent 70, medium-sized districts, Midwest, 2005). Yet, as difficult as these groups are, superintendents recognize that they cannot resist or ignore them. They must attempt to build positive relationships with them, if at all possible. "We need to work with teachers rather than against them" (Superintendent 72, medium-sized districts, Midwest, 2005).

As difficult and as narrowly focused as individuals and groups such as teacher unions can be, no one group generated more discussion than school boards, the superintendent's employer. "Board members can say whatever they want to you because they pay your salary" (Superintendent 3, mostly small-sized districts, Midwest, 2006). As a result, one of the greatest challenges of the superintendency is establishing positive, productive relationships with every school board member. School board–superintendent relationships are a common concern for some superintendents throughout the United States. In fact, some superintendents clearly perceived school boards as their number one stumbling block. "If I'm really honest, it seems that I have spent the majority of my time in my particular situation working with the board to see the bigger picture, not having the luxury of focusing on kids" (Superintendent 22, small-sized districts, Midwest, 2004). Rather than partnering with the superintendent, some boards view themselves as independent of the administration. As a result, they are easily influenced by outside individuals and groups. Superintendents often find themselves justifying their actions rather than feeling a level of support from board members.

> I find it frustrating when your school board and administration is in a reactive phase dealing with teachers because somebody in the community is unhappy. There's nobody who knows greater what's happening in those classrooms, or should know, than the administration, and they should be addressing that. (Superintendent 38, small-sized districts, Midwest, 2004)

Superintendents also discussed the effects of constantly responding to questioning from the board members. "The care and feeding of school boards is another thing that drains the energy of many superintendents and sometimes distracts from the job that they need to do" (Superintendent 51, medium-sized districts, New England & Mid-Atlantic, 2006). Superintendent 44 commented,

> Sometimes the hardest point is selling the board of education that these are some changes that need to take place. If they get complaints from parents who don't understand, or get complaints from anyone, they tend to react to those constituencies pretty quickly. (mostly small-sized districts, Southwest & West, 2004)

The types of individuals who seek school board positions influence this process. Although superintendents work to build and maintain positive relationships with board members and encourage them to do so among themselves, not all board members choose to do so.

> I'm not saying all board members are bad, but unfortunately we've got more of the acid-type people that are invading, and they are splitting boards 4/3s,

5/2s, where we used to have a maybe 6/1. You could have that radical but you could isolate them. Now, you have no idea what you're dealing with on any given night because who's gotten to who. (Superintendent 53, medium-sized districts, New England & Mid-Atlantic, 2006)

Relationship building is clearly important and integral to the day-to-day responsibilities of superintendents. In the complex social and political environments that characterize public education nationally, these challenges will likely increase. Yet, superintendents see themselves up to the task even if, at times, they feel less than appreciated. "Leadership is all about ... [having] ... what is really good for kids and right for kids. You have [to have] the courage" (Superintendent 10, mostly small-sized districts, Midwest, 2006). In the end, superintendents widely believed that children must come first. "You gotta keep kids first and foremost. Kids are all inclusive. That means all our children" (Superintendent 55, medium-sized districts, Midwest, 2005).

## PRINCIPALS' VOICES

As important as relationship building is to superintendents, it is equally so for principals. Principals recognize that building positive relationships with certain stakeholders, especially with teachers and students, is a prerequisite to creating a cohesive, productive school culture. As elementary school Principal 14 pointed out, "I think the biggest thing for me was the developing of culture. Really realizing how much of an impact the building leader has on the culture of the building" (Midwest, 2004). As part of this focus, principals discussed several areas they considered essential to their personal and the school's success. The first subtheme includes the link between relationship building and organizational success through in-district collaboration, trust, and support. The second includes the stumbling blocks to relationship building that principals regularly face.

Principal after principal spoke about the absolute value of creating a collaborative school culture, especially if they hoped to increase student achievement. Most principals focused first on teachers. Clearly they see teachers as critical to the school improvement process. To build teacher investment, principals stressed shared decision making. "I think that whenever possible, you share decision making" (Principal 46, high schools, Southwest & West, 2005). Elementary school Principal 23 noted,

I do think that people need to have a voice in decision making in order to feel valued. I think that if they feel like their creativity ... if they are able to voice their opinions and that people listen to them, then they are more likely to buy into what your goal is and all people will have a common goal. (Southeast, 2005)

The value of being listened to was echoed by others. "They are more likely to be members of the team [if] they have a voice" (Principal 3, elementary schools, Midwest, 2005). Being invited into the decision-making process enhances cooperation while building investment. "If a [teacher] is allowed to share their input, the likelihood of cooperation in the future is enhanced" (Principal 3, elementary schools, Midwest, 2005).

In contrast, principals cautioned against being disingenuous. Asking for input without caring about the responses can undermine the school culture and discourage collaboration.

> There is nothing more insulting to people [than] to say, "Let me hear your opinion," and if they walk away, they are feeling they weren't really heard or their opinion did not really count. It can have a negative effect on the whole process. (Principal 66, middle schools, Midwest, 2006).

At the same time, administrators explained that collaboration does not equate with universal group decision making. Principals acknowledged the critical importance of broad-based involvement but also recognized that administrators must be, at times, independent decision makers. "A good leader probes everybody, uses their opinions, and ultimately does what is best for the most" (Principal 69, middle schools, Midwest, 2006). As elementary school Principal 3 said, "No matter how great collaboration or teamwork is, there are always some decisions that are made without them, and that you have to prepare for those as well" (Midwest, 2005). Principals recognized that for their schools to move forward, they must find the proper balance between collaboration and administrative decision making. "There are times where there is input from the faculty, and then there are times ... you have to make a decision [quickly]. Then you don't consult anyone and you just make the decision" (Principal 85, high schools, Midwest, 2006).

Principals reported that teachers equate an invitation to participate with respect from the administration. So much of what happens in schools is connected to whether teachers respect their principals. One way principals earned teacher respect was to ask them to express their opinions. In fact, teachers "want to know that you respect them enough to ask them" (Principal 24, elementary schools, Southeast, 2005).

Principals themselves want to feel respected by their superintendents. Several discussed the importance of being treated with respect by their superintendents. They were convinced that their superintendent's support was a prerequisite for their success. Some noted that superintendents who fail to show support undermine their own support with their administrative team. Principal 13 shared an early memory of this lack of support from a superintendent: "[During] my first interaction with [my superintendent, he said], 'I just want you to know that I'm the leader and you are the managers,' and basically, it kind of rubbed me the wrong way" (small-sized districts, Southeast, 2006). Elementary school Principal 36 said, "If you don't have district support, you really can't make the rest happen" (Southwest & West, 2006). Principals truly valued relationship building and recognized that their success revolves around their people skills. They understood that they are responsible for building a positive school culture; winning the trust of their teachers; and creating a collaborative, focused environment. Yet, they, too, felt a need for similar encouragement from their superintendents.

Principal after principal spoke about putting children first. They see themselves as student-centered leaders. Establishing good relationships with children is a very important priority for them. "I really like children and I really want to do this job because I like kids. Then, the rest of the stuff can come into place" (Principal 51, elementary schools, Southwest & West, 2006). Whereas the broader discussions about teachers and superintendents included both successes and challenges, those about students were almost exclusively positive. As elementary school Principal 10 said, "The thing that I enjoy the most about [administration] is my interaction with all children instead of just the 25 or 26 in a classroom" (Midwest, 2004). Principals believe that students should be encouraged, similar to other stakeholders to share their ideas and opinions. "I think about things I've done for kids, like hold fireside chats with them and let them feel empowered that you're listening to them" (Principal 57, elementary schools, Midwest, 2005). High school Principal 84 summarized the importance of student–principal relationships: "I'm gonna talk about the relationship piece.... Once you've got that relationship, you can teach'em anything" (Midwest, 2006).

## PRINCIPALS' PERSPECTIVES ON STUMBLING BLOCKS TO RELATIONSHIP BUILDING

Principals, as did superintendents, reported stumbling blocks they face as they work to establish positive and productive relations with those both in and outside their schools. These challenges appear integral to the work of school-based leaders. Principals understand that they are unavoidable. The stumbling blocks are lack of principal autonomy; disconnections between principals and central office administrators; and relationship challenges with parents, teachers, and school board members.

The most often mentioned stumbling block noted was principals' relationships with central office administrators, especially the superintendent. Although some principals described central office administrators with whom they have felt a sense of partnership, many more discussed relationship concerns. One, in particular, was a lack of principal autonomy. Principals said that they are more than willing to assume responsibility for school results but need the autonomy to be true school leaders. As high school Principal 26 said, "I think the principal should have more power to make decisions for his or her school" (Southeast, 2005). Principals noted that at times central office administrators can be too directive, which limits principal autonomy. "There are things that I know that the way [they are] presented to me from the central office, you know, I can pretty much read if I am going to have a choice here or not" (Principal 22, elementary schools, small, Southeast, 2005).

The lack of autonomy speaks to principals' desires to be included as part of the district administrative team. Some said that they are treated by central office administrators as subordinates. This leads to feelings of organizational disenfranchisement. "In our district, there is almost an absence of principal dialogue in decision making. It's all made at the central office and handed down to us" (Principal 5, elementary schools, Midwest, 2005). Principals want to feel as much a part of the district administrative team, as they believe teachers should be school team members. "We're in the middle … [Sometimes we] just feel like nobody trusts [us] … to work … then [we] go to a principals' meeting and [superintendents give] some directive" (Principal 33, elementary schools, Southwest & West, 2006).

Others described frustrations with central office administration's isolation. "That's my frustration. It does seem like … there are people at the central office [who] are not aware of what's going on in schools" (Principal 23, elementary schools, Southeast, 2005). When district-level administrators are not visible in schools or show little, if any, direct interest in day-to-day school operations, principals feel unsupported.

> [The] last 3 or 4 weeks, there have been a number of things that have come out of central office that looks like they don't look at our schedule. That's my frustration. It does seem that there are people at the central office that are not aware of what's going on in schools. (Assistant Principal 31, high schools, Midwest, 2005)

This lack of connectedness leads to a middle-manager mentality. "I would just add that we are middle managers, trying to appease our superiors" (Principal 80, high schools, Midwest, 2005).

Principals also believe that superintendents have an important role in working with principals to keep a districtwide focus on children first.

"From my experience, I can't begin to tell you how important the role of the superintendent is for doing what's best for kids, as well as just setting a healthy culture or not healthy culture in the district" (Principal 73, middle schools, Midwest, 2006). When principals and superintendents work well together and share this common focus, much can be accomplished. "If you don't have district support, you really can't make the rest happen" (Principal 36, elementary schools, Southwest & West, 2006). When principals do not have the support of the superintendent, then other central office administrators assume a less supportive role, which in turn hurts relationship building among all district administrators. "[I] hit a roadblock with my special education director. She has been so completely frustrating because, in my eyes, this is what I thought was best for this child and, because of bureaucracy and paperwork, that's not what happened" (Principal 10, elementary schools, Midwest, 2004).

Beyond relationships with central office administrators, principals find that interactions with parents, teachers, and school board members can become stumbling blocks to their success. "We have to see the big picture and remember that parents and teachers are more tunnel vision" (Principal 1, elementary schools, Midwest, 2005).

What is especially frustrating for principals is how willing others are to work around them for whatever they want.

> We're trying to do what's best for children.... We are looking at all the information ... and talking with parents. We're trying to get them to listen, but they've made up their mind and they call central office, and we get a phone call. (Principal 5, elementary schools, Midwest, 2005).

Part of this disconnect is viewed by principals as symptomatic of poor relationships between the district administration and school board, which ultimately affects them at the school level. "I feel a disconnect between district administration and the school board" (Principal 1, elementary schools, Midwest, 2005). One principal related an incident representative of the disconnect principals feel with the support they receive from the school board:

> I have two board members who are parents on my campus. Last year, I needed to get some of the wrong people off the bus and did so in a manner that was approved by my district. But these teachers went to the board members who are also parents and ... neighbors, and, of course, they badmouthed me. I was the hated principal. (Principal 41, elementary schools, Southwest & West, 2005)

Stumbling blocks to relationship building are clearly on principals' minds. They discussed relationship issues they had experienced interacting with an array of stakeholders, including central office administrators, especially their superintendents; board members; parents; community members; teachers; and other employees. They believed that these impacted their ability to improve their schools and, most importantly, increase student achievement.

## SIMILARITIES AND DIFFERENCES

As both superintendents and principals offered their suggestions on the critical importance of relationships to school and district success, they expressed more similarities than differences. As school leaders, they recognize that little is accomplished without the involvement and support of others.

### Similarities

When superintendents and principals spoke about leadership, many mentioned collaboration. Because education is a people-centered business, building collaborative relationships is essential to organizational success. In fact, these leaders described how collaboration is at the very foundation of school culture building. In establishing a culture of collaboration in the district and school, they discussed several key elements. One was the importance of stakeholders, especially school district employees, having voice in decision making. Whether this was at the district or school level, they recognized that stakeholders associate having voice with trust and support. Yet, they cautioned that asking others to share their opinions or participate in decision making was not sufficient itself. Administrators must be genuinely interested in hearing what others have to say. Otherwise, stakeholder support and involvement can quickly erode.

Another common element they discussed was a commitment to team building. Superintendents and principals understood that accomplishing what needed to be accomplished was the result of the collective efforts of many. Each argued the importance of administrators working diligently to help stakeholders feel a part of the district or school team. At the same time, the school leaders noted how this may actually be more of a goal than an accomplished fact. They pointed to the challenges inherent in team building. Because of the diversity of personalities, differing interests, and varying levels of organizational investment, not everyone is likely to buy in to the team. Both superintendents and principals described the many challenges they face with boards of education, parents, and other stakeholders. The superintendent conversations tended to focus more on the broader community and school board relations than those of principals, who typically discussed parents and parent groups. Each presented its special team-building challenges.

As part of this discussion, superintendents and principal in the focus groups seemed to believe that those not in administrative roles are frequently concerned with what is best for themselves rather than the organization. For parents, this is what is best for their own child. Some teachers, unions, and community groups present a similar perspective. Administrators saw this self-focus as a true challenge to successful relationship building and teamwork. Finally, both groups stressed that collaboration and voice do not equate with democratic decision making. They discussed how successful administrators identify which decisions others should make and those they must make themselves. In making this point, they agreed that an administrator's skill in managing the decision-making process can either contribute to or detract from successful stakeholder–administrator relationships.

## Differences

Although superintendents and principals held parallel views on relationship building, some differences were apparent. Principals saw periodic disconnects between what superintendents espoused and how they led their school districts. Although both groups argued the value of collaboration, some principals pointed out that at times superintendents talk about teamwork but do not fully engage in it. In these instances, superintendents tended to be controlling rather than collaborative. Several principals described their superintendents as district rather than school focused. They suggested that principal–superintendent relationships could be enhanced if superintendents spent more time on school-level issues. Also, principals who worked with very district-focused superintendents tended to question the cohesiveness of the district administrative team. They also reported feelings of isolation within the school district and a decrease in their personal investment.

Another difference centered on leadership focus. Even though both superintendents and principals spoke strongly of the need to put children first, some principals lamented that their superintendents were more focused on adult relationships. They reported that their superintendent rarely visited their schools. Rather, they directed most of their energies to school board and community members, as well as district issues. Also, principals spoke of the power of culture in school and district success. Finally, some principals described superintendents who espoused culture building but supported nonresponsive district cultures. In these instances, principals tended to see their central office administrators as obstacles to success.

## DISCUSSION AND CONCLUSIONS

In this chapter, we explored the relationship dimension of school leadership from the perspectives of superintendents and principals across all regions of the United States. The central theme that framed the chapter's content was the ability of superintendents and principals to build and maintain positive relationships with stakeholders, such as parents, students, teachers, central office staff, and school board members. These positive relationships were a key factor in their personal success as well as the school districts' success in improving schools. Several subthemes that emerged from the data provided specific information related to the importance of (a) collaboration, (b) trust and support, (c) student interactions, and (d) establishment of relationships beyond district personnel in building and maintaining positive school and district relationships. Superintendents and principals noted the challenges in working with diverse constituents as the stumbling blocks that sometimes inhibited their ability to build and maintain these positive relationships.

Several conclusions can be drawn from this research. The first conclusion is that both superintendents and principals recognized the importance of collaboration in their personal success as well as district success in building and maintaining positive relationships. These collaborative relationships were achieved by giving voice to stakeholders in the decision-making process, developing trusting relationships, and taking the time to listen to stakeholders. Team building was an essential element in building a culture of collaboration. To this end, superintendents and principals understood that a collective effort of many was needed to accomplish the school and district improvement goals. Superintendents and principals argued the importance of administrators' inclusive approaches to involve stakeholders. However, these leaders acknowledged the "messy" process of doing what's best for all children when dealing with diversity of personalities and perspectives. They often encountered conflict of values over choice, equity, excellence, and quality. Finding ways to get buy-in from school board members, parents, and other stakeholders with competing interests remained a challenging and a complex process. In building positive collaborative relationships with all stakeholders, these leaders' actions appeared to reflect what Gross and Shapiro (2005) described as democratic ethical educational leadership in that they "sustained a process of open dialogue, right to voice, community inclusion, and right of participation toward a common good" (p. 1).

A second conclusion is that superintendents and principals described developing positive relationships among administrators and key stakeholders as essential to organizational success and a strong school culture. Positive school cultures consisted of dynamic work environments, which were inclusive and participatory. Inclusive practices involved listening to the voices and opinions of all stakeholders related to important decisions that impacted teachers, students, and parents. Principals appeared to include teachers and parents in the school improvement process as a way to gain their buy-in and support. Positive school cultures seemed to be developed through collaborative teamwork and by gaining trust and support from all teachers, parents, and community members. Principals understood the importance of trust and support from campus-level staff and parents, but they also felt a need for support and trust from their superintendents. Principals wanted to feel respected, valued, and supported by their superintendents. This type of trust and support was perceived by superintendents who gave principals autonomy and freedom to serve as the instructional leader on their campuses.

The final conclusion is that executing democratic leadership in building and maintaining positive relationships within schools and across the district is an essential task, although not easily accomplished. These superintendents and principals encountered many stumbling blocks, such as lack of principal autonomy to make decisions for the school, competing interests among key stakeholders that inhibited doing what's best for all children, lack of district support, and top-down state and federal mandates. One of the ways superintendents and principals chose to deal with these stumbling blocks was their use of personal or referent power, which is highly associated with building and sustaining relationships. These findings are supportive of French and Raven's (1959) research on social influence theory.

## IMPLICATIONS AND RECOMMENDATIONS

In order to build and sustain positive relationships among stakeholders and develop strong school and district cultures, superintendents and principals must practice democratic leadership, which exemplifies an environment that supports participation; sharing of ideas; and the virtues of honesty, openness, flexibility, and compassion. Leaders must be intentional in their efforts to institutionalize structures, forums, and communication processes that promote participation and team building. Within the climate of top-down accountability and high-stakes testing mandates, leadership preparation programs must prepare aspiring school leaders for democratic leadership. We recommend that these preparation programs (a) provide guidance to transform positive aspects of accountability and democracy into a comprehensive school improvement strategy that recognizes the necessity of serving the needs of all children and (b) build the capacities of our future leaders to become more politically astute in leadership practices so that they can successfully navigate the political terrain of schools and organizations.

The ability to build and sustain positive relationships with all stakeholders and to develop strong school cultures was dependent on the leadership actions reported by these superintendents and principals. The long-term success of school leaders requires supportive, skilled leadership at all levels of public education. As a result, states, districts, and schools must adopt well-coordinated policies and practices that help leaders meet the daily demands they face. The Wallace Foundation (2006) report, *A Wallace Perspective: Leadership for Learning: Making the Connections Among States, Districts, and School Policies Practices,* confirmed,

> States and district must address (a) standards that specifically state what leaders need to know and be able to do to improve organization success, (b) develop training to ensure that school leaders have the skills and capacities to meet the demands of their job, and (c) provide the needed resources (people, time and money) to meet the needs of all students. (pp. 2–3)

In addition, superintendents and principals must understand that the culture of an organization contributes to relationship building, commitment of stakeholders, and the level of trust and support that exists among campus and district support staff. Thus, these educational leaders must gain insight into both the culture of the school organization and the various racial, ethnic, and religious cultural groups that make up the larger social culture of their community. To sustain positive relationships among all cultural groups, educational leaders are challenged not only to understand these groups but also to develop strategies to connect with these groups (Green, 2010).

## REFERENCES

Collins, J. (2001). *Good to great: Why some companies make the leap ... and others don't.* New York, NY: Harper Collins.

Cooper, J., & Croyle, R. T. (1984). Attitudes and attitude change. *Annual Review of Psychology, 35,* 395-426.

Covey, S. R. (1989). *The seven habits of highly effective people.* New York, NY: Free Press.

Elmore, R. E. (2000). *Building a new structure for school leadership.* Washington, DC: The Albert Shanker Institute.

French, J., & Raven, B. H. (1959). The bases of social power. In D. Cartwright (Ed.), *Studies in social power* (pp. 150-167). Ann Arbor, MI: Institute for Social Research.

Fullan, M. (2004). *Leading in a culture of change.* San Francisco, CA: Jossey-Bass.

Gall, J., Gall, M., & Borg, W. (2005). *Applying educational research.* Boston, MA: Pearson Allyn & Bacon.

Gladwell, M. (2000). *The tipping point: How little things can make a big difference.* New York, NY: Little, Brown.

Goodyear, R., & Robyak, J. (1981). Counseling as an interpersonal influence process: A perspective for counseling practice. *Personnel and Guidance Journal, 60,* 654-657.

Green, R. L. (2005). *Practicing the art of leadership: A problem-based approach to implementing the ISSLC standards* (2nd ed.). Upper Saddle River, NJ: Merrill Prentice Hall.

Green, R. L. (2010). *The four dimensions of principal leadership: A framework for leading 21st century schools.* New York, NY: Allyn & Bacon.

Gross, S. J., & Shapiro, J. P. (2005, Fall). Our new era requires a New DEEL: Toward democratic ethical educational leadership. *UCEA Review, 47*(3), 1-4.

Kersten, T. A. (2010). *Stepping into administration: How to succeed in making the move.* Lanham, MD: Rowman & Littlefield Education.

Leithwood, K., Seashore Louis, K., Anderson, S., & Wahlstrom, K. (2004). *How leadership influences student learning.* New York, NY: Wallace Foundation.

Martin, R. P. (1978). Expert and referent power: A framework for understanding and maximizing consultant effectiveness. *Journal of School Psychology, 16,* 49-55.

Marzano, R., Waters, T., & McNulty, B. A. (2005). *School leadership that works: From research to results.* Arlington, VA: Association for Supervision and Curriculum Development.

Maxwell, J. C. (2003). *Thinking for a change: Eleven ways highly successful people approach life and work.* Nashville, TN: Center Street.

Spillane, J. P., Halverson, R., & Diamond, J. B. (2001). Investigating school leadership practice: A distributed perspective. *Educational Researcher, 30*(3), 23-28.

Wallace Foundation. (2006). A *Wallace perspective: Leadership for learning: Making the connections among states, districts, and school policies and practices.* Retrieved from http://www.wallacefoundation.org/knowledge-center/school-leadership/district-policy-and-practice/Pages/Wallace-Perspective-Leadership-for-Learning.aspx

CHAPTER 9

# PRESSURE OF OUTSIDE FORCES, STRESS, AND FINDING BALANCE

## Thomas L. Alsbury and Kathryn S. Whitaker

Superintendent and principal decision making is influenced by a wide variety of internal and external pressures. In this chapter, we highlight outside forces that have changed the landscape of the superintendency and principalship in recent years, the stress conveyed by these forces, and how leaders navigate those stresses in practice. Dilemmas related to increased accountability from state and federal mandates, including the No Child Left Behind Act (NCLB, 2002), have certainly contributed to the changed landscape. Additional challenges include highly political environments that encompass coalitions and alliances, greater social diversity in ethnicity and race, conflict internal to school districts, and increasingly complex expectations for schooling (Malen, 1995).

While all U.S. administrators likely share common external forces and stresses, it could be argued that these may vary based on the size of school district, the complexity of the district organization, the unique culture of the community and school, and even geographic location. These contextual variations can effectively lead to a wide disparity in the role of school and district administrators, the specific stresses they face, and how they

*Snapshots of School Leadership in the 21st Century:*
*Perils and Promises of Leading for Social Justice,*
*School Improvement, and Democratic Community,* pp. 169–187
Copyright © 2012 by Information Age Publishing

169

effectively deal with these stresses. Indeed, a major theme that emerged from the superintendent and principal data collected in the UCEA Voices 3 study related to how these forces and stresses influence decision-making processes and how leaders in various district contexts navigate through these stresses. Here we hope to report on some of the stresses faced by superintendents and principals and how leaders in various district and community contexts grapple with the balance between increasing external influences and accountability on all phases of education.

## LITERATURE REVIEW

### Heightened Demands

In the past 15 years, external pressures and demands for accountability on school districts and their leaders have increased. The push for improved performance and the expectations for school leaders to produce those improvements have risen dramatically (Queen & Queen, 2005). For example, Cuban (2001) found that school districts are affected by the communities in which they reside, whether the voices in the community are powerful ones or not. The reality is that public schools are not only expected to achieve academic outcomes but are also tasked as a foundation of our democracy and expected to instill civic and social attitudes and skills that shape how graduates lead their lives in communities. Schools are expected to build respect for differences in ideas and cultures (Cuban, 2001). Added to this external community pressure is the drive by NCLB (2002) to reduce the achievement gap and produce Adequate Yearly Progress (AYP) from *all* students. Concurrent with NCLB is a move for state and federal standardization in school curriculum and assessment, presenting even more stress on school principals and superintendents, who then must negotiate demands from faculty and local citizens to maintain local control over their own children's education (Goldstein, 1992; Richardson, 1998).

While teaching students to be better citizens, other democratic values are also becoming more critical, such as the importance of responding to ever-widening and pluralistic voices from external constituents. The challenge for district and school leaders is balancing the demands of sometimes disparate and incongruent external voices in the community, federal and state policy, and what they believe is best for students. Increasingly, administrators are asked to listen to the voices of diverse stakeholders and interest groups, sometimes referred to as leading through community (Furman & Shields, 2003). Underlining the importance of superintendents working with community groups, Grogan (2000) noted,

> They are expected to have in-depth knowledge of the groups and know what their issues are and who the major figures are. Superintendents must devote a great deal of time and energy to build coalitions among their constituents and forge ties between schools and local communities. (p. 118)

In addition to demands from community, federal, and state entities, superintendents and principals face numerous stresses associated with the occupational demands. Principals cite inadequate compensation and overwhelming management duties coupled with expectations to function as leaders rather than as managers (Whitaker, 2003). Emergent demands to reduce achievement gaps, increase test scores, dramatically increase time spent on personnel evaluation, and find and keep highly qualified teachers are proffered with no additional time to accomplish these tasks. Superintendents also face stressors including challenging school board relations, heavy workloads, public demands and community politics that sometimes conflict with state and federal academic mandates, increasing demands from special interests, competition from alternative private and homeschooling, an increasingly litigious public, and personnel issues (Glass, Bjork, & Brunner, 2000; Queen & Queen, 2005; Richardson, 1998). In fact, a study conducted with over 250 superintendents in Texas reported that job expectations had become unrealistic and that educators are less interested in becoming a superintendent (Lowery, Harris, Hopson, & Marshall, 2001). These job expectations have contributed to increasing superintendent turnover in many sections of the country and namely in school districts with more disadvantaged student populations (Cooper, Fusarelli, & Carella, 2000; Fuller et al., 2003; Glass, 2000; Glass & Franceschini, 2007). Some research (Litchka, Fenzel, & Procaccini, 2009) has shown that school superintendents and principals may even experience higher levels of stress than do other executives with respect to role overload and the level of responsibility their position carries. In addition, superintendents and principals in large school districts and those who are younger and have fewer years of experience report higher levels of stress (Glass, 2000; Litchka et al., 2009; Schmidt, Kosmoski, & Pollack, 1998).

## Coping With the Stress

Researchers over the years have demonstrated that school superintendents and principals experience considerable work- or role-related stress that can have deleterious effects on personal well-being and job effectiveness (Brimm, 1983; Glass, 1992; Glass & Franceschini, 2007; Gmelch, 1995). Glass and Franceschini (2007) suggested that the amount and types of occupational stress that superintendents and principals face can be excessive and overwhelming to the point of leading to "a disabling condition affecting behavior, judgment, and performance" (p. 47). Because of the potential for the high levels of debilitating distress as a result of the high levels of challenge and difficulty many superintendents and principals experience in their jobs, their ability to cope effectively with the stress and overcome adversity becomes critical to their personal and professional success, and even their survival. Often school leaders, because of the considerable pressures they are under, tend to devote more time to managing the stress rather than focusing on the task of furthering the development of the school district. Effective coping strategies need to be put into place before the demands of the job overwhelm the executive's capability to carry out his or her responsibilities effectively.

## STUDY METHODS

Results presented in this chapter derive from two researchers' reviewing all the UCEA Voices 3 study superintendent and principal transcripts relevant to the broad themes of outside forces, stress, and finding balance in the roles of superintendent and principal. Each researcher reviewed the transcripts twice to uncover emergent themes, agreed upon through collaboration on the coding results. Having analysts code separately and then examining the commonalities between them provides a more reliable method of analysis than with a single observer and coder (Stewart & Shamdasani, 1990). Specific quotes were selected from superintendent and principal data that represented the themes of this chapter. Once emergent themes were identified, the constant comparative method was used to determine similarities and differences in responses between superintendents and principals relative to the themes of outside forces, stress, and finding balance. What follows is a reporting of those emerging common themes expressed by superintendents and principals regarding outside forces, stress, and finding balance.

## SUPERINTENDENT AND PRINCIPAL PERSPECTIVES

### External Forces and Pressures on the Superintendency

The major subthemes in the focus group data from superintendents included the pressures related to NCLB, dealing with boards of education and teacher unions, and attempting to do what is best for students in light of the politics within school districts. In the arena of decision making, superintendents overwhelmingly spoke of the necessity of giving voice to others in the school community, while acknowledging that there are so many different groups within a district, the politics of decision making can be stressful. Several superintendents commented on the toll the role takes on their personal life amid the stresses and external pressures inherent in the job.

### Dealing With NCLB

Superintendents in these focus groups pointed out several positive outcomes of the NCLB legislation. They spoke in positive terms about how NCLB had brought more focus to curriculum and instruction and held principals and teachers more accountable. The law has mandated a greater focus on the use of student achievement data. Concomitantly, superintendents praised the positive outcomes of increased professional development for teachers and the emphasis on enhancing academic growth among specific subgroups. For example, Superintendent 51 highlighted the benefits of focusing on minority students: "Parents in this community didn't really care about poor kids and minority kids. Before, they could just be left behind and people didn't have to focus on them— and now you do" (medium-sized districts, New England & Mid-Atlantic, 2006).

Although superintendents agreed with the intent of NCLB, they were dissatisfied and frustrated with the implementation of the law. Components of the law such as AYP, particularly related to special education, and highly qualified teachers posed difficulties for superintendents. Lack of funding to implement NCLB was another stressor for superintendents. In pointing out the dilemmas with AYP, Superintendent 11 from a small district commented,

> In the county, we did not make AYP in math. If we'd had one less student as being identified as being disadvantaged, or more students passed the test, we would have been home free. One student made the difference. If we could have averaged the percentages, we would have made it, but they don't let you do it that way. (Southeast, 2006)

The impact of NCLB on special education was another frustration for superintendents. Superintendent 63, with a district enrollment of over 2,000, went to his high school teachers and plainly stated, "You guys are going to be identified as a low-performing school because kids with disabilities don't do as well as the other kids" (medium-sized districts, New England & Mid-Atlantic, 2005). A rural superintendent echoed the problems with NCLB and special education:

> NCLB and special education are both federal laws and they contradict each other. In special education, kids have to be 2 years behind to qualify as learning disabled. With NCLB, every single kid has to pass at grade level. (Superintendent 72, medium-sized districts, Midwest, 2005)

In the area of meeting the mandate related to hiring only "highly qualified" teachers, these small district superintendents provided examples of how this NCLB provision was not realistic. A female superintendent with an enrollment of 1,980 remarked,

> NCLB is an unfunded mandate and many parts aren't realistic. You find me a district that is not looking for a math teacher who is highly qualified. There are schools that are looking for 14 math teachers right now. To say they are going to have all those in place and ready to go by the time school starts is not realistic. (Superintendent 31, medium-sized districts, Southwest & West, 2005)

### Dealing With the School Board

A significant pressure for superintendents included the dilemmas associated with working with different community groups and the impact on decision making. Superintendents spoke of dealing with power groups in the community who were interested in doing what was best for their own kids or a certain segment of the community, whereas superintendents themselves had to focus on what was best for *all* children. A rural superintendent commented,

> There are so many special interest groups out there. Not just the academic type or the money type, but now the cultural type issues are emerging as well. For those in larger districts, the demands from different ethnic groups are unbelievable. (Superintendent 70, medium-sized districts, Midwest, 2005)

Superintendents also faced power issues with members of their boards of education. Terminating employees seemed to cause a lot of angst for small-district superintendents in terms of their relationship with boards and communities. Superintendent 28 recounted a situation where he had to dismiss an employee: "Those decisions turned out to be very unpopular with the board, to the point they would ask that I compromise my principles and I refused to do so. Consequently, I was not offered a second contract" (medium-sized districts, Southeast, 2005). Superintendent 44, a female superintendent from the Southwest and West region, had to terminate a principal. She recalled the anxiety this decision created: "I told my spouse I heard rumblings about secret meetings to get rid of me. We received hate mail and it was a living hell" (mostly small districts, 2004). Fortunately, the board supported her decision in the end.

Several superintendents discussed the relationship between board members and members of the community and the difficulty this relationship can cause in making decisions. Superintendent 64 described the frustration of what he referred to as shadow boards: "A shadow board is a group of people who are dissatisfied with what the board and the schools are doing and has a powerful impact on the health and well-being of a school district" (medium-sized districts, New England & Mid-Atlantic, 2005). Superintendent 67 from the same focus group added,

> One individual in our system can say things that aren't really accurate, maybe half truths at best, and distract the organization. There's a lot of power that an individual with ill will or good will can take and just grab. They can have a lot of power in a system. (medium-sized districts, New England & Mid-Atlantic, 2005)

Veteran Superintendent 53 from the Mid-Atlantic region echoed the dilemmas within the decision-making arena:

> It's the classic problem of the superintendency: You're either going to be on the right side of the issue or the popular side. And on a daily basis as a superintendent, you have to make that decision on everything that hits your table. If you waffle, your career is usually pretty short. (medium-sized districts, 2006)

### Dealing With the Teachers' Union
Other superintendents reflected on the difficulties and frustrations with teachers' unions in the context of making decisions in the best interests of students. A female from a suburban district recounted a story about a feud with the teacher's union over a 2-week vacation at Easter. She asked the union to split the vacation time so the kids wouldn't lose instructional time. The teacher's union insisted on the 2-week vacation and the superintendent broke the contract, which caused a huge dispute with the union. She elaborated, "When the union president says to me, 'I don't care about kids; it's only about what's good for teachers,' I thought, where are we going?" (Superintendent 51, medium-sized districts, New England & Mid-Atlantic, 2006).

Superintendent 70 from a Midwest district echoed the frustration with teacher unions.

> One of the biggest roadblocks in doing what's best for kids is our unions. We can't do this or we can't do that because of the contract. And you continually have union issues coming up that change the way you like to do things. When union people come talk to you, they're not coming to talk to you about what's best for kids; they're coming to talk to you about what's best for teachers. (medium-sized districts, 2005)

### Dealing With the Search for Balance

A final subtheme emerged related to dealing with the stress of the role and trying to find balance between personal and professional lives. As expressed by superintendents in the various focus groups, the role is a "24-7 job." As Superintendent 17 stated,

> I can't count the number of times that I've been awakened at 2:00 in the morning by the sheriff's department because the alarm is going off in the elementary school and the principal can't be reached. We are expected to be out in front on every issue. (small districts, Southeast, 2006)

Some superintendents worried about the profession getting bashed due to a few superintendents who embezzled funds or committed some other illegal act, which creates a generalization that superintendents are "crooks," as stated by one superintendent.

Superintendents expressed concern about their colleagues getting burned out and wounded in the role. Superintendent 60, a superintendent who was new to the role, remarked, "The people that we have that are so good just won't continue to do it. They are going to burn out, so I worry about who will replace them" (medium-sized districts, Midwest, 2005). Some focus groups conversed about the superintendent being the target of all that goes wrong in a district. Superintendent 22, a female from a small Midwest district, summed it up,

> Last year I had an article about me that was just full of lies, just out-and-out lies. Other superintendents tell me the same has happened to them. And your character can be put in question, your integrity—it goes deeper. People can be so cruel when you are the superintendent. It's an attack that goes clear to your soul. It happens a lot, and nobody wants to talk about it, and I think they need to start talking about it. (2004)

### Dealing With Gender Issues

Gender issues continue to be a consideration in the role of superintendent. In these focus groups some superintendents wondered about how the role impacted their family lives. Superintendent 25 "questioned how much time I spend with my own kids. Even when I am with the family, I feared not really being there because my thoughts are constantly about the job" (small districts, Midwest, 2004). Superintendent 22 also noted concerns about females in the superintendency:

> I watched some of them [females] exit. I know two young women who just left. I know they are good superintendents; I know they had the talent, and I know why they left. They just don't have the support at home like guys do. (small districts, Midwest, 2004)

The feeling of being wounded was expressed by male and female superintendents alike. A few interviewees spoke about the need to support one another because the superintendency is a very lonely job. Female Superintendent 31 discussed at length her frustration:

> You spend so much time dealing with what you really didn't get into the profession to deal with and it's draining. It is physically and mentally draining. You do it as long as you can and it's just that you get beaten down and it shouldn't be that way. (medium-sized districts, Southeast, 2005)

Despite the stress inherent in the role and the frustrations with scarce resources, NCLB, and community and board conflicts and power struggles, superintendents tended to focus on the positives about their jobs. First and foremost, most superintendents felt they were making a positive contribution to society by focusing on the most important aspect of their jobs—doing what was in the best interests of the students they served.

## External Forces and Pressures in the Principalship

### Dealing With NCLB

All levels of principals, elementary, middle, and high school, spoke freely about the dilemmas associated with the implementation of NCLB. Although most principals acknowledged that the law had good intentions and admirable goals, they struggled with the implementation of the law. Positive aspects of NCLB included an emphasis on accountability, the positive goal of improving educational outcomes for all children, a heightened focus on the academic growth of special education students and English language learners, increased attention on curriculum and assessments, and enhanced professional development for teachers. As high school Principal 80 stated, "On the positive side, it has allowed us to focus on some populations that we've ignored and helped us put emphasis on some kids that we hadn't paid attention to in the past" (medium-sized districts, Midwest, 2005).

Principals of all three levels had the most difficulty with the actual implementation of NCLB. They spoke about the conflict between the efficiency and accountability aspects of NCLB and the focus on human factors and doing what's best for kids. Elementary school Principal 10 shared her frustration:

> These people sitting over in Washington, DC, [should] come into a classroom and see the children who go home and have no one at home, no food at home. The least of their worries is whether they are going to pass the [standardized] test come February. (medium-sized districts, Southeast, 2004)

Most principals stressed the lack of resources to implement the pieces of NCLB in conjunction with doing what's best for students. Middle school Principal 66 commented, "Sometimes we have to make decisions based on fiscal responsibilities that may not be best for kids. That really presents a challenge to the administration, I believe" (medium-sized districts, Midwest, 2005). Elementary school Principal 23 recalled,

> I think the stress can be very damaging to teachers if all they see is the negative and they don't see how well they have done with other things. You have to work very hard with them to get through all that. (medium-sized districts, Southeast, 2005)

The provision in NCLB related to AYP caused significant anxiety among principals. This provision creates more focus on diversity issues and academic achievement among subgroups, but most principals emphasized that meeting AYP for all subgroups was virtually impossible and has produced several unintended consequences. For example, middle school Principal 67 summed up some of the difficulties with meeting AYP:

> Eight subgroups in our district didn't make AYP. There were 400 kids in eighth grade in one building, and this is the 3rd year they didn't make AYP, so they had to offer transfers. They started with special ed[ucation] kids because they get first choice. So guess what school now has the special ed[ucation] kids? It's really affecting us quite a bit. (mostly small districts, Midwest, 2006)

A second provision within NCLB that caused a great deal of tension for principals was meeting the mandates associated with highly qualified teachers. High school Assistant Principal 31 with an enrollment of 1,150 provided an example of this dilemma:

> Teachers have gotten so stressed out because they think they aren't going to be highly qualified. They are thinking they are going to have to go back and take courses and units and they aren't considering the experience of a teacher who has been teaching math for 30 years. (medium-sized districts, Southeast, 2005)

Elementary school Principal 38 expressed,

> I wonder if those people who made that rule ever sat in on a middle school teacher interview. Before, we used to hire great teachers, but now you lose out and you may have to pass up a great teacher because you have to hire a "highly qualified" math teacher who may not be a good teacher at all. (small districts, Southwest & West, 2005)

These examples point to the conflict between the development of NCLB rules by bureaucrats with no experience in education versus the reality of implementing such rules by well-seasoned educators with experience.

### Dealing With Competing Stakeholder Input

In addition to NCLB pressures and dilemmas were issues related to finding the balance between giving "voice," soliciting input from others when making decisions, and making the right decisions in regard to what's best for students. Principals often struggled with their desire to solicit input and the simultaneous political pressures of community members or board members wanting decisions to go their way. Coupled with pressures from boards and community members was working with the teachers' unions within the decision-making arena.

High school Principal 84 with a school enrollment of 800 summarized the dilemma of reacting to what the public wants, reflecting,

> We are always reacting to what the public wants of us. Every time you go for a bond issue, everybody's out there to vote because it's something they feel they have control over. Everybody walks into our school and feels like they know about education because they've been a part of education. (mostly small districts, Midwest, 2006)

High school Principal 83 recalled a situation where the school made a decision to raise the grading scale. The board initially voted in favor of it, then overturned the decision when influential community members "screamed and made noise" (mostly small districts, Midwest, 2006). Further, a male elementary school principal stated,

> Too often board members want to control the outcome of decisions and when they get elected, bring their own personal agendas, such as getting rid of a particular teacher. And principals have to look at issues globally in terms of what's best for their students and their school community rather than the agenda of a particular board member. (Principal 48, small districts, Southwest & West, 2005)

### Dealing With the Teachers' Union

Principals of all three levels spoke about the multitude of changes brought on as a result of special education, lack of resources, changing community and family dynamics, and NCLB. Although these changes were stressful, the principals also addressed the need for change within their schools. These perceived changes related to reconfiguring school structures and processes, curricular changes, and changes needed in how teachers teach. Often when principals desired a particular change, they faced conflict with the teachers' union. Principal 20, an experienced principal, expressed the conflict she perceived between teacher rights and site-based decision making. She provided the example of the need to make changes to the teacher handbook. It was decided to do the work for half a day over the summer, and one teacher complained about working in the summer for no pay (medium-sized districts, Southeast, 2005).

High school principals from the Midwest discussed the tough balancing act as middle managers in trying to appease superiors while working on a daily basis with the union. Principal 79 related a story about meeting with the elected faculty forum once per month, only to discover that each forum member had his or her own following, and the 140 faculty members were essentially divided up into 10 "packs," with each pack developing their own resolution to issues (medium-sized districts, Midwest, 2005). Needless to say, the situation quickly got out of control. High school Principal 80, in a school of more than 1,300 students, recapped a situation where the school needed to make a time change with the schedule:

> It had to go to a vote because of the union contract. Eighty percent of teachers had to agree on the change, and only 65% voted for it. The union set the bar so high that the recommended change could not possibly pass. (medium-sized districts, Midwest, 2005)

In addition to the tensions created by external pressures, principal focus groups shared the strains associated with the changing role of the principal. Middle school Principal 71 stated,

> I think when young people come into leadership they have to look at the position as it has changed over the years in terms of time commitment and accessibility. That wasn't the same when I first began. It changed and took its toll on the family. (mostly small districts, Midwest, 2006)

### Dealing With Finding Balance

Principals struggled with the demands of both the management aspects of their jobs and the leadership dimensions. In discussing the differences between educational leadership and management, Elementary Principal 14 commented,

> If we want true educational leaders, we also need educational managers, because the management stuff has to get done. It does consume you, because you're doing educational leadership from 7:30 a.m. to 5:30 p.m. and your management stuff from 5:30 p.m. to 8:00 p.m. (medium-sized districts, Southeast, 2004)

The demands of both management and leadership created significant stresses for principals. For example, elementary principals from the Southwest and West regions had a lengthy conversation about the stress associated with the role. Principal 45 noted,

> Talking about the number of tasks—just the amount of supervision. I was in the military for 20 years and if my span of control was over seven people, things got reorganized and I had two people working for me. Those of you with 20 or 30 teachers, I don't know how you do it. (small districts, Southwest & West, 2005)

Principal 41 shared examples of overwhelming health issues faced by administrators in her district:

> In our district, nearly every administrator has had cancer. And that's more than 30 people. We don't look at the toll this job has had on us physically. I would love to see a research topic on health and the toll it takes on our bodies. Let them go home at 5:00 on some days, don't require them to be at all these meetings, because we're losing them. (small districts, Southwest & West, 2005)

In handling the day-to-day pressures of the principalship, elementary, middle, and high school principals conversed about the importance of support groups and their relationships with colleagues. They noted the importance of using colleagues as sounding boards and an occasional shoulder to cry on. Given that they spend so much of their time working and thinking about work, finding outlets such as athletic and recreational activities is crucial.

## SUPERINTENDENTS AND PRINCIPALS: COMPARISONS AND CONTRASTS

In reviewing the focus group transcripts from principals and superintendents, similarities and differences in responses emerged within the theme of external pressures. Similarities between responses include positive aspects of the NCLB legislation, frustrations in the implementation of NCLB, valuing input in decision making while recognizing the interference of politics, and the overarching belief that doing what's best for students is a top priority. Differences between superintendent and principal responses encompassed principals' beliefs that they know kids better than superintendents, the differences in responsibilities of district leadership versus school leadership, and the lonely nature of the role of superintendent.

Both principal and superintendent interviewees agreed that although NCLB created a great deal of external pressures, the goal of the legislation was admirable. Both groups cited positive outcomes of NCLB, such as an increased focus on accountability and achievement data; enhanced professional development for teachers; a greater emphasis on minority and other subgroups; and a heightened concentration on curricular, instruction, and assessment issues.

Although both principals and superintendents valued broad input in decision making, they both shared that politics often interferes with input in decision making. Both groups mentioned the delicate nature of involving community members in decisions, especially when powerful parent groups and community members have special agendas. Coupled with these political realities, both groups cited political issues with teacher unions when attempting to make decisions in the best interests of students. These political issues created many external pressures and stresses for both principals and superintendents and sometimes caused termination of contracts. Despite the political realities and external pressures, principals and superintendents indicated a desire to focus on making decisions in the best interests of all students.

Both principals and superintendents alluded to the stress inherent in their roles. Principals and superintendents felt that they were consumed by their professional roles, causing personal issues with family life on occasion and a struggle to find balance between their personal and professional lives. Both groups expressed concern that the frustrations and stress inherent in their roles caused some to want to leave the profession. Similarly, they wondered about the impact of external pressures and stress on individuals desiring to enter the principalship and superintendency. Both groups commented on the need for support systems for the two roles.

Despite similar themes and subthemes expressed by principals and superintendents in the area of external pressures, stress, and finding balance, a few differences emerged from the focus group data. Several principals expressed that they felt like they knew students better than superintendents and that superintendents were more removed from the daily lives of students in schools. There seemed to be a feeling on the part of principals that they knew what was best for students in their individual schools.

Although there were more similarities than differences between principal and superintendent responses in regard to NCLB, there were also a few subtle differences in responses. For example, principals spoke more about their frustrations with AYP and highly qualified teachers, whereas superintendents spoke more globally about the pressures created by NCLB. Principals provided more examples of the stress NCLB created for teachers in their buildings, whereas superintendents discussed the punitive nature of

NCLB and their belief that public education was being bashed generally. Additionally, superintendents talked about external pressures from state legislation and the role of state legislators in issuing unfunded or under-funded state mandates, which is not surprising, since superintendents interact more frequently with state legislators than do principals.

Superintendents often cited issues with school boards that created pressures and frustrations, particularly as community power struggles became intermixed with politics within boards. Principals seemed less likely to understand the complexity of the superintendent's role with boards while also working to satisfy entire communities. Principals were most concerned with their specific school's parent community and sometimes did not understand why a superintendent or board made a certain decision regarding students and teachers. Less discussion occurred about school boards from the principals, although one principal provided an example of being caught in the middle between the school board and the community.

Also in line with differences between macroviews held by superintendents and more microviews held by principals, superintendents alluded to the overwhelming pressures of being responsible for everything in the entire district, whereas principals were responsible for their individual schools. Superintendents spoke of the time spent on board relations and communication with community members, whereas principals mostly focused on communication with the superintendent and their own parent community within their school. Whereas superintendents remarked about stressors with boards, several principals discussed frustrations with central office and alluded to central office administrators' not understanding the enormity of the job of principal. Additionally, several principals cited the managerial nature of the principal's job, with too many tasks to be accomplished and not enough time.

## IMPLICATIONS FOR PRACTICE, LEADERSHIP PREPARATION AND RESEARCH, AND POLICY

It is evident from these Voices data that superintendents and principals face a daunting combination of personal and professional stressors, including politics, heavy workloads, faculty and school board relations, federal and state reform mandates, personnel problems, unions, and public demands and criticisms. School and district leaders shared that these stressors can bring on anger; frustration; resentment; anxiety; and feeling powerless, devalued, unappreciated, and lonely (Richardson, 1998). Leaders also shared a number of methods they use to cope with balancing the stress of the position, some more effective than others. Less effective coping mechanisms included withdrawing, acquiescence, negative self-talk, and maintaining mental distance. Although these coping strategies could have short-term effectiveness, they lacked sustainable and satisfying resolution to the stressors.

Recommendations for coping with these stresses at a personal level include stress-reduction activities, like meditation, relaxation training, physical exercise, health and wellness programs, and time-management training. Indeed, school leaders reported that the most effective coping mechanisms included physical exercise, talking with friends, and venting to their spouse. From an organizational level, districts could develop programs to increase and improve recognition and feedback for school leaders.

In addition to coping mechanisms at a personal care level, studies have indicated that school leaders who use more effective problem-solving approaches can lower the damaging effects of stressors (Fenzel, Litchka, & Procaccini, 2009). In fact, studies have reported that the use of effective problem-solving techniques by school leaders moderates occupational stressors significantly (Moos & Billings, 1982; Skinner, Edge, Altman, & Sherwood, 2003). Patterson and Kelleher (2005) called for a goal of training future leaders to develop a more resilient character. This character involves both competence in interpreting adverse events and tackling problems, as well as a heightened sense of personal efficacy.

If coping skills can alleviate some of the negative outcomes of occupational stress, leadership preparation programs need to consider providing this training. In fact, virtually no preparation program requires coursework for potential leaders on how to handle the political dimensions of the job, strategies on how to effectively cope with stress, education on understanding the sources of stress, or leadership techniques that can diminish the stressors. For example, Queen and Queen (2005) noted that administrators may be causing their own stress by setting unrealistic deadlines for task completion, engaging in poor communication techniques, and failing to set clear guidelines and responsibilities for themselves and their faculty. In addition, training programs need to differentiate common stressors and coping mechanisms for superintendents and principals and for leading in different district contexts (small to large, urban to rural, and affluent to poor).

Additional systemic stress reducers may include the use of collaborative and distributive leadership styles. Providing social support time for faculty and staff and fostering more effective mentor–mentee relationships across the district can lessen the onset of stress (Whitaker, 2003). Whitaker (2003) also suggested that seeking broader input in goal setting and decision-making can lessen stress because leaders know they have broader buy-in and are less likely to be surprised by staff or community opposition. Despite the logic of this claim, most leaders in this study pointed to experiencing considerable challenge, and in fact stress, in dealing with input from a broader constituent base. We suggest that while collaborative decision making may lessen one type of stress, it may simultaneously heighten another form of stress. Therefore, the use of shared decision making may not be a recommended technique to lower overall leadership stress. Stress-reduction efforts must occur not only at the school but also at the district level. Superintendents need to set clear and realistic role expectations for principals, and board members need to be held accountable for clearly delineating and evaluating superintendents on reasonable and measureable duties.

Finally, policy makers at every level should consider a re-evaluation of position responsibilities for the superintendent and principal position, providing improved administrative infrastructures and supports akin to private business. Professional development for leaders in the field should be provided on identifying and coping with outside influences and stressors that accompany them. When considering only principals, systemic issues like the decreasing ability to recruit, hire, and retain high-quality teachers is a major stress producer. For superintendents, a key to stress is high school-board turnover and strained relationships with their board members (Alsbury, 2008). Given that outside influence and stressors can emanate from a wide variety of sources, every facet of the district organization, educational policy, and even the governance structure of schools should be considered.

Indeed, some of the top-performing countries in the world cite the use of alternative governance structures as responsible for their improvement. Most notable, perhaps, is Finland, where many of the operations, personnel, and support responsibilities are removed from the superintendent and placed under the responsibility of an elected municipal board. In their system, the board hires the superintendent, and shifted responsibilities leave the elected school board only instructional matters to consider. They report that this system, by shifting responsibilities that are mostly noninstructional to a partnering board, has diminished undue outside influences and the stresses of both the superintendent and principal positions and has helped focus their effort more toward improving educational systems. In fact, even pervasive national testing like we see in the United States is no longer used as an accountability tool, because it is believed to have produced a great deal of damaging stress on the students and faculty, while not resulting in significant improvements in student achievement (M. Risku, personal communication, October 28, 2010).

## CONCLUSIONS AND RECOMMENDATIONS

It seems evident that the positions of superintendent and principal present stressors that affect both personal and professional life and have led to these positions being referred to as "undoable" (Queen & Queen,

2005, p. 10). Indeed, in the absence of appropriate coping mechanisms, administrators are at a high risk of exhaustion and burnout, including long-term physical ailments (Queen & Queen, 2005). Although some may choose to downplay concern for the personal impact on school leaders, notable is the fact that studies have indicated that effective district and school leadership is critical to high levels of district success. Glass (1992) indicated that school leaders under great and sustained stress generally do not perform well when they are preoccupied with handling stress rather than focused on advancing student achievement. This makes it imperative to seriously consider recommendations for not only reducing stress through role redefinition but also providing adequate training to cope with stressors, as well as considering resiliency as a critical leadership disposition. Our hopes for deep and lasting school reform depend on it.

## REFERENCES

Alsbury, T. L. (2008). School board member and superintendent turnover and the influence on student achievement: An application of the dissatisfaction theory. *Leadership & Policy in Schools, 7*, 202-229.

Brimm, J. L. (1983). What stresses school administrators? *Theory Into Practice, 22*, 64-69.

Cooper, B., Fusarelli, L., & Carella, V. (2000). *Career crisis in the superintendency?* Arlington, VA: American Association of School Administrators.

Cuban, L. (2001). *How can I fix it? Finding solutions and managing dilemmas: An educator's road map.* Williston, VT: Teachers College Press.

Fenzel, L. M., Litchka, P., & Procaccini, J. (2009, April). *The stress process among school superintendents: Analysis and implications.* Paper presented at the meeting of the American Educational Research Association, San Diego, CA.

Fuller, H. L., Campbell, C., Celio, M. B., Harvey, J., Immerwahr, J., & Winger, A. (2003). *An impossible job? The view from the urban superintendent's chair.* Seattle, WA: Center on Reinventing Public Education.

Furman, G. C., & Shields, C. M. (2003, April). *How can educational leaders promote and support social justice and democratic community in schools?* Paper presented at the meeting of the American Educational Research Association, Chicago, IL.

Glass, T. E. (1992). *The study of the American school superintendency: America's education leaders in a time of reform.* Arlington, VA: American Association of School Administrators.

Glass, T. E. (2000). Where are all the women superintendents? *School Administrator, 57*(6), 28-32.

Glass, T. E., Bjork, L., & Brunner, C. C. (2000). *The study of the American superintendency, 2000. A look at the superintendent of education in the millennium.* Arlington, VA: American Association of School Administrators.

Glass, T., & Franceschini, L. (2007). *The state of the American superintendency: A mid-decade study.* Lanham, MD: Rowman & Littlefield Education.

Gmelch, W. G. (1995). Administrator stress and coping effectiveness: Implications for administrator evaluation and development. *Journal of Personnel Evaluation in Education, 9*, 275-285.

Goldstein, A. (1992). Stress in the superintendency: School leaders confront the daunting pressures of the job. *School Administrator, 49*(9), 8-13, 15-17.

Grogan, M. (2000). The short tenure of a woman superintendent: A clash of gender and politics. *Journal of School Leadership, 10*, 104-30.

Litchka, P., Fenzel, L. M., & Procaccini, J. (2009, February). *Stress and the superintendency.* Paper presented at the meeting of American Association of Colleges for Teacher Education, Chicago, IL.

Lowery, S., Harris, S., Hopson, M., & Marshall, R. (2001, November). *Take this job and LOVE it! A study of why superintendents stay or leave.* Paper presented at the meeting of the University Council for Educational Administration, Cincinnati, OH.

Malen, B. (1995). The micropolitics of education. In J. D. Scribner & D. H. Layton (Eds.), *The study of educational politics: The 1994 commemorative yearbook of the Politics of Education Association (1969–1994)* (pp. 147-167). Philadelphia, PA: Falmer.

Moos, R. H., & Billings, A. G. (1982). Conceptualizing and measuring coping resources and processes. In L. Goldberger & S. Breznitz (Eds.), *Handbook of stress: Theoretical and clinical aspects* (pp. 212-230). New York, NY: Free Press.

No Child Left Behind Act of 2001, Pub. L. No. 107-110 (2002).

Queen, J. A., & Queen, P. S. (2005). *The frazzled principal's wellness plan: Reclaiming time, managing stress, and creating a healthy lifestyle.* Thousand Oaks, CA: Corwin Press.

Patterson, J., & Kelleher, P. (2005). *Resilient school leaders.* Arlington, VA: American Association of School Administrators.

Richardson, L. M. (1998, November). *Stress in the superintendency: Implications for achieving excellence.* Paper presented at the meeting of the University Council for Educational Administration, St. Louis, MO.

Schmidt, L. J., Kosmoski, G. J., & Pollack, D. R. (1998). *Novice administrators: Psychological and physiological effects.* Retrieved from ERIC database. (ED427386)

Skinner, E. A., Edge, K., Altman, J., & Sherwood, H. (2003). Searching for the structure of coping: A review and critique of category systems for classifying ways of coping. *Psychological Bulletin, 129*, 216-269.

Stewart, D. W., & Shamdasani, P. N. (1990). *Focus groups: Theory and practice.* Newbury Park, CA: SAGE.

Whitaker, K. S. (2003). Superintendent perceptions of the quantity and quality of principal candidates. *Journal of School Leadership, 13*, 159-180.

CHAPTER 10

# SOCIAL JUSTICE IN MIDDLE PASSAGE

## The Voyage From Frustrations to Hopes

**Ira Bogotch**

Within this book, we are being pointed in the right direction. That is, we are learning how to listen and make sense of the administrative voices in and around public schools. But as with most complex educational discussions, the term *journey* is an apt metaphor, for it allows us to track progress in our own learning. The first task is to understand and create meanings from the focus group voices of principals and superintendents. We know from research that leaders create meanings for their followers and they do so primarily through the use of words (Bogotch & Roy, 1997; Gronn, 1983). For many years, well-known leadership educators such as Roland Barth, Gordon Donaldson, Richard Ackerman, Pat Maslin-Ostrowski, and others, some of whom have been affiliated with principal centers around the world, have argued that *listening* is an important leadership skill. To be sure, listening itself is not an easy skill to master. Even when we think we understand the words, phrases, acronyms, contexts, and cultures through which principals and superintendents speak, we all too

*Snapshots of School Leadership in the 21st Century:*
*Perils and Promises of Leading for Social Justice,*
*School Improvement, and Democratic Community,* pp. 189–208
Copyright © 2012 by Information Age Publishing

quickly have experienced how contexts change with demographics, the assignment of letter grades to schools, Adequate Yearly Progress outcome measures, and the personality differences that come each and every time an administrator is replaced. So we begin here by listening carefully and actively.

The next question to ask is what should we be listening for? My response is that we are listening carefully for any evidence of socially just ideas and actions on the part of these principals and superintendents. Our listening for social justice, however, is made more difficult because the words themselves, *social justice*, are not part of the spoken or written language of most public school administrators. That was certainly true for these focus group participants. But the absence of the words does not necessarily mean that there are not socially just ideas and behaviors in and around our nation's public schools. It becomes our responsibility as educational leadership researchers to translate the voices and data into socially just concepts to determine how, when, and where the *possibilities for social justice* might emerge as part of school leadership practice, policy, and research. Among the many possibilities, sadly, is that socially just ideas and actions are not present in today's school leaders' world. I don't think that is the case here, but it remains as an empirical question worthy of more research.

The starting point for this chapter analysis has to be the words themselves. But as I listened and read a subset of the administrator transcripts and the eight empirical chapters written by researchers, it became obvious that what I was hearing was not one voice, but rather three distinct, almost disconnected, leadership voices. The first voice was the words and phrases spoken by the school administrators themselves. The second voice came from the professor-authors of the empirical chapters. The third set of voices was from the ever-present external influences on both the public school administrators and the professor-authors. This third voice is often heard as the boisterously loud opinions expressed by politicians, businessmen and women, and philanthropists. It represents the dominant national discourse not only on school leadership as a profession but also on the entire enterprise of public schooling. As such, it reflects the cynical mood of the nation; the current out-of-favor political status of public education; and the belief that choice, competition, and privately initiated options are superior to state-run schools. This third voice also reflects the expanding role of the federal and state governments in ways not envisioned by our nation's architects and school system builders. For a social-justice researcher, this paradigm shift calls for careful examination to see how a centralized system within the U.S. cultural dynamics affects socially just ideas, actions, and programs (Bogotch, 2011b).

How then should we be listening to these three disconnected voices? The very fact that education speaks with disconnected voices does not hold great promise for developing social justice as an educational leadership construct. Nevertheless, our focus on words, phrases, language, translations, and communications may arguably be the right and only step, at this particular time in middle passage, where we need to search for evidence of and possibilities for social justice.

None of the three sets of voices is difficult to hear; what is difficult is communication among all the participants in public education that may lead to shared meanings and understanding. How should we make sense of the voices from the different perspectives within the field of educational leadership? We know that what makes sense to school administrators in their current situations is different from what makes sense to professor-authors living and working in universities. In turn, both perspectives are different from the points of view held by educational policy makers. This fragmented institutional reality, resulting from different situations and experiences, speaks to the need for an integrated or common language among educators, for its absence leads to political, moral, and methodological limitations to whatever contributions educational leaders at all levels are hoping to make for our nation's school systems. These communicative limitations result in continuing choruses of frustrations, which were loudly and repeatedly expressed throughout the Voices data. Thus, until we can reunite these voices communicatively so that the groups stop talking past each other and begin to challenge the dominant discourses collectively, the possibilities for educational leadership and social justice will remain limited.

Yet, in spite of these various limitations, the voices heard here come from individuals who are fully engaged and fully competent in the practice of their chosen professions. The problem is that whenever the voices are heard outside the context of their different institutional settings, there is a communicative disconnect that results in tensions and conflicts, which then are expressed first as frustrations (by practitioners, professor-authors, and policy makers), followed by distinct statements of hope for the future. These hopes are the "if only" realities of educational leadership today. As researchers, we ought to study whether the possibilities for social justice result from frustrations, from the "if only" realities, or from a combination of the two. Central to any and all social justice discussions is that we should be witness to the dynamic struggles of ideas in each and every school leadership idea, action, or program.

## "IF ONLY" REALITIES

I found no space in the Voices data for nostalgia, romance, or critique, for it takes every ounce of energy from these individuals to make public education in U.S. schools and universities work as well as it does. These are trying times (though not necessarily a national crisis), as the mandated school reforms themselves take time and energy away from the professional work of curriculum development, innovative and creative teaching, new learning, and new leadership. That would not be the case if all school reforms were first grounded in the professional activities of teachers, administrators, and professors and then realigned through communicative discourses, rather than externally imposed upon school administrators by policy makers. Hovering over the voices of these focus group principals and superintendents and professor-authors is a dominant discourse that has disciplinary powers to influence the words and actions of the participants in this book. Thus, the voices we hear are moderated, domesticated, and disciplined via tangible rewards and sanctions, by governmental authorities and their proxies—and sometimes, we ourselves serve as proxies. School reform has become a full-time and, for a few individuals, a profitable industry, one that robs educators of the time they need to do their best work. Each group—practitioners, professor-authors, and policy makers—has never worked harder. Yet, their busy lives have been redefined and redirected by disciplinary and governmental authorities, not by good research, theories, or best practices.

This is true for school administrators in terms of monitoring curriculum alignment, calculating accountability measures, complying with unfunded mandates, and navigating the subsequent rules and regulations that result. It is also true for educational leadership professor-authors in terms of rewriting leadership preparation programs to keep meeting the latest federal, state, or district standards or national accreditation indicators. Professor-authors are also driven by the rewards and sanctions imposed by their universities and the promotion and tenure process. And it is just as true for professional policy makers in terms of persuading the public, primarily through words, that public education is our nation's number-one domestic priority—which by any objective measure (i.e., dollars and cents/sense), it is not and they know it is not. Thus, policy makers who know that public education is not our nation's number-one domestic priority use words to conceal that reality. And in so doing, they too expend their energies, which are needed to explore new and different ideas about schools. The bottom line is that each group—practitioners, professor-authors, and policy makers—should come together to decide collectively what is worth fighting for (Fullan, 1997).

Thus, we have, at best, the "if only" responses, the hoped-for realities, to today's school reforms. That is, school administrators and professor-authors think they know what they could accomplish by working with those around them (i.e., collaborative leadership) "if only" they had the following policies and structures in place:

- more latitude through government waivers;
- more funding to meet the demands of mandated programs;
- more workplace autonomy to tap the creativity of teachers and staff;
- collaborative voices of teachers, parents, and community members participating in messy decision-making processes;
- permission as well as freedom to break rules when necessary; and
- the courage to lead.

Professor-authors have research studies, hypotheses, and tentative theories to support the above list, which they continue to offer to practitioners as unsolicited advice and in a language (e.g., American Psychological Association [APA] style) that is unique to the professoriate. Policy makers believe they could accomplish their top-down reforms with fewer headaches of implementation "if only" everyone else would just do what they say and stop making excuses.

There are conflicting perceptions inside the "if only" realities. For example, on the one hand, school administrators stated that the No Child Left Behind Act (NCLB) has given them the leverage to focus on poorly performing students and teachers and to do what is best for children; at the same time, the very same law conscripts everyone in public schools to adhere to rigid standardized testing, curriculum alignment, and Adequate Yearly Progress goals, which school administrators know is not best for children. Listening to the school administrator voices, we can hear their understandings of the contradictions as they talk about their frustrations and stress over the tensions and complexities of just doing their everyday jobs, which are compounded by the dictates of central office politics and personnel. It is all so real in the present that it has become almost impossible to recognize that we are still in a middle passage of a long and arduous journey through public school history, a journey that historically has traveled through many real crises in terms of separate and unequal schools for Black and White children; programs to educate impoverished immigrants; the political realities of regional as well as world wars; and the periodic economic downturns that result from unregulated market forces, including unemployment, poverty, and homelessness.

The question is how we can collectively, not individually, figure out ways to turn these frustrations into the "if only" ideas listed in terms of new governance structures, new leadership practices, democratic theories of action, and new policies governing public schools. In other words, although neither you nor I can identify social justice explicitly in these voices and data sets, we still may be able to find within the *middle passage* the "if only" realities, the communicative connections to leadership, learning, caring, and critique (Starratt, 1991). To do so may likely require a beginning again in developing new research methods for translating distinctly different institutional discourses. It may also require theoretical bridge building in school leadership along the lines suggested by Tooms and Boske (2009) and Boske (in press). But our task here and now is to stay within the data.

## LOOKING INSIDE THE VOICES DATA

As a researcher, I align myself with the professor-authors' voices in this book. Like many others in the professoriate, I doubt whether I could do the job of principal or superintendent as well as many who are doing it today. There are, of course, professorial exceptions (those who have worked successfully as administrators), among them Theodore Sizer, Larry Cuban, Jane Clark Lindle, and A. William Place. Thus, it is with admiration and respect that I look upon all practitioners. But that does not stop me from being a critical friend to any and all voices in this book. Probably, I am most critical of the professor-authors, for it is within their set of voices that I also hear myself.

With respect to research methods, I used the same qualitative methodologies on the administrator data subset as I did on the professor-author data set. And the very same methodological limitations that I see in this book, I too am guilty of here. Specifically, I read eight transcripts of the focus groups, listening to what principals and superintendents said. I then read the coeditors' introduction to better understand how they designed and conceptualized the organization of this book. Then I read the conclusions, summaries, and implications of the eight empirical chapters written by the professor-authors. My purpose was to listen and understand prior to translating what I learned.

To both data sets, I brought forward a list of social justice words and phrases that speak to the problems, possibilities, and issues of social justice (Bogotch, Beachum, Blount, Brooks, & English, 2008). These *a priori* codes included the following terms taken from published social science literatures on the topic of justice and social justice: *poverty, health* and *healthcare, jobs, the economy, nutrition, politics, ideology, justice, ethics, morality, home visits, transparency,* and *corruption.*[1] Lastly, I synthesized the professor-authors' concluding sections and conducted a second analysis of the word data followed by a critique of the contexts of both data sets.

Using the lens of social justice for analyzing these two data sets is admittedly ambiguous, if not also contentious, at least for educators.[2] The phrase *social justice* was not used at all by the principals or superintendents in their focus group interviews. The term was used only in passing by one or two professor-authors. What does that tell us about the relationship between educational leadership and social justice other than what we already knew? And that is the contentious meanings and subsequent actions of social justice are not on the minds and lips of our most committed and dedicated school leaders.

## Principal and Superintendent Voices

Because my chapter comes at the end of the book, it allows us to draw conclusions from the eight empirical chapters. This is as true for you as the reader as it is for me as a professor-author. The question for us to keep in mind is whether we should expect school leaders to be civic leaders and social justice advocates, or is that asking too much of these busy, overstressed individuals?

The data here do not approach the "yes, but" tone identified by Marshall and Ward (2004) in their sample of administrators. In that study, the "yes" represented administrators' awareness of ethical and socially just actions; the "but" represented their risk assessment, which prevented them from taking action on their ideas. We are all aware of principals, superintendents, and central office administrators who are engaged in promoting social justice overtly. For example, Anthony Smith, not one of the participants in these focus groups, but rather the current superintendent in Oakland, California, when he was deputy superintendent in San Francisco, was quoted as saying, "Schools have been a place of dehumanizing alienation for our kids" (Eslinger, 2007, para. 1). Nowhere in the Voices 3 focus group data were there any similar statements. Neither could I find the kind of advocacy promoted by central office administrator Laurel Schmidt (2009), who works in the Santa Monica-Malibu Unified School District and who wrote in *Educational Leadership* the following paragraph:

> In an era of homogenized, shrink wrapped, germ-free curriculum, social justice is the renegade. It doesn't just push the envelope—it's several leagues outside the box. For a start it has few right answers. Study geography, and you know you're dealing with topography and climate. Yet history has some solid content among the questions and interpretations. Social justice is amorphous. It's an unscripted mixture of politics, economics, laws values, humanitarian crises, and issues that pit common sense against the common good. (para. 1)[3]

What might account for the absence of these connections between schooling and society in the Voices data here? As a researcher, the first place to look is with the instrument and methods. What were the specific questions asked of these school administrators? First, I noted that all the questions were open ended, allowing individual administrators to choose any pathway to school improvement, democratic community, or social justice. Second, I wondered about the effects of the focus group format on responses. Would that inhibit school administrators? Maybe. We know from critical theory that consensus, not dissensus, and convergence, not divergence, are conditioned responses in school leadership research with principals and superintendents. Third, I looked specifically at how respondents described "what's best for kids."[4] I found that the clause "what's best for kids" when used as the subject of a sentence was not always followed by a predicate. That is, it was used often as a stand-alone response as if it explained intentions and actions without specifying what those intentions or actions look like in practice. When the phrase was followed by a modifier or predicate, its meanings varied from being used as an umbrella term of art to references to specific actions that included (a) shared decision making, (b) staff development for teachers, (c) making personnel moves, and (d) individualizing instruction. These adult, managerial behaviors, all appropriate for improving instruction or the culture and health of a school, did not explain explicitly why and how it was connected to "what is best for children" or to social justice as an educational construct.

What I did find in the data set by looking at the *a priori* codes were discrete references to the following terms: *politics*, *health*, and *jobs*. This positivist approach to qualitative data analysis is flawed methodologically as the *a priori* concepts posit the utterance and minimize the larger sociocultural context. That said, it is hard to dispute the specific meanings that this sample of school administrators assigned to these terms. Principals 63 and 66 both mentioned the word *politics*. In the first instance, the politics of school grades gave the principal some protection from central office interference. In the second instance, the reference referred to the disappointing reality of "central office politics." In these two examples and elsewhere when administrators spoke about the politics of inclusive and messy decision making, the term had to do with internal school or district dynamics and relationships. At no time in the eight transcripts I read did these school administrators introduce references to the local or national politics in terms of taking political actions in the community.

The same internal dynamic can be seen in how the term *health* was used by the participants. Again, what makes the responses problematic was that the school administrators were asked open-ended questions. Therefore, instead of talking about the "health" of children, their families, or the nation, the term was used in the context of within-school dynamics as in adding an elective health course to the curriculum or as in working in a healthy organizational culture. When these examples were extended to the context of the responses, I observed that health was associated with the difficulty of doing their jobs as administrators. Thus, bringing "health" into the curriculum involved negotiating with teachers, administrators, and community to make this curriculum decision. "Health" as a function of a school culture involved getting faculty and the school board to agree to restructure the class schedule to include a health class; the principal described this as a "fairly exhaustive process." Thus, curricular change became for this individual a frustrating reality in today's environment. In the second example, middle school Principal 73 expressed relief that she was now working in a district that had a healthy culture, which she described as follows:

> I can remember the very first day I went over to the superintendent and asked how many times a day I was to check in with him. And he looked at me and said, "I'll see you once a week at our meetings." "Oh, you mean I can really do my job?" "Yep, that's why you were hired." (Midwest, 2006)

While reading this example, I didn't know whether to smile along with this principal or to cry over the fact that there are school administrators who have to check in daily with their supervisors. In either case, the context of "health" is far away from issues facing children and their families regarding their health, well-being, nutrition, diet, hunger, and the health-care needs of citizens living in this nation.

The third example taken from the *a priori* code was the term *jobs*. Here the discussion, primarily among superintendents, revolved around the pressures of being a superintendent today. Thus, the context was their own feeling of stress, not the stress felt by children, teachers, parents, or communities. There was not any overt expression of the concern for jobs that do or do not pay living wages, or for the changing landscape of jobs across the nation, or asking exactly how we might align curriculum to what our children may be expected to do to earn a living. Instead, the context was on the stress of being a superintendent. That is, to be sure, an important topic, just as the internal micropolitics of schools and school districts are important topics. Building healthy school cultures is an important topic. But the theory of social justice, as I will outline shortly, cannot revolve around closed-system thinking of schools and school systems or about roles. Terms such as *politics, health,* and *jobs,* which all are integral to the lives of school administrators, have to identify the problems and possibilities in the 21st century, and how educational leaders can play a dominant role in creating better futures for this and coming generations.

## Professor-Author Data

The coauthors of Chapter 2 (No Child Left Behind as School Reform: Intended and Unintended Consequences) framed the theme of the voices:

> Superintendents and principals see benefits in NCLB having focused attention on the academic success of all children. It gave school leaders legitimacy to talk about equity in terms of not only equality of opportunity but also equality of outcome. It gave them leverage over individuals and groups who resisted change. In other words, the political power of NCLB indirectly influenced changes in school and district culture. But it failed to give them all the support they needed to sustain reform, and some of its unintended consequences actual work against leadership for reform.

I concur, and so did each of the professor-authors in this book. But the question of social justice remains the same for me; that is, how should we take the words of the school administrators and translate them into possibilities for social justice in and outside of schools? The various theories that framed each of the chapters, although as important as the practitioners' uses of *politics, health,* and *jobs,* miss the target of establishing one particular theory as being the appropriate theory to understand and translate problems of school administrators. There was very little traction in the ensuing discussion sections of the chapters; instead, professor-authors fit specific problems under a theory here or a theory there, depending on how they interpreted the Voices data. All of the theories being offered were meant to be helpful and hopeful. They included school improvement, shared decision making, critical leadership, and collaborative and democratic decision making. But without contextual details in the actual transcript data, the named theories, presented as fully developed answers, become non sequiturs to the actual everyday problems of the practitioners. Without traction, there is no lift off from today's one-dimensional student achievement measures to educational accomplishments that reflect deeper understandings of knowledge (as described in Chapter 6, Assessment). The hope for critical leadership or socioemotional theories butts up against high-stakes assessments. Thus, critical leadership and socioemotional theories become non sequiturs and do little to respond to administrators' general frustrations. Where in practice are we "integrating individualized caring for students with student achievement" (Chapter 3, Growth and Development of Children)? Where is the research on how to integrate critique into school practices? And how exactly does caring connect to critique and justice (Starratt, 1991)? The non sequiturs of our research hypotheses are not answers to specific school reforms. They could be, however, if we promoted discussion and dialogue among the participants. The professor-authors themselves acknowledged that socioemotional concerns are not built into high-stakes assessments. So that bit of helpful advice remains a non sequitur, another disconnect with the realities and frustrations of practicing school administrators.

Professor-authors like me want to be helpful. Truly. We have knowledge of many sociocultural and organizational theories, and we want to offer them as answers to problems. But I'm not sure we know whether what we are writing is helpful. Is our offering of unsolicited written advice (i.e., interpretations) helpful? I'm not sure how helpful conceptual frameworks are to practitioners. I'm not sure how our research designs are helpful to practitioners. And I know from listening to practitioners that our academic writing style is not at all helpful. If we believe in the viability of our new ideas, then we need to communicate them by translations and bridges to practice and policy.

What I found most helpful in the professor-author chapters was their efforts to stay inside the tensions, contradictions, complexities, frustrations, and stress of practitioners. In that light, I found particularly helpful the chapters that divided the various tensions into what is negative and what is positive. The negative tensions came from unfunded mandates, the narrowing of curriculum based on which subjects were to be tested, the difficulties of hiring quality teachers in minority schools, the lack of autonomy throughout the system from principals to teachers, and the scripting of lessons. Each eroded bit by bit the professional workplace pride of the individuals who have chosen public education as their life's work. On the positive side, there was the discussion in Chapter 2 (No Child Left Behind as School Reform: Intended and Unintended Consequences) of the political levers of NCLB. Chapter 6, Assessment, then, expands upon that notion by talking about disaggregated data that let administrators and teachers hone in on problems of specific groups of children. Of course, the problem itself is a contradiction, as it was created by our profession not developing curricula for the child, that is, what is best for the child, in the first place. We deliver an already developed curriculum and are told to align it with what we do. Nevertheless, the activity described as curriculum alignment gets listed, by default, as a positive tension, for it remains the one area with the potential of creativity.

Chapter 3, Growth and Development of Children, tells us, "Superintendents reported that they did not push aside inclusive social justice practices to achieve school improvement goals, but instead the two unfolded and were integrated together into their daily professional practices." Chapter 3 made a couple of other mentions of social justice, as did Chapter 5 (Leadership Practices and Processes That Impact Personnel, Professional Development, and Teacher Professionalism and Influence

School Improvement) and Chapter 7 (Decision-Making Processes, Giving Voice, Listening, and Involvement). But in general, there is little mention of the concept of social justice in this book. As close as we can get to doing collaboration is that we hear how difficult, time consuming, messy, and conflictual collaboration can be. That's the everyday situation for school administrators. The "as if" realities of collaboration become the frustrations of doing collaboration.

I am not trying to complicate what is in the minds and on the lips of these participants. They themselves see the complexities, tensions, and contradictions involving today's schools. In Chapter 6, Assessment, for example, reaching NCLB goals is described as "impossible." The theme of "frustration" for all educators involved appeared throughout this book in discussions of NCLB. Such expressions indicate more than just the words; they communicate the political and social dynamics beyond the words themselves.

## BEYOND THE VOICES DATA: SOCIAL JUSTICE IN MIDDLE PASSAGE

Whenever I think about the concept of social justice, I do so not from the disconnected institutional perspectives of schools, universities, or government agencies, but rather from the ideals and purposes of education and society. This sociocultural foundation is helpful for two reasons: (a) It explicitly connects the workings or situations of school administrators with roles and situations of professor-authors as well as educational policy makers, and (b) it forces me, as an educational researcher-professor-author, to adopt a lens or a particular theory of education that may better serve the needs of children, adults, and societies than the practices, research methods, and policies dominating today's schools.

This theoretical position on education has helped me to arrive at *social justice* as that one particular and most appropriate theory for school leadership, for it opens the role of school leadership to civic, social, political, and moral dimensions. As such, it requires us to rethink and redefine school leadership in terms of what we see as the purposes of education and the intellectual role of professor-authors. Education itself is not only greater than any one social science discipline but also historically prior to the development of disciplinary thinking across fields of science, social science, and the humanities. Education as growth and development is what makes systematic analysis in any academic discipline possible. It is what makes reasonable and practical decision making, in schools, universities, and governments, possible. It is what makes some civilizations flourish.

At the level of instruction, education is more than factual acquisition, for it provides participants and citizens with opportunities for developing thinking and literacy skills as well as the dispositions to participate in life's endeavors with *others*. Likewise, education is more than transmitting a single culture as it "provides alternative views of the world and strengthens the will to explore them" (Bruner, 1966, p. 117). Critically, education as the consequences of theory and practice is more than words and protests (Fine, 2004; Noguera, 2003). The most serious underlying challenge for education as a field and for educators is to come to the realization that education is *more than* the limited field it has been presupposed to be in today's era of accountability, that is, teaching, learning, and testing. This realization, however, must first begin with educators themselves before it can be communicated and translated to one another and to others outside education.

Thus, it is through education that both the individual and the collective aspects of life (namely, family, race, ethnicity, religion, and culture) are nurtured. It is through education that one's self struggles to be heard as a voice and not ignored, marginalized, or erased by another set of voices. Education cannot let one's life devolve into either selfishness or total obedience to authorities. Education strives to make one's life connected to larger social, political, and moral issues beyond any one institutional setting, such as a school, university, or government agency. Thus, the educator is always engaged in teaching, learning, and leading so as to redefine the world in terms of how individuals learn to interact with others for the purposes of better solutions and better futures for themselves and for others. If education is more than schooling or doing research in isolation, then social justice is more than distributing resources socially or economically (Young, 1990). The combination of education and social justice leads to understanding of *individuals with others* in this world, with socially just ends as one immediate possibility (Bogotch, 2006).

The field of educational leadership evolved historically and culturally with three separate and unequal gaps: (a) the gap between administrators and teachers regarding management, hierarchies, and organizational theories; (b) the gap between business elites and school administrators regarding educational policies; and (c) the gap between professor-authors, school practitioners, and policy makers, referred to as the theory–practice gap. There were many reasons why the transitions from teachers to head teachers to principals to superintendents, from superintendents to professors, and from school leaders to educational policy makers broke down into separate and unequal voices. But the overall effect has been communications' problems that are not being addressed by any of the three disconnected voices.

The data sets of principals and superintendents make numerous references to these dynamics in terms of the micropolitics, organizational cultures, reforms, and decision making. With respect to the theory–practice gap between school administrators and professors, the dynamics have been driven by the epistemological assumptions (a) that good theory is practical and (b) that practitioners apply theories to practice. There have been many efforts to bridge all of these gaps. Some of the efforts are referred to as reflective practice, theories-in-action, pedagogical knowledge, practical knowledge, practitioner knowledge, and leadership for learning. These hybrid approaches to theory–practice have an embedded professional assumption; that is, educators, whether teachers, administrators, or professors, have more in common that they have differences. Unfortunately, the evidence in the Voices data does not bear out these epistemological assumptions.

In teaching leadership, I make the assumption that change begins with the leader, either in terms of finding ways to make the work meaningful to others or in making the initial changes in difficult interactions so as to elicit and model changes for others. Problems in the workplace have much to do with how the leader speaks and acts (and also writes) and how the leader is perceived by others. Thus, unless leaders (as school administrators, professor-authors, and policy makers) are willing to make changes first, how can we or they expect others to make real changes beyond following directions, policies, or mandates (Bogotch, 2011a)?

## Communicative Strategies

What about a common written and spoken language to address the separate but unequal voices? What would that language have to include? The first criterion of a language is that it be able to describe the world around us. There needs to be descriptive vocabulary linked to an active grammar that captures the static and dynamics elements of the surroundings. These elements might be referred to as lived experiences. The first step in the communications process would be to share the lived experiences, orally and in writing, with others so that a level of understanding can develop. This can never lead to perfect understanding, but it can lead to understandable voices. Those organizations, communities, and societies that do this openly are called transparent (a relative measure). It is harder to "get over" on another in a communicative, transparent climate. It makes it possible, not easy, to build trust. And with trust, there are further possibilities for equity, health, and ethical behaviors.

But what about situations in which there are institutional differences (e.g., schools, universities, and government agencies) in structures, belief systems, cultures, and work lives? What are the effects of these institutional differences across school administrators, professor-authors, and policy makers? It depends. If we, as leaders, reform education as a community, that is, with members who have more in common with one another than differences, then institutional differences could be renegotiated and realigned by transparent language, defined here as translations and bridge building. The immediate follow-up question is how do we begin? And that, for me, is where this book begins again. That is, by giving all the members a voice to remake the rules and regulations governing education in our society. Here I am using the term *voice* not as words alone, but rather as participants in active decision making related to education.

How different would this reality be from the one of separate and unequal voices, where the structural hierarchies hide the political and social dynamics of superintendents, for example, from principals and teachers, and vice versa? What should a superintendent do or know that should not be known and commented upon by a teacher or a parent? A restructuring of communicative behaviors would have to include educational policy makers who would be subject to (i.e., required to listen to and communicate with) the voices of other educators. Today, with so many nonparallel voices within the field of educational leadership, we have conceptual, behavioral, attitudinal, and methodological limitations. It takes away from our abilities to deal effectively with the "impossible" and to work around and through our "frustrations." How such a common language would include, or not, social justice discourses would be decided by communicative processes from all stakeholders. Voices therefore become the vehicle for developing theory, perhaps a theory of social justice as an educational construct.

Historically we have documented evidence of generations in which it was expected that all teachers adapt curriculum and instruction materials for use in a classroom. Curricula, whether yesterday or today, have to fit the needs of the children in the classroom, the school, and communities. This, sadly, is not the school practice of today. Instead, we hear the words of principals and superintendents as they laud the reform called curriculum alignment: in other words, alignment to already developed standards. Today's curricular environment emphasizes very different skills, those that laud alignment over inquiry and development. The latter takes a great deal of time and effort and in today's fast-paced world would create different conflicts, tensions, and frustrations from the ones we heard in the Voices data here. Our goal is not to eliminate frustrations, tensions, or even contradictions in a system that is built upon the "if only" scenarios described above. Teaching and administrating are fraught with frustrations, tensions, and contradictions that do not allow professionals to adjust to today's discourses of standards and accountability without curricular debate.

And what should be the professor-authors' responses? How should professor-authors support and serve administrators and policy makers? Should not our communicative strategy have changed beyond the scholarly writing that relies on citations of previous authors (which are variably known to some in the reading audience) to establish validity and historical authenticity? Professor-authors use citations to supplement and expand meanings and make the words they use real. But to practitioners, this language of APA formatting with citations has little to no meaning-making capacity and structurally becomes a barrier to comprehension itself.[5]

Thus, even prior to writing in a common language, each of the separate and unequal voices would have to engage in its own grammatical housecleaning. Can this happen? As we watch how social networking and media change languages and discourses around the world, and as we accept the fact that our work has not impacted schools in ways we deliberately intended, then we need to become educational leaders in a different modality. Separate and unequal discourses do not serve the profession. Leaders, regardless of their fields or disciplines, are distinguished from other organizational members by their or our willingness to take risks and demonstrate the courage to question established customs and tradition. They go outside the boundaries to create new discourses. Shouldn't we in educational leadership model this courageous leadership?

Whose dominant discourses influence everyday practices? The Voices data include federal, state, and district mandates, rules, and regulations—all of which demand obedience, compliance, and alignment. How then should we disrupt the dominant discourses of the voices?

## Next Steps

I prefer to begin this concluding section by looking inward toward professor-authors. What might we say or write regarding social justice that a practicing administrator and an educational policy maker are likely to take to heart? With respect to our shared history, how best should I/we communicate that previous generations of school practitioners were at the forefront of *all political struggles* to protect democracy, to Americanize immigrants, and to support national priorities in times of political and economic crises? Politically, how best should I/we remind school leaders that the federal government funds public education at less than 4% of the national budget and that philanthropists "play school" (Barzun, 1959, p. 200) while handing out pennies on the dollar of their wealth to influence school reforms across the nation? How do we collectively break through the dominant language of standards and accountability in order to inject ethics, morality, voice, and public service into administrative discourses? How do all sit down together and examine these historical, economic, or political connections?

So long as the three voices remain disconnected, educational leadership as a profession will continue to come up short on all input and outcome measures. Either we find ways to translate our disconnected institutional contexts or we continue in the middle passages of frustrations and "if only" hopes. What I learned from reading of the Voices data reinforced what I had already known and felt, that we are fortunate to have men and women willing to serve as principals and superintendents, who have dedicated their lives to public education. We have the kind of caring and critical professor-authors we need. And I have to believe that among educational policy makers, there are individuals who want to hear the voices of school administrators and professor-authors.

## Beginning Again: Social Justice Takeaways

Each of us plays an important role in beginning again. We get to redefine the situation of "if only" hopes in response to today's frustrations. So the first translation I propose is that the work of school leadership may be frustrating, complex, even contradictory, but it still has to connect to democracy, the purposes of public education, and social justice. For that to happen there must be a questioning or a struggle of ideas in school leadership. Until then, we remain in middle passage. These larger constructs of democracy and social justice are, according to my second translation, more significant than the objectives of institutions, whether schools, universities, businesses, or government. Thus, the concept of education is needed to connect across institutions and their respective cultures.

The third translation comes directly from leadership theory. That is, leadership gives meanings to voices. This is the most basic translation in that we have to work with people as we find them, not as we want them to be. The process of building relationships and leadership capacity begins with words and actions, our words, our actions. We should remember the fourth translation, that while we are living in the middle passage, the present, including NCLB, has no historical precedents. Thus, as leaders, it is our responsibility to take the wheel, read the compass, and set a course consistent with what is best for children and the society, not as a distant goal, but for today and for this generation. The school leaders of the past refused to accept the realities of poverty beyond a single generation. They definitely did not accept it as a cycle or a culture of poverty, or as inevitable for the children's children. There was a direct connection between what was done in the present with changes that followed immediately. At the level of practice, Translations 5, 6, and 7 and going forward, we need to bring leadership substitutes to such shortsighted practices as standards, accountability, curriculum alignment, and APA genres. Our goal is not just communicative competencies across educational institutions, but rather to work for a society that is educationally fluent.

## AUTHOR NOTE

I want to thank my colleague Dilys Schoorman for her suggestions along with those from doctoral students in school leadership at Florida Atlantic University: Jacqueline Akerina, Ginger Featherstone, Traci Porter, Maria Rodriguez, Scott Smith, and Tommy Tucker.

## NOTES

1.   I did not include democracy or community as I understood those were assigned as separate chapters in this book to be written by different professor-authors.
2.   Other professions, in particular social work, have made social justice one of the profession's core values. In quoting from the National Association of Social Workers (2008) *Code of Ethics,*

> Social workers should promote the general welfare of society, from local to global levels, and the development of people, their communities and their environments. Social workers should advocate for living conditions conducive to the fulfillment of basic human needs and should promote social, economic, political, and cultural values and institutions that are compatible with the realization of social justice.... Social workers should promote conditions that encourage respect for cultural and social diversity within the United States and globally. Social workers should promote policies and practices that demonstrate respect for difference, support the expansion of cultural knowledge and resources, advocate for programs and institutions that demonstrate cultural competence, and promote policies that safeguard the rights of and confirm equity and social justice for all people. (§ 6.01, 6.04[c])

3.   So as not to interrupt the narrative argument I am struggling to make, I ended the quote after the first paragraph. For those of you who want to read more, Schmidt (2009) continued,

For every earnest cause, dozens of well-educated and well-funded countervailing voices explain why the situation can't or shouldn't change. So you and your students must grapple with this question: Are there some behaviors or conditions that we simply must address, no matter how difficult or unpopular our work will be?

There's so much to do, even in our own neighborhoods. Some projects are simple fixes, but many turn out to be a tiny first link in a long, arduous chain of effort. Think of the thousands of discrete actions required over the decades to achieve civil rights for minorities in the United States. So your students may never have the thrill of seeing a bill signed into law, a shelter renovated, or even a municipal code modified to create a publicly funded meals program for homeless people. They may solve one part of a problem, only to discover that they've uncovered a greater injustice or need. Social activists face disappointment and frustration every day, but they keep on trying.

Social activism is also potentially dangerous. A veteran educator explained how one of his students warned him, "You know, Mr. Kohl, you could get arrested for stirring up justice!" You have only to look at the history of the civil rights movement to know how right he was.

So social justice is untidy, exhausting, discouraging, even dangerous work—which may be the reason why it's not on the top ten list of social studies projects in many schools. Better to have kids build a model of a *rancho* (a group of huts for housing ranch workers) or recreate a *potlatch* (a festival ceremony practiced by the indigenous peoples of the Pacific Northwest) and be done with it. (para. 2–5)

4.  It should be noted that the editors used the phrase "what's best for students," whereas the school administrators variously translated that to "what's best for kids" and "what's best for children."
5.  As I write this chapter I have no solution to the reading comprehension problem, as APA formatting has become natural to my writing and thinking. I would have to retrain myself over time and distance myself from the dominant scholarly discourses imposed by the Academy.

## REFERENCES

Barzun, J. (1959). *The house of intellect*. New York, NY: Harper Torchbooks.
Bogotch, I. (2006, November). *Social justice as an educational construct: Problems, possibilities, leadership, and research*. Paper presented at the meeting of the University Council for Educational Administration, San Antonio, TX.
Bogotch, I. (2011a). Democracy is little "l" leadership: For every day at any time. *The Scholar-Practitioner Quarterly, 5*(1), 93-98.
Bogotch, I. (2011b). U.S. cultural history: Visible and invisible influences on leadership for learning. In T. Townsend & J. MacBeath (Eds.), *International hand-*

book of leadership for learning (pp. 29-50). Dordrecht, The Netherlands: Springer.

Bogotch, I., Beachum, F., Blount, J., Brooks, J., & English, F. (2008). *Radicalizing educational Leadership: Dimensions of social justice.* Taiwan: Sense.

Bogotch, I., & Roy, C. (1997). The context of partial truths: An analysis of principals' discourse. *Journal of Educational Administration, 35,* 234-252.

Boske, C. (Ed.). (in press). *Educational leadership: Building bridges among ideas, schools and nations.* Charlotte, NC: Information Age.

Bruner, J. (1966). *The process of education: Towards a theory of instruction.* Cambridge, MA: Harvard University Press.

Eslinger, B. (2007, December). *School district adds superintendent for social justice.* Retrieved from http://www.sfexaminer.com/local/school-district-adds -superintendent-social-justice

Fine, M. (2004). The power of the *Brown v. Board of Education* decision: Theorizing threats to sustainability. *American Psychology, 59,* 502-510.

Fullan, M. (1997). *What's worth fighting for in the principalship?* New York, NY: Teachers College Press.

Gronn, P. (1983). Talk as the work: The accomplishment of school administration. *Administrative Science Quarterly, 28*(1), 1-21.

Marshall, C., & Ward, M. (2004). "Yes, but … " Education leaders discuss social justice. *Journal of School Leadership, 14,* 531-563.

National Association of Social Workers. (2008). *Code of ethics.* Retrieved from http://www.socialworkers.org/pubs/code/code.asp

Noguera, P. (2003). *City schools and the American dream: Fulfilling the promise of public education.* New York, NY: Teachers College.

Schmidt, L. (2009). *Stirring up justice.* Retrieved from http://www.ascd.org/ publications/educational-leadership/may09/vol66/num08/ Stirring-Up-Justice.aspx

Starratt, R. (1991). Building an ethical school. *Educational Administration Quarterly, 27,* 185-202

Tooms, A., & Boske, C. (Eds.). (2009). *Bridge leadership: Connecting educational leadership and social justice.* Charlotte, NC: Information Age.

Young, I. (1990). *Justice and the politics of difference.* Princeton, NJ: Princeton University Press.

CHAPTER 11

# THE ASKERS AND
# THE TELLERS

## Larger Messages From the Voices 3 Project

**Tony Townsend**

In April 2003, as I was coming to the end of a year's visiting professorship at the University of Michigan, I was interviewed by one of the network television stations in Flint, Michigan. They were interested in my perspective on American education. I was asked if I had heard of No Child Left Behind (NCLB), and then I was asked what I thought of it. My response at the time was, "The best you can hope for is zero progress." Kerachsky (2009) has reported minimal progress on the National Assessment of Educational Progress since 2004. In short, there has been a 4-point rise in reading for 9-year-olds (from 216 to 220, about a 2% increase), a 3-point rise in reading for 13-year-olds (from 257 to 260, just over a 1% increase), and a 3-point rise in reading for 17-year-olds (from 283 to 286, about a 1% increase). In the period 2004–2008, there has been no significant change in the gap between White students and Black students or between White students and Hispanic students. For mathematics, the actual numbers are different, but exactly the same trend has occurred overall. This

*Snapshots of School Leadership in the 21st Century:*
*Perils and Promises of Leading for Social Justice,*
*School Improvement, and Democratic Community*, pp. 209–235

suggests that NCLB has had some impact on improving the scores of all students, especially at the elementary level, but has had virtually no impact on reducing the gap at any level. Over a longer period, 1971–2008, there has been a 6% improvement in scores for reading for 9-year-olds and a 2% improvement in 13-year-olds, but no improvement in 17-year-olds since 1971. However, there has been a significant reduction in the gap in reading at all three levels. Again, for mathematics, the actual numbers are different, but exactly the same trend has occurred overall.

So, it could be argued that all the reform efforts that have happened in the United States in the last 40 years, NCLB included, have at best made some reduction in the gap between White students and those traditionally seen as disadvantaged, especially at the elementary level, but that there has been virtually no increase in performance by students by the time they left school. So if we measure the impact of the American education system by the performance of students at the end of their compulsory years at school, then NCLB has had virtually zero impact on performance. My comment of 2003 was close to being an accurate prediction of what has in fact happened in the United States over that time. Of course, none of the other reforms that have been implemented since 1971 have had any significant impact, either.

However, the data collected in the Voices 3 project add a new dimension to our understanding of NCLB and its impact. Chapter 6, Assessment, reported on Peterson and West's (2003) view that the first goal of NCLB was to close the achievement gap between minority and nonminority students and between educationally disadvantaged children and their more educationally advantaged peers, with the second goal being to create and implement an assessment regime with significant consequences by holding schools and school systems accountable for those who fail.

The collected evidence tells us that the first goal has failed to achieve what it set out to do and the United States is no closer to the goal of having "all students in the United States reach the level of 'proficient' on state assessments in reading and mathematics by 2014" (Chapter 6, Assessment). However, the second goal has been well and truly achieved; there is an accountability system, one that focuses on blame and failure, that all people involved in education have now come to fear. The impact of the success of the second goal has been to make everyone associated with education to be under stress. Quotes from this book demonstrate the stress levels of administrators at both system and school-building levels. For example, Chapter 9, Pressure of Outside Forces, Stress, and Finding Balance, reminds readers of research showing "school superintendents and principals may even experience higher levels of stress than do other executives with respect to role overload and the level of responsibility their position carries." Some research has shown that it is not only the adults who are stressed: "For many students, high-stakes testing does cor-relate with academic success, but it also provides for discomforts that include test anxiety, nausea, and inhibited concentration and recall, which lead to poor test performance" (Chapter 3, Growth and Development of Children).

So, my comment of "the best you can hope for is zero impact" takes on a new poignancy. On average, there has been zero impact in student achievement; students in some schools have improved, some are much the same, but there are also many schools that are doing worse now than they were previously, so the question now becomes, at what cost? Zero impact in total would have been no improvement in student achievement but no real change in the lives of the people involved in the activity as well. What we have seen is a substantial change in the day-to-day lives of superintendents, principals, teachers, and students. All have been impacted by this law in a negative fashion.

Some of our worst fears have come true. Schools in some areas struggle to find highly qualified teachers. This causes further problems at the school level as principals try to balance what is required with what they need. Those who are teachers are choosing not to become principals, and superintendents are finding that making tough decisions in even tougher times sometimes has unfortunate consequences.

But it is not only the United States that has found it difficult to shift levels of student achievement. The 2006 report of the Programme for International Student Assessment (PISA) makes the following statement about the Organisation for Economic Co-operation and Development (OECD):

> It is now possible to track change in reading performance over a 6-year period. The results suggest that, across the OECD area, reading perfor-mance has generally remained flat between PISA 2000 and PISA 2006. This needs to be seen in the context of significant rises in expenditure levels. Between 1995 and 2004 expenditure per primary and secondary student increased by 39% in real terms, on average across OECD countries. (p. 48)

So why are measures of student attainment showing a relatively flat tra-jectory despite a substantial increase in funding and all sorts of reform efforts? The answer is not as simple as looking at a few numbers on a cou-ple of pages. And perhaps it is here that we start to recognise the weak-nesses inherent in the systems currently in place. It could be argued that systems that use raw achievement measures to judge the quality of school-ing (both PISA and NCLB do this) have been implemented for political purposes. After all, what do these systems do except allow politicians to make simplistic statements, such as, "My country is better than yours in mathematics" or, "My state has improved its reading scores more than any other state"? Underneath those numbers is a very complex set of reasons as to why this might be the case, but these broad statements disguise the fact that in a single country, not all states perform equally well; within a state, there is variation in student achievement from district to district; and, even within a single district, there is wide variation in the performance of schools.

In order to understand the level of complexity that educators must face from day to day, a complexity that is referred to time and time again in the Voices 3 data, I want to focus on two main issues that have underpinned my own work for the past 20 years. The first is the development of an understanding of school effectiveness and school improvement, and the second is the rapidity and the complexity of change, which has created an environment for teachers and learners that is nothing like what it was when we went to school. And I will also make further comments about how the research discussed in the chapters of this book helps to contribute to our understanding of how we might move forward.

## EDUCATIONAL EFFECTIVENESS AND SCHOOL IMPROVEMENT

The past 20 years has seen a substantial focus on making judgements about what a good school is (how we define an effective school) on the one hand, and how we make more schools effective (what elements lead to school improvement) on the other. The first of these foci has been shaped by a comparatively new research field called school effectiveness and the second focus by school improvement, a field that grew out of the need to improve schools' effectiveness. However, by the early 1990s, it became clear that these two areas of research were connected and needed each other to find a way that would improve the outcomes of students. As Smink (1991) pointed out,

> School effectiveness is concerned with results. Researchers try to describe certain variables for school success in measurable terms. On the other hand, school improvement places the accent on the process; here one finds a broad description of all the variables that play a role in a school improvement project. Both approaches need the other to successfully modernize the system. (p. 3)

The school effectiveness movement, as with all scientific areas of study, has changed over the years and, despite criticism from sociologists who argued that there were methodological and conceptual difficulties (Slee & Weiner, 2001; Thrupp, 2001), it is now seen as a viable and fruitful means of looking at schools. Reynolds, Sammons, De Fraine, Townsend, and Van Damme (2011) argued that there have been five distinct phases of research into what is now being called educational effectiveness. The first emerged as a reaction to the seminal studies of Coleman et al. (1966) and Jencks et al. (1972), who concluded that schools had little effect upon the outcomes of their students in comparison to the effects of their own ability and social backgrounds. The attempt to rebut this view included the empirical studies in the United States of Weber (1971) and Edmonds (1979) and, in the United Kingdom, of Rutter, Maughan, Mortimore, and Ouston (1979) and Smith and Tomlinson (1989).

The second phase, from the mid-1980s, saw studies that considered the scientific properties of school effects, such as the stability over time and differential effects of school upon students of different backgrounds and size of school and long-term effects on students. The third phase, in the 1990s, saw numerous attempts to explore the reasons *why* schools had different effects, with studies by Teddlie and Stringfield (1993) in the United States and Sammons, West, and Hind (1997) in the United Kingdom. My own work in Australia (Townsend, 1994) found that the expectations of school communities varied, not only from school to school but also from district to district. It showed that, in a district that was predominantly middle class, many parents, teachers, and students felt that the major role of school was academic (to prepare people for further education), whereas in a more working-class district, parents, teachers, and students were much more supportive of the role of the school being vocational (to prepare people for work). These differences suggested that a definition of an effective school should be broader than having a simple academic focus and not only consider systemic concerns but local ones as well:

> An effective school is one that develops and maintains a high quality educational program designed to achieve both systemwide and locally identified goals. All students, regardless of their family or social background, experience both improvement across their school career and ultimate success in the achievement of those goals, based on appropriate external and school-based measuring techniques. (Townsend, 1994, p. 48)

The fourth phase, which began in the middle to late 1990s, saw the internationalization of the research, together with further collaborations between school effectiveness and school improvement researchers and practitioners, led by people such as Fullan and Hargreaves (1991, 1992), MacBeath (1999, 2006), MacBeath et al. (2007), Stoll (1997), Stoll and Fink (1996), and Caldwell and Spinks (1988, 1992, 1996). School improvement was more concerned with the processes that lead to improvement within the school, rather than just seeking to know which aspects of school activity made a difference to student achievement. They were concerned with discovering *how* we could develop teachers so that they would have high expectations of students, *how* we involved parents, and *how* various styles of leadership might support school development, rather than simply knowing that these things made a difference. The school effectiveness and school improvement research, together, created the impetus for much school reform in many parts of the world, especially during the last decade of the 20th century.

The fifth phase started in the late 2000s and involved a change in terminology from *school effectiveness* to *educational effectiveness*, which is considered to be a dynamic, not static, set of relationships. This work considered that the effectiveness of a school was impacted by factors at a number of levels: the student, the teacher, the school, and the system (Creemers & Kyriakides, 2008). In order to really understand how schools became more effective we needed to better understand how each of these levels interacted with the other. If we look at the Voices 3 study, we can see that the different levels of activity from the nation, state, district, school, and classroom all impact on the level of learning that students actually achieve. However, we have known for quite some time that if we really wanted to improve student learning, the closer we get to the student, the better (i.e., Hattie, 2009; Hill, 1998; Wang, Haertel, & Walberg, 1993).

## CHANGE AND ITS IMPACT ON EDUCATION

Recently I argued,

> When educating teachers for an increasingly complex and rapidly changing world, one simple way to open their eyes is to ask the question, "What can a 15-year-old do or experience today that you could not do when you were 15?" Given a few minutes to think about this, they will come up with a series of responses such as "iPhones," "Facebook," "laptop computers," and so on. It is clear that teachers recognize that there has been substantial change in the types of technology available to young people today, most of which we as adults feel less comfortable about than they do. However, when they are probed further, they come to recognize that it is not just technology that has changed, but pretty much everything else too.... We could argue that virtually everything has changed and that children today think, act and understand things differently to what their parents did. (Townsend, 2011, p. 121)

There are two quotations that, taken together, demonstrate the importance of understanding how change impacts on human development and, in turn, on education. First, Drucker (1993) argued,

> Every few hundred years in western history there occurs a sharp transformation. We cross ... a divide. Within a few short decades society rearranges itself, its world view; its basic values; its social and political structure; its arts;

its key institutions. Fifty years later, there appears a new world.... We are currently living through such a transformation. (p. 1)

Twenty years earlier, however, Toffler (1971) had argued the amount of time that we have to respond to change has collapsed: "I coined the term 'future shock' to describe the shattering stress and disorientation that we induce in individuals by subjecting them to too much change in too short a time" (p. 12).

Of course, 40 years later, future shock is now a state of life. If we put these two quotations together, we start to get an understanding of how the world is changing at the moment, with quite substantial changes, changes that shift how we think about things and how we behave, now coming much quicker than ever before in history. Two examples of this, just in the past decade, are the War on Terror and how it has changed how we move about the planet, and Facebook, and how that has changed how we interact with each other. With the world changing so fast and so dramatically, the question then becomes, how do educators keep up?

At a recent conference in Dubai, Baroness Susan Greenfield (2010) made the point that by the end of their primary school years, students have spent substantially less time in school than they have in their local communities and, to an even lesser extent, online or in front of their computers. If this is the case, then how important will school be in comparison to other forms of learning that students undertake? How many new ways to learn are there now, than when we were in school? Yet, when we look at the way in which we educate them, how much has changed (Townsend, 2011)?

The research suggests that most teachers have never played a computer game. How are they able to communicate with students who spend more time on computers, using Facebook or Twitter, or just playing games, than they do with their teachers?

I used an S-curve model (Townsend, 2009, 2011) to describe what I considered to be four changes in the way in which we have thought about education over history. The first S-curve in education, Thinking and Acting Individually, lasted from the time when education was first conceived until around the 1870s. Most people were not educated at all, except by their parents. Then, communities started to take responsibility for educating their populations. This was the second S-curve in education, Thinking and Acting Locally, where most people (at least in the Western countries) received some education, and this phase of education lasted for about 100 years. Around the 1970s and 1980s, education started to be identified as being of economic value as well as of social importance. Governments started to make demands of local education systems to ensure that all students be educated to the levels required. The third S-curve, Thinking

Nationally and Acting Locally, had begun. The authors of Chapter 6, Assessment, argue that the coming of Sputnik in 1957 started the process of national thinking about education.

By the mid-1990s, the advent of the Trends in International Mathematics and Science Study and PISA led to the fourth S-curve, Thinking Internationally and Acting Locally. International comparisons were being used, and countries were sharing knowledge about curriculum, pedagogy, and the administration of schools; but individual schools were still seen as the locus of change. NCLB is a perfect example of how individual schools are expected, individually, to take responsibility for developing world-class students. The system of punishment for those that don't make Adequate Yearly Progress was referred to in Voices 3 over and over again.

Hedley Beare (1997) used three metaphors, the "preindustrial metaphor" when education was "for the few and the privileged," "the industrial metaphor" where "the factory-production metaphor [was] applied to schooling," and the "postindustrial metaphor" when "enterprise" became "the favoured way of explaining how education operates" and when "schools are being talked of as if they are private businesses or enterprises" to describe similar changes in educational thought (pp. 4–13). Following Beare, we could suggest that the metaphor for Thinking Internationally and Acting Locally is accountability, and this has been instituted through the use of education as a market, using the same underlying principles, those of privatization, competition, and choice. I argued,

> Governments, especially those in the west, seem to have accepted that they cannot afford to educate everyone to high levels of skill … and have adopted the rather facile approach of supporting private enterprise practices as the means of achieving this goal. Put simply (perhaps crudely), western governments are saying "If you don't like the school you are in, go to another one. If the government system can't provide for you, there is a private school that will." … This has allowed governments to keep education budgets within what they consider to be reasonable bounds, based on other increasing demands for funding (from a rapidly aging … population of "seniors" and those who will soon join them, on the one hand, to the burgeoning budget for terrorism surveillance on the other), but this has been done by shifting the cost of education from governments to individual families and one outcome seems to be an increasing gap between those who do well and those who struggle at school. (Townsend, 2011, p. 124)

This claim resonates with some Voices 3 respondents who suggested that the purpose of NCLB was to destroy public schools.

I argued in the first paragraphs of this chapter that the evidence suggests these different ways of thinking about, and acting on, education have not brought about the levels of improvement that we were hoping for. I argued it was time for the next S-curve, to Think and Act Both Locally and Globally (Townsend, 2009), where the metaphor changes from accountability to responsibility, where we do what is necessary to deliver a quality education to all students. I argued we cannot have education just for the few who are rich and privileged (preindustrial), or see schools as factories (postindustrial) or businesses (enterprise), and we cannot expect the market to solve our problems (accountability), but we must instead see education as a global experience, where the full range of human capabilities are fostered and students are seen as more than just future economic units.

I argued (Townsend, 2009) that this has implications not only for education policy and the way in which schools are structured but also for classroom practice, for curriculum, for pedagogy, and for assessment. This changes the way we need to conceive of teaching and teacher preparation, and this also requires a change in the way we see educational leadership and the preparation of educational leaders (Townsend, 2011).

Given that one focus of this book is how we might need to change what happens in terms of leadership preparation, I want to spend a little time outlining my view of this area in order to provide a background to commenting on how this book has changed my thinking. Table 11.1 is how I see we operate now (by thinking globally but acting only locally), and how I think we might move forward to thinking and acting both locally and globally.

It is clear that school leaders can have a powerful, if indirect, influence on student achievement (Leithwood & Jantzi, 2000) through their ability to influence the quality of teaching (Fullan, 2001; Sergiovanni, 2001). What is being argued in Table 11.1, however, is that the combination of the recognition of the importance of the school leader with the current urgent need to improve student achievement in a very narrow way has narrowed the focus of the task of the school leader. Many of the respondents in the Voices 3 data expressed a level of concern about the narrowness of the curriculum now offered after NCLB.

School improvement goals have narrowed the education of children to routines of learning content that matches a minimum-standards test while failing to provide for their social and emotional needs (Kohn, 2005; Popham, 2001). In many cases this has meant a more managerial approach to leadership than perhaps previously has been required. This becomes obvious when we look at the case of Florida, where of "the 91 specific skills identified as part of the new statewide FELE [Florida's Educational Leadership Examination], 44 of them (48%) refer to a knowledge and understanding of state or federal legislature" (Townsend & Bogotch, 2008, p. 225). Here:

**Table 11.1.   Changing our Understanding of School Leadership**

| Current Thinking for School Leaders: Thinking Globally | Current Action: Acting Locally | Alternative: Thinking and Acting Both Locally and Globally |
|---|---|---|
| International recognition that the role of the school leader is becoming increasingly important in establishing the conditions for high levels of student learning. Leaders now have to respond to rapidly changing economic, social and environmental conditions. | Strong focus on those elements of management that promote instructional leadership, including the need to understand the law, finance, policy, data analysis, and personnel development. | Recognition that an outstanding leader relies upon the people that he or she works with and that managing the school can only be successful if team leadership and relationship skills are also developed. Leaders think and act strategically to distribute their leadership within the school and to develop a focus on learning for all aspects of school activity. |

*Source:*   Townsend (2011, p. 131).

Of the 16 skills that are identified under the standard of Managing the Learning Environment, 15 refer to state legislation or standards, and of the 13 skills related to Human Resource Development, 12 refer to Federal or state laws or regulations. All 4 of the ethical leadership skills do the same. Clearly, an ethical leader is one that obeys the local rules. Four of the six-skills related to Community School Partnerships can likewise be accomplished through memorizing state statutes. (Townsend & Bogotch, 2008, p. 225)

However, the case I now wish to make is about not a narrowing of leadership but an expansion of it, so that leaders of schools strategically work their way through the substantial changes they are facing. On the one hand this means that we need to develop school leaders with a strategic approach to the task (Pisapia, 2009), but on the other we need to recognize that the task ahead of us is too big for one person to oversee.

Others also see the task of leadership expanding dramatically in the future, both in terms of focus and scope. The recent Australian Council for Educational Leaders Capability Framework (n.d.) has three major sets of roles for school leaders:

• leads self for learning,
• leads others for learning, and

- leads the organization for learning.

Within these three areas, there are 11 different specific capabilities with 34 separate indicators designed to enable school leaders to map their own level of performance. School leaders can judge their own current capability using a rubric with four different ways of considering their performance:

- influencing within and beyond classroom,
- influencing within and beyond team,
- influencing within and beyond school, and
- influencing within and globally beyond school.

From this massive set of expectations about what might happen for leadership within schools in the future, we also need to recognize that the task of educational improvement can no longer be given to just one individual, the "heroic leader" turning around failing schools, if we expect schooling for all students to be successful in this rapidly changing environment. This notion of the heroic leader was mentioned by eight of the authors who wrote a chapter for the recent *International Handbook on Leadership for Learning* (Townsend & MacBeath, 2011), yet none of the authors felt that this was a viable concept in today's schools. It is important to notice the terminology used in the Australian Council for Educational Leadership (n.d.) framework, and it is this point that I want to spend some time on in the next section. The task of the leader in the future is to lead self, others, and the organization for *learning*. It is focusing on building the capacity of everyone in the organization to become a learner.

Yet this seems to be the direct opposite of what is happening in the United States. Elmore (2007) argued that recent events have created a system that creates problems even in terms of student learning.

> [In] state accountability systems in the U.S. and the U.S. national policy (No Child Left Behind), accountability for performance is considered to be the leading instrument of policy and human investment is considered to be a collateral responsibility of states and localities, which can be exercised according to their preference. In the U.S. ... this situation has resulted in a disastrous gap between capacity and performance—the states and the federal government exert increasing pressure on schools to perform, but have essentially defaulted on their responsibility for human investment, leading to an increasingly large number of low-performing schools that continue to operate at low capacity. (p. 2)

This gap between expectation and capacity has a constant presence in all the chapters. On the one hand is the focus on what schools should be doing, and on the other hand is the level of resources that they have to do it. From the curriculum perspective, the education of the whole child has suffered since the implementation of NCLB, which, Elmore (2003) argued, "focuses primarily on measuring growth in school performance against fixed standards—the so-called adequate yearly progress requirement—and only incidentally on building capacity of individual educators and schools to deliver high-quality instruction" (p. 6). Two sentences from this volume ring true in this regard. The first reads,

> Although school superintendents and principals desire to provide students with an education that focuses on their academic, social, and emotional needs, the competing demands of school improvement, defined as higher scores on state achievement tests, often create barriers for school leaders that disconnect what they know from what they do.

The second asks, "How do superintendents and principals maintain a focus on the education of the whole child when what gets measured is a narrow range of minimum student achievement standards developed by each state?" (See Chapter 3, Growth and Development of Children.)

Perhaps even more damaging is the likelihood that, in order for leaders to achieve the best possible outcome within the school, some students now get even less attention than they did prior to NCLB being implemented. Chapter 3 also describes educators "focusing on the borderline students, those students who are within 10 points of a passing score, resulting in students at the lower end of the performance range lagging further behind and high-performing students declining in achievement."

A second issue is the gap between expectations and resources. Noddings (2005) argued, "NCLB is an underfunded mandate that makes costly demands without providing the resources to meet them" (in Chapter 6, Assessment). This has led to what researchers have argued is an unhealthy, test-driven focus on learning.

The Voices 3 data tell us that both system and building leaders in the United States are faced with delivering a broad range of national and community expectations, with a limited budget, but with success being judged only by a very narrow range of standardized, measurable outcomes. It is the school leader who is expected to deal with these ambiguities, and again, this is not something unique to the United States. MacBeath and Townsend (2011) provided a plethora of quotes about the difficulties facing school leaders in South Africa, where "there is little wriggle room for head teachers who are directly in the firing line of political pressure" (p. 1241). In China, principals described their work lives as "uncomfortable, increasingly uncertain, and fraught with tensions" (Qian

& Walker, 2011, p. 210). Here, the "dominant tension across the principals' narratives was between delivering High Exam performance and promoting more holistic student development" (Quian & Walker, 2011, p. 218).

In the United States, there are "miserable" and "frustrated" principals (Fink, 2011, p. 587). One of them commented, "Everything has a number to it. I have to make sure all those numbers are increasing, that the trend is upward on all pieces of data except for things like suspension rates" (Reitzug & West, 2011, p. 169). In Canada, a "blizzard of initiatives" flowed into schools, which are constrained by high-stakes tests and accountability and a whole raft of factors that "lie outside the control of even the most skilled local leaders" (Leithwood, Reid, Pedwell, & Connor, 2011, p. 349). In Australia,

> the ability to focus on leading learning and, on the other hand, the ability to manage the multiple accountability demands determined by the policy environment [are] considered a significant challenge in the Australian quest to prepare and support school leaders more effectively. (MacBeath & Townsend, 2011, p. 1242)

The source of these tensions might be considered as the difference between "sollen" (duty, what you "must" do) and "wollen" (aspiration, what you "want" to do), terms used by Schley and Schratz (2011) to depict the leadership dilemma in Austria, where government interventions cause an overload problem "by piling disconnected policies one upon another, leading to a sense of confusion and uncertainty" (p. 268). This condition is brought about when "close interconnections between education and economic growth are apparent" (Dimmock & Goh, 2011, p. 226). A "real and seemingly irresolvable problem for principals is the disconnection between what the curriculum reform proposes and what the exam system demands" (Qian & Walker, 2011, p. 219), thus leading school leaders to be "forced to engage in both frontstage and backstage performances when they play out their role of leaders for learning" (p. 210). The Voices 3 data provide a number of instances where both superintendents and school leaders walk this tightrope between doing the "right thing" by the state and doing "the right thing" for the students.

We see a further layer of complexity for school leaders. "More and more, those not in administrative roles are frequently concerned with what is best for themselves rather than the organization" (Chapter 8, School and District Relationships). The outcome of this dichotomy between working for students and working for self is frustration. "Superintendents shared frustration with working with the school boards who did not always have students as the focus of their decisions" (Chapter 6,

Decision-Making Processes, Giving Voice, Listening, and Involvement). This walking of the tightrope comes at a price.

If we accept that the concept of the "heroic leader" cannot work in this increasingly diverse and rapidly changing environment, and we are having difficulty finding such people anyway, then the concept of leadership has to change, from one to many leaders within the institution. O'Brien (2011) argued, "High leadership density, it is claimed, is important to an effective school where a shared sense of purpose allows people to feel that they belong" (p. 86). We need to encourage more people to accept that part of the role of being a teacher is also to be a leader: a leader of learners within the classroom but also a leader outside the classroom, of parents, of colleagues, of the wider community. It is this notion of capacity building for leadership that may be the way forward. Elmore (2007), in his analysis of the Victorian (Australia) approach to leadership development, argued that one of the things that "distinguishes the Victorian approach among its peers is the presence of a strategic view of school improvement" (p. 2). Another was its focus on capacity building.

> From the ministerial level, through the department level, to the operating level of the public schools office, into the regions and then into the schools, there is broad agreement on the essential message that the strategy is fundamentally about investing in the knowledge and skill of people. (Elmore, 2007, p. 2)

The above suggests that one of the key activities of school leadership is developing the potential of other people in the school to adopt a leadership perspective in everything they do. This suggests that if we think and act both locally and globally (Table 11.2), then the commencement of the task of learning about leadership does not come when one is thinking about leaving the classroom; it is implicit in everything that we do as teachers.

Thus, undergraduate students should learn about leadership (of their classroom), and more experienced teachers should understand how to lead others in curriculum, in pedagogy, and in relationships, so that they no longer see leadership as being administration of departments or schools, but as part of what we do as a teacher. In order for this to happen current school leaders have a responsibility to foster both leadership understanding and leadership practice in all the people they work with. This has a two-fold benefit; the first is that the onus on the school leader will be lessened as more people have the skill and the will to take part in decisions that affect them and their students, and the second is that when the school leader moves on, either to another school or retirement, there will be no discontinuity of leadership within the school. Collectively, all the people who have become leaders, even if it is only in small ways, can

**Table 11.2.   Changing our Understanding of Leadership Preparation**

| *Current Thinking for Leadership Preparation: Thinking Globally* | *Current Action: Acting Locally* | *Alternative: Thinking and Acting Both Locally and Globally* |
|---|---|---|
| Recognition that the job of school leader is now too complex and difficult for a single person to achieve. There are now a number of international research activities comparing school leadership in various countries. | Formal educational leadership preparation programs focus on developing school leaders who are capable of operating within the school system that trains them.<br><br>Training is mostly associated with preparing formal school leaders that manage their schools and the operations within them. | School leadership programs offer opportunities for a range of leadership development activity from junior staff to senior leaders in an effort to both spread the responsibility for leading the school and establish a succession planning model in schools. |

*Source:*   Townsend (2009, p. 372).

have the knowledge previously only available to one person in the school. The school can continue performing as if the identified leader were still there, because the leadership still is.

## WHAT HAVE WE LEARNED FROM VOICES 3?

It is clear from the commentaries provided that NCLB in itself has a range of positive components, and these have been identified by both superintendents and principals in the Voices 3 data. First, it has provided a focus for school improvement. So NCLB was based on a sound set of principles. It "brought more focus to curriculum and instruction and held principals and teachers more accountable. The law has mandated a greater focus on the use of student achievement data" (Chapter 9, Pressure of Outside Forces, Stress, and Finding Balance). It also made it clear that it wasn't just the average performance of a school that would count, but subgroups all had to perform well, too. However, the implementation strategy and the environment in which NCLB came about have meant that both superintendents and principals have little chance of success. These two main factors, the narrow focus and the lack of funding, have been the basis of substantial "pressures of retaining individual school culture, good relationships, and high morale amid standardization" (Chapter 2, No Child Left Behind as School Reform: Intended and Unintended Consequences).

So, NCLB provided a framework for improvement that people in the study agreed with in theory. Many of the underlying concepts, of equity, social justice, and achievement, are hard to argue with. But we need to recognize that a policy framework is an enabler, not a guarantee that something will happen. The purpose of policy is to set up conditions that will enable things to happen, that will provide an understanding of the rationale for and possible avenues for improvements to occur. But the implementation of policy relies on many things: the resources that are available to activate the policy, the people who will implement the policy, and the acceptance or otherwise of the policy by the people who will be impacted. What we have seen with NCLB is not so much a failure of policy, but a failure of implementation. It is to this failure of implementation that I want to turn in my final comments.

## NCLB AND INSTRUCTIONAL LEADERSHIP

I think there are elements associated with NCLB that have led to the view that instructional leadership is the way American school leaders should undertake the task of leading. This has taken pride of place for the last 30 years, and now the importance of instructional leadership is referred to in almost every state standard for leadership. The emergence of the term *instructional leadership* dated from around the 1980s (Hallinger & Heck, 1996, 1998; Hallinger & Murphy, 1985). Proponents proposed three dimensions in this leadership role: (a) defining the school's mission, (b) managing the instructional program, and (c) promoting a positive school learning climate. Northouse (2010) suggested that leadership is a process whereby an individual influences a group of individuals to achieve a common goal. It contains three dimensions: the people, the power relationship between them, and the task to be accomplished. It could be argued that the same sorts of conditions apply to virtually every human interaction. I put it this way: "There are three dimensions to human relationships, the way in which we interact, the content of the interaction, and the circumstances in which the interaction occurs" (Townsend, 2009, p. 376). Defining the school's mission looks at the content of the interaction, managing the instructional program considers the way in which people interact, and promoting a positive school learning climate can be equated with the circumstances in which the interaction occurs.

Although instructional leadership has a great deal of research backing it, the word *instructional* gives us a hint as to how this term might be applied. To give an instruction is to tell people to do something, so instructional leadership stretches the definition of instruction in a way that limits both leaders and teachers. Although there may be many areas that need to be discussed in order to improve the quality of schooling, those areas that *can* be discussed are defined by the law itself and the level of resources available to schools to deliver their program. In an environment of scarce resources, those resources likely will be spent ensuring that the mandated (and measured) part of the curriculum is delivered. Only when there are resources left over after these aspects have been attended to can other things be considered. In the United States, this emanates from the federal government telling everybody what to do (NCLB) but only providing resources if these are directed to this purpose; the states then tell school districts what to do, school boards tell superintendents what is required, and school superintendents tell principals how they are going to be judged, all of which results in the principal telling teachers how to do their work. The teacher telling the students what to do is the end of the chain. The people most responsible for the learning outcomes of the U.S. education system (the students) and the person most likely to guide, encourage, and teach them (the teacher) are, ironically, the least powerful people in this chain. They have no flexibility, can ask no questions, and can do nothing that is not mandated by someone further up the chain. This is supported by the data from Voices 3 on numerous occasions.

The data revealed that on some occasions "stakeholders wanted to be involved in the decision-making process, but not necessarily responsible or accountable for the decision-making outcome," and on other occasions "teachers do not want to give up their time to participate in decision making because they are well aware of the time involvement," leading to the conclusion that "shared decision making is a messy process" (Chapter 6, Decision-Making Processes, Giving Voice, Listening, and Involvement). One cannot help but think, however, when reading these commentaries, that it is sometimes easier for school leaders to simply think that the excuses given above are legitimate, especially in a hierarchical system, and choose not to try and change people's perceptions so they *are* prepared to take the time to make the correct decisions and then take responsibility for them. In a hierarchical system it is always easier to make the decision yourself than to get others involved in the process.

Let me take you right back to paragraph 1 where I said, "The best you can hope for is zero progress." Only compliant people do what they are told to do without thinking. Furthermore, every piece of our learning and perhaps all the learning for the entire human race have come about not because we are told things, but because we ask questions. Clinch (2001) argued there are two types of teachers: the askers and the tellers. He suggested that it is in those classrooms where most of the time teachers use questioning and explaining as a mechanism for getting the message across that learning really happens. If we extrapolate to the school and district levels, we might suggest that school leaders who question the policy and question the processes, rather than simply relaying them to the people below, might have a better chance of developing a learning community than those who do not. So, the first element of instructional leadership is how we manage information. We either ask people questions and help them move toward the answers, or we simply tell them the answer and ask them to memorize it. It seems pretty clear that the system described by both superintendents and principals is one where messages from above are shaped marginally by the next level and then passed down to the one below it.

The types of question we use or, alternatively, what we tell people can also be different in nature and form. It can be about individual facts, tasks, or a bit of information, or it can be about the broader processes or concepts we use as human beings. The difference between individual facts and concepts is huge. An individual fact (or a specific task) is not necessarily connected to anything else, so the answer to "What is 4 + 4?" or "When do you start bus duty?" doesn't really go much further. But we use our concepts and processes daily to help us manage our lives. The ways in which we respond to a situation depend on the current concepts that we have associated with that situation. So discussing the concept of addition is much more enriching than remembering the answer to a simple addition; the concept of student safety is much more challenging than bus timetables. The individual fact may help us to understand our concept, but if we spend all our time on facts and little time on concept development, then not much learning will take place. The Voices 3 data are littered with references to the narrowness of what is being delivered to American students. Much of the instructional leadership literature focuses on specific tasks that leaders might do to ensure their teachers promote high levels of student achievement. Hallinger and Murphy (1985) talked about "10 instructional leadership functions." Viewed uncritically, this can too easily result in a series of what might be called recipes for success that fail to take into account the uniqueness of every school. As McGaw, Banks, and Piper (1991) argued, "There is no definitive how of effective schools and so there can be no one recipe for every school to try. Schooling is too complex a business for a recipe" (p. 15).

The third element that is associated with instructional leadership, especially under the conditions of NCLB, is the environment in which all this activity takes place. This can either be positive or negative, and again the overall environment in which schools are operating is, in part, determined by people outside the school and is enacted or overseen by leaders inside the school. Essentially in regards to this aspect of human behavior, the simple way of differentiating is to ask ourselves the question, "Do we trust our school leaders and teachers to do the job of educating our students or not?" It is pretty clear that in many parts of the world at the moment, we don't trust our teachers and school leaders to do the task, and the result of this is a constraining of the level of freedom allowed at the school level. This in turn leads to unfortunate outcomes, such as a narrowing of both curriculum and the teacher's ability to make decisions.

As discussed previously, the process of enabling teachers and school leaders to make decisions at the local level, based on what they know about their students, is severely curtailed when the only way in which school leaders, teachers, and schools themselves are judged by the public is on the basis of a narrow range of curriculum activities tested under conditions that are antithetical to learning. Ruff and Gieselmann (Chapter 2, No Child Left Behind as School Reform: Intended and Unintended Consequences) argued the data showed, "with an average of 3 weeks out of a 9-month school year consumed with testing, that schools were spending too much time assessing students." Thus, much of the time that used to be spent learning new things is now used to study a narrow range of things by which school success is measured. This seems to be directed more toward teachers and students in schools that have usually been identified as failing in the first place than in schools that are achieving.

It is interesting to note that in the Finnish education system, identified by many politicians as the benchmark because of their performance on PISA, there is no standardized testing until the completion of secondary school. Unlike many other education systems, consequential accountability accompanied by high-stakes testing and externally determined learning standards has not been part of Finnish education policies (Sahlberg, 2007).

## FROM INSTRUCTIONAL LEADERSHIP TO LEADERSHIP FOR LEARNING: THE TELLERS AND THE ASKERS

In the *International Handbook on Leadership for Learning*, MacBeath and Townsend (2011) discussed the differences between instructional leadership and leadership for learning. My view of the difference between instructional leadership and leadership for learning is that instructional leadership has a tendency to atomize a very complex set of interactions into specific competencies or activities, then tells teachers how to do them, within an environment that suggests neither teachers nor school leaders can be trusted to make decisions by themselves. On the other hand, leadership for learning promotes the notion that successful organizations are driven by questions. "How well are we doing?" "How do we know?" and "What do we do next?" are three classic questions that underpin school self-evaluation (MacBeath, 1999). "Who is not learning?" "Why are they not learning?" and "How can I help them learn?" are three classic questions that teachers should be asking themselves every single day.

Second, leadership for learning focuses on developing concepts and processes, such as professionalism, cooperation, and how to develop a professional learning community. We have seen in Voices 3 that school leaders have attempted to do this, but the underlying framework for undertaking this exercise is still that narrow base of outcomes judged as being important by NCLB. Finally, leadership for learning requires trusting the people involved to do the job. It makes sure that teachers and school leaders are well trained and resourced, and it is assumed that they are dedicated enough to act professionally in all aspects of their work. If we put the three elements together—asking and telling, facts and concepts, and supportive or oppositional environment—we come up with eight different types of leadership behavior. If we use one form of behavior consistently, it is likely that teachers will learn to respond in a particular way. Table 11.3 provides a tentative breakdown of the types of interactions that can be initiated by leaders and the responses that are likely to emerge from teachers because of that interaction, adapted from Townsend (2009). I made the following case for how the relationship develops (Townsend, 2009):

> If the principal tells a teacher what to do in a confrontational way and the task is something very specific, then all the teacher gets to do is memorize the task and the principal is made happy. There may be times when this is appropriate, where for instance the teacher has failed to comply with a very specific departmental regulation. From another perspective, if the principal asks the teacher questions about ways in which processes or concepts are associated with the teaching task and provides the teacher with support and feedback to assist them, then the likely outcome will be a better understanding by teachers of how to do their jobs. (p. 377)

Are there some overlaps between the two approaches to leading? Of course; it would be inappropriate for me to suggest that instructional leaders currently never ask questions, never consider the bigger issues, and never trust their staff, or vice versa. But it is the extent to which one form or the other for each of the three dichotomies is being used. Since much of the environment in which school leaders work under NCLB is determined by those outside the school, by those in government or at state or district levels, then if the negative sides of the issue start here, it becomes hard for school leaders not to act in this way, too. The Voices 3 data demonstrate conclusively that the current implementation of NCLB has created a negative atmosphere, which can, in the worst-case scenario, lead to cheating as standard procedure (Chapter 6, Assessment).

**Table 11.3.   Leaders' Actions and Likely Responses**

| Management Approach | Environment | Content Focus | Teacher Response |
|---|---|---|---|
| Leader asking | Leader supporting | Concepts, processes | Understanding |
| Leader asking | Leader supporting | Facts, tasks | Knowledge |
| Leader asking | Leader managing | Concepts, processes | Self-doubt |
| Leader asking | Leader managing | Facts, tasks | Guilt |
| Leader telling | Leader supporting | Concepts, processes | Self-belief |
| Leader telling | Leader supporting | Facts, tasks | Clarity |
| Leader telling | Leader managing | Concepts, processes | Unquestioned belief |
| Leader telling | Leader managing | Facts, tasks | Memorization |

*Source:*   Townsend (2009).

Keeping learning at the very center of everything in the face of myriad other pressures and everyday "busyness" requires the ability, in David Hargreaves's words, to "fly below the radar" (Bangs, MacBeath, & Galton, 2010, p. 149). It requires both the will and skill to pursue what is valued rather than simply what is measured. So it is hard, yes, but not impossible.

## THE ESSENCE OF LEADERSHIP FOR LEARNING

MacBeath and Townsend (2011) teased out how leadership for learning might move to restore the priority of leadership over managing the narrow task of maximizing student achievement, arguing,

> Whereas much of the instructional leadership literature reduces learning to "outcomes," leadership for learning embraces a much wider, developmental view of learning.... It sees things through a wide angle lens, embracing professional, organisational and leadership learning. It understands the vitality of their interconnections and the climate they create for exploration, inquiry and creativity. (p. 1250)

Whereas instructional leadership seems to focus on "student outcomes" to "support growth with a focus on results" (Pedwell et al., 2011, p. 613), leadership for learning is concerned about learning beyond the student body. It could be argued that leadership for learning is designed to create learning at all levels within the system: student learning, teacher learning, organizational learning, and leadership learning all at once. The task is to look at where the school is now; make some decisions about where it wants to be; and then to enable these to "unfold from within the fabric of school life, reflect and respond to the conditions that prevail in the school, and be authentically connected to the daily work of teachers and students" (Mitchell & Sackney, 2011, p. 977).

## THE WAY FORWARD

We might suggest that schools as they are currently structured, managed, and operated are not sustainable. NCLB has not delivered on closing the gap between advantaged and disadvantaged students, and it is not approaching its goal of all students being proficient by 2014. However, it has created an environment and a system that encourage teachers to think more about all students and not simply to think that if a student is not successful, it is the student's fault. It has provided the impetus for much more teacher interaction, for the development of professional conversations. It has provided teachers with the knowledge and skills they need to look at data, analyze data, and make sensible decisions about how to proceed.

There seems, however, to be one major obstacle to overcome, the widely held belief that if schools were more businesslike in their approach to education, then success must follow. NCLB tries to manipulate the conditions within schools to make education a fail-safe activity when it isn't. Schools don't necessarily have quality ingredients to work with and can't ignore those that are not. A teacher once said at a presentation,

> We take them big, small, rich, poor, gifted, exceptional, abused, frightened, confident, homeless, rude, and brilliant. We take them with attention deficit hyperactivity disorder, junior rheumatoid arthritis, and English as their second language. We take them all. Every one. And that is why it's not a business. It's a school. (Cirone, 2011, para. 10)

Instructional leadership under NCLB places priority on task, achieving a narrow range of student outcomes, whereas leading for learning places the focus on people and the development of everyone through a focused learning process. It could be argued that focusing on learning for all rather than on outcomes is the best way to improve those outcomes anyway, because it relies on interacting with one's environment rather than simply remembering discrete elements of it. It moves from atomism to holism, from remembering to understanding, and from a focus on failure to a focus on success.

So how might we move forward? How might we use the power of the policy of NCLB to improve American education? NCLB has helped teachers to develop new understandings of what they need to do and perhaps better understandings of how to go about doing it. What has happened is that teachers and school leaders *know* so much more than they did in 2000, but it might also be true that they are being held back by the focus on too narrow a task. The real question for the future is do we trust our teachers? If we removed the high-stakes, punitive nature that underpins NCLB, do we trust our teachers enough to expect them to continue to use what they have learned in the last decade, to continue to focus on all students, but to encourage a broader range of outcomes that better suit the needs of a diverse range of students? Do we trust them enough to use their new knowledge of data collection, analysis, and decision making for the benefit of all, rather than some? If we trusted our leaders and teachers, then NCLB could be repealed, and what has been learned in the past decade could continue, but not in the environment of fear.

This may mean a move from where school leaders and teachers are being told what to do to one where they are being asked the hardest questions of their lives. The tasks may be more daunting, but the people will not be the same. The relationships between leaders and teachers and between those in the school and those outside it would be different, ideally more positive. To do this leaders will need to be courageous; they may need to challenge authority and may need to be subversive (MacBeath, 2008). The Voices 3 project has shown that school leaders are concerned about both tasks and people. But, it is the interchanges between one way of looking at schools and the other, where task and people become equally important, that the interesting developments, especially related to leadership of the future, may lie.

## REFERENCES

Australian Council for Educational Leadership. (n.d.). *The ACEL leadership capability framework*. Retrieved from http://www.acel.org.au/index.php?id=1163

Bangs, J., MacBeath, J., & Galton, M. (2010). *Reinventing schools, reforming teaching: From political visions to classroom realities*. London, England: Routledge.

Beare, H. (1997). Enterprise: The new metaphor for schooling in a post-industrial society. In T. Townsend (Ed.), *The primary school in changing times: The Australian experience* (pp. 3-20). London, England: Routledge.

Caldwell, B. J., & Spinks, J. M. (1988). *The self-managing school*. London, England: Falmer Press.

Caldwell, B. J., & Spinks, J. M. (1992). *Leading the self-managing school*. London, England: Falmer Press.

Caldwell, B. J., & Spinks, J. M. (1996). *Beyond the self-managing school*. London, England: Falmer Press.

Cirone, B. (2011). *Story about blueberries shares important message about teaching*. Retrieved from http://www.noozhawk.com/article/060111_bill_cirone _blueberries_and_teaching/

Clinch, R. (2001). *Secret kids' business*. Melbourne, Australia: Hawker-Brownlow.

Coleman, J. S., Campbell, E., Hobson, C., McPartland, J., Mood, A., Weinfeld, F., & York, R. (1966). *Equality of educational opportunity*. Washington, DC: Government Printing Office.

Creemers, B. P. M., & Kyriakides, L. (2008). *The dynamics of educational effectiveness: A contribution to policy, practice and theory in contemporary schools*. Abingdon, England: Routledge.

Dimmock, C., & Goh, J. (2011). Transforming Singapore schools: The economic imperative, government policy and school principalship. In T. Townsend & J. MacBeath (Eds.), *The international handbook of leadership for learning* (pp. 225-242). New York, NY: Springer.

Drucker, P. F. (1993). *The ecological vision: Reflections on the American condition*. New Brunswick, NJ: Transaction.

Edmonds, R. (1979). Effective schools for the urban poor. *Educational Leadership, 37*, 15-27.

Elmore, R. F. (2003). A plea for strong practice. *Educational Leadership, 61*(3), 6-10.

Elmore, R. (2007). *Educational improvement in Victoria*. Melbourne, Victoria, Australia: Office for Government School Education, Department of Education.

Fink, D. (2011). The succession challenge: Warm bodies or leaders of learning? In T. Townsend & J. MacBeath (Eds.), *The international handbook of leadership for learning* (pp. 589-602). New York, NY: Springer.

Fullan, M. (2001). *Leading in a culture of change*. San Francisco, CA: Jossey-Bass.

Fullan, M. G., & Hargreaves, A. (1991). *Working together for your school*. Hawthorn, Victoria: Australian Council for Educational Administration.

Fullan, M. G., & Hargreaves, A. (1992). *Teacher development and educational change*. London, England: Falmer.

Greenfield, S. (2010, November). *Developing UAE citizens for the modern world: The human/technology balance*. Paper presented at the Education Competitiveness Conference, Dubai.

Hallinger, P., & Heck, R. H. (1996). Reassessing the principal's role in school effectiveness: A review of the empirical research, 1980–1995. *Educational Administration Quarterly, 32*(1), 5-44.

Hallinger, P., & Heck, R. H. (1998). Exploring the principal's contribution to school effectiveness: 1980–1995. *School Effectiveness and School Improvement, 9*, 157-191.

Hallinger, P., & Murphy, J. (1985). Assessing the instructional management behavior of principals. *The Elementary School Journal, 86*, 217-248.

Hattie, J. (2009). *Visible learning: A synthesis of over 800 meta-analyses relating to achievement*. London, England: Routledge.

Hill, P. W. (1998). Shaking the foundations: Research driven school reform. *School Effectiveness and School Improvement, 9*, 419-436.

Jencks, C. S., Smith, M., Ackland, H., Bane, M. J., Cohen, D., Gintis, H., ... Michelson, S. (1972). *Inequality: A reassessment of the effect of the family and schooling in America*. New York, NY: Basic Books.

Kerachsky, S. (2009). *NAEP 2008 trends in academic progress*. Retrieved from the National Center for Education Statistics website: http://nces.ed.gov/whatsnew/commissioner/remarks2009/4_28_2009.asp

Kohn, A. (2005). *Unconditional teaching*. Retrieved from http://www.mantleoftheexpert.com/studying/articles/AK%20-%20Unconditional%20Teaching.pdf

Leithwood, K., & Janzti, D. (2000). The effects of transformational leadership on organizational conditions and student engagement with school. *Journal of Educational Administration, 38*, 112–129.

Leithwood, K., Reid, S., Pedwell, L., & Connor, M. (2011). Lessons about improving leadership on a large scale: From Ontario's leadership strategy. In T. Townsend & J. MacBeath (Eds.), *The international handbook of leadership for learning* (pp. 335-352). New York, NY: Springer.

MacBeath, J. (1999). *Schools must speak for themselves: The case for school self-evaluation*. London, England: Routledge.

MacBeath, J. (2006). *School inspection and self-evaluation: Working with the new relationship*. London, England: Routledge Falmer.

MacBeath, J. (2008). Leadership moments: How to lead. In T. Townsend & I. Bogotch (Eds.), *The elusive what and the problematic how: The essential leadership questions for school leaders and educational researchers* (pp. 119-134). Rotterdam, The Netherlands: Sense.

MacBeath, J., Gray, J. M., Cullen, J., Frost, D., Steward, S., & Swaffield, S. (2007). *Schools on the edge: Responding to challenging circumstances*. London, England: Paul Chapman.

MacBeath, J., & Townsend, T. (2011). Thinking and acting both locally and globally: What do we know now and how do we continue to improve? In T. Townsend & J. MacBeath (Eds.), *The international handbook of leadership for learning* (pp. 1241-1259). New York, NY: Springer.

McGaw, B., Banks, D., & Piper, K. (1991). *Effective schools: Schools that make a difference*. Hawthorn, Victoria: Australian Council for Educational Research.

Mitchell, C. & Sackney, L. (2011). Building and leading within learning ecologies. In T. Townsend & J. MacBeath (Eds.), *The international handbook of leadership for learning* (pp. 993-1012). New York, NY: Springer.

Noddings, N. (2005). What does it mean to educate the whole child? *Educational Leadership, 63*(1), 8-13.

Northouse, P. G. (2010). *Leadership: Theory and practice* (5th ed.). Thousand Oaks, CA: SAGE.

O'Brien, J. (2011). Leadership for learning in the United Kingdom. In T. Townsend & J. MacBeath (Eds.), *The international handbook of leadership for learning* (pp. 81-88). New York, NY: Springer.

Pedwell, L., Levin, B., Pervin, B., Gallagher, M. J., Connor, M., & Beck, H. (2011). Building leadership capacity across 5,000 schools. In T. Townsend & J. MacBeath (Eds.), *The international handbook of leadership for learning* (pp. 601–616). New York, NY: Springer.

Peterson P., & West, M. (2003). *No Child Left Behind: The politics and practice of school accountability*. Washington DC: Brookings Institution.

Programme for International Student Assessment. (2006). *PISA 2006: Science sompetencies for tomorrow's world*. Retrieved from http://www.oecd.org/dataoecd/15/13/39725224.pdf

Pisapia, J. (2009). *The strategic leader*. Charlotte, NC: Information Age.

Popham, W. J. (2001). *The truth about testing: An educator's call to action*. Alexandria, VA: Association for Supervision and Curriculum Development.

Qian, H., & Walker, A. (2011). Leadership for learning in China: The political and policy context. In T. Townsend & J. MacBeath (Eds.), *The international handbook of leadership for learning* (pp. 209-224). New York, NY: Springer.

Reitzug, U. & West, D. (2011). A developmental framework for instructional leadership. In T. Townsend & J. MacBeath (Eds.), *The international handbook of leadership for learning* (pp. 169-188). New York, NY: Springer.

Reynolds, D., Sammons, P., De Fraine, B., Townsend, T., & Van Damme, J. (2011). *Educational effectiveness research (EER): A state of the art review*. Paper presented at the meeting of the International Congress for School Effectiveness and Improvement, Cyprus.

Rutter, M., Maughan, B., Mortimore, P., & Ouston, J., with Smith, A. (1979). *Fifteen thousand hours: Secondary schools and their effects on children*. London, England: Open Books.

Sahlberg, P. (2007). Education policies for raising student learning: The Finnish approach. *Journal of Education Policy, 22*, 173-197.

Sammons, P., West, A., & Hind, A. (1997). Accounting for variation in pupil attainment at the end of key Stage 1. *British Educational Research Journal, 23*, 489-511.

Schley, W., & Schratz, M. (2011). Developing leaders, building networks, changing schools through system leadership. In T. Townsend & J. MacBeath (Eds.), *The international handbook of leadership for learning* (pp. 267-296). New York, NY: Springer.

Sergiovanni, T. (2001). *The principalship: A reflective practice* (5th ed.). San Antonio, TX: Trinity Press.

Slee, R., & Weiner, G. (2001). Education reform and reconstruction as a challenge to research genres: Reconsidering school effectiveness research and inclusive schooling. *School Effectiveness and School Improvement, 12*, 83-98.

Smink, G. (1991). The Cardiff conference, ICSEI 1991. *Network News International, 1*(3), 2-6.

Smith, D. J., & Tomlinson, S. (1989). *The school effect: A study of multi-racial comprehensives*. London, England: Policy Studies Institute.

Stoll, L. (1997, June). *Successful schools: Linking school effectiveness and school improvement*. Keynote presentation at the Successful Schools Conference, Melbourne, Australia.

Stoll, L., & Fink, D. (1996). *Changing our schools*. London, England: Open University Press.

Teddlie, C. & Stringfield, S. (1993). *Schools make a difference: Lessons learned from a ten year study of school effects*. New York, NY: Teachers College Press.

Thrupp, M. (2001). Sociological and political concerns about school effectiveness research: Time for a new research agenda. *School Effectiveness and School Improvement, 12*, 7-40.

Toffler, A. (1971). *Future shock*. London, England: Pan.

Townsend, T. (1994). *Effective schooling for the community: Core plus education*. London, England: Routledge.

Townsend, T. (2009). Third millennium leaders: Thinking and acting both locally and globally. *Leadership and Policy in Schools, 8,* 355-379.

Townsend, T. (2011). Thinking and acting both locally and globally: New issues for teacher education. *Journal of Education for Teaching, 37,* 121-137.

Townsend, T., & Bogotch, I. (Eds.). (2008). *The elusive what and the problematic how: The essential leadership questions for school leaders and educational researchers.* Rotterdam, The Netherlands: Sense.

Townsend, T., & MacBeath, J. (Eds.). (2011). *The international handbook on leadership for learning.* Dordrecht, The Netherlands: Springer.

Wang, M. C., Haertel, G. D. & Walberg, H. J. (1993). What helps students learn? *Educational Leadership, 51*(4) 74-79.

Weber, G. (1971). *Inner city children can be taught to read: Four successful schools.* Washington, DC: Council for Basic Education.

# ABOUT THE CONTRIBUTORS

**Michele A. Acker-Hocevar**'s work background spans over 35 years, with an interdisciplinary PhD in organizational studies and school leadership. Her experiences as a teacher, consultant for a national publishing company, sales and marketing key accounts executive for a Fortune 10 company, school administrator, research assistant, and faculty member led her to focus on organizational theory and behavior, especially around decision making, power, change, and culture. She is one of the coinvestigators of the Voices 3 study and was named recently the coeditor of the *Journal of Research on Leadership Education*.

**Betty J. Alford** is a professor, doctoral program coordinator, and chair of the Department of Secondary Education and Educational Leadership at Stephen F. Austin State University (SFASU) in Nacogdoches, Texas. In 2008, she received the SFASU Foundation Faculty Achievement Award for Research. Her previous awards include the department's Teaching Excellence Award and the SFASU Chapter Phi Delta Kappa Educator of the Year award. Her doctoral degree in educational administration is from The University of Texas at Austin. Her experiences in public school include service as a school principal; a school counselor; and an elementary, middle, and high school teacher.

**Thomas L. Alsbury** is currently professor in the Department of Educational Leadership at Seattle Pacific University. His research focuses on school boards, superintendents, and district governance, and he directs the UCEA Center for Research on the Superintendency and District Governance. His book, *The Future of School Board Governance: Relevance and Revelation,* and over 50 publications on board and superintendent research have made him a regular keynote speaker at state and national school board and superintendent conferences.

**Julia Ballenger,** associate professor, teaches in the doctoral program in the School of Education at Texas Wesleyan University. Julia's research agenda includes leadership for social justice, gender equity, principal preparation program effectiveness, and culturally responsive pedagogy. Julia serves on several professional boards. She currently serves as cochair of the Research on Women and Education Special Interest Group of the American Educational Research Association (AERA) and is a council-at-large board member of the Southwest Educational Research Association. In addition, she is the associate editor of the National Council of Professors of Educational Administrators Yearbook and serves as assistant editor of several national and international journals.

**Ira Bogotch** is professor of school leadership at Florida Atlantic University. In 1990s, Ira facilitated the development of leadership standards in Louisiana. He is coediting an international handbook on social justice scheduled for publication in 2013. Ira serves as the associate editor for the *International Journal of Leadership and Education*. His most recent books are *Radicalizing Educational Leadership: Dimensions of Social Justice* (2008) and *The Elusive What and the Problematic How: The Essential Leadership Questions for School Leaders and Educational Researchers* (2008). He has published recently in *The Scholar-Practitioner Quarterly* and *Intercultural Education*. He may be reached via e-mail at ibogotch@fau.edu.

**Sharon Gieselmann** is an associate professor at the University of Evansville where she prepares educators for success in the classroom. She has been an elementary school principal, staff developer, and elementary school teacher. Her research interests include social justice issues in public schools. She has presented her work internationally at conferences in Paris, France, and Moscow, Russia.

**Sally Hipp** teaches graduate classes in teacher leadership in the College of Education at Grand Valley State University. In addition she is the program coordinator for the Graduate Teacher Certification program. Before coming to Grand Valley State University, Sally served as a principal, counselor, and elementary and secondary teacher in urban schools. Her research interests are curriculum and instruction, urban education, and technology in education.

**Gary Ivory** is associate professor at New Mexico State University. He has taught in Grades 5–8 and at the community college level. He has been coordinator of research, testing, and evaluation in a district of 50,000 students and academic department head at New Mexico State University. He is editor of *What Works in Computing for School Administrators* (Scarecrow

Education) and coeditor (with Michele Acker-Hocevar) of *Successful School Board Leadership: Lessons From Superintendents* (Rowman & Littlefield Education).

**Thomas A. Kersten** is associate professor and Educational Leadership Program director at Roosevelt University in Chicago, Illinois. Prior to university appointment, he served as an Illinois public school administrator for 28 years, during which he was an assistant principal, elementary principal, middle school principal, assistant superintendent, and superintendent. He has authored two books: *Taking the Mystery out of Illinois School Finance* and *Stepping Into Administration: How to Succeed in Making the Move*.

**Kristin Kew** serves as an assistant professor in the Department of Educational Management and Development at New Mexico State University. Her teaching and research interests include educational change, school reform, and the principalship. She has taught at all levels of schooling. She worked in educational management, opening new charter schools in inner cities throughout the United States, and assisted in the creation and management of networks. She was managing editor of the *Journal of Educational Change* while completing her dissertation at Boston College, *The Effects of Educational Change on Traditional High Schooling*.

**Jacquelyn Melin** teaches graduate classes in educational differentiation, curriculum development, and assessment practices for the College of Education at Grand Valley State University. Formerly, she was a public school teacher, gifted-and-talented coordinator, and principal. She also does educational consulting in various topics, mainly differentiated instruction and formative-assessment practices. Her published books include *Passport to Learn* (Zephyr Press, 2001) and *Performance Appraisal Made Easy* (Corwin Press, 2005).

**Elizabeth Murakami-Ramalho** is an associate professor in Educational Leadership and Policy Studies at The University of Texas at San Antonio. She received her PhD in Educational Administration and International Development at Michigan State University. She teaches graduate-level courses in school leadership, school change, and principal preparation in urban areas. Her research focuses on urban and international educational leadership, including organizational learning and ecology, leadership dynamics, hybrid identities and communities, social justice, race, and gender.

**Miriam M. Muñiz** is an associate professor in the Department of Education at Sul Ross State University, Rio Grande College, which serves Del

Rio, Uvalde, and Eagle Pass, Texas. She teaches a wide spectrum of undergraduate and graduate education courses, including educational administration, educational foundations, and reading. Originally from the Rio Grande Valley, Miriam and her husband, Fernando, have lived in Del Rio, Texas, for nearly 25 years. She is actively involved in church and community organizations.

**A. William Place** has been a teacher, teacher-association representative, and administrator. He has publications in prestigious journals, as well as the recent book *Principals Who Dare to Care*. He is director of doctoral studies and teaches research, school public relations, and personnel courses at the University of Dayton. He was elected to the executive board of the National Council of Professors of Educational Administration. He is a past president of the Mid-Western Educational Research Association and the Ohio Council of Professors of Educational Administration. In 2005, he received the School of Education and Allied Professions Teaching Award.

**Fernando Z. Quiz** has been an associate professor of education at Sul Ross State University, Rio Grande College for 8 years. He is currently serving as a school trustee for the San Felipe Del Rio (Texas) Consolidated Independent School District. He obtained his PhD in Educational Leadership as a Kellogg Fellow at New Mexico State University.

**Mariela A. Rodríguez** is an associate professor in the Department of Educational Leadership and Policy Studies at The University of Texas at San Antonio. Her scholarly research focuses on the role of school principals who support English language learners in dual-language education programs. Her work has been published in the *Journal of School Leadership* and the *International Journal of Leadership and Education*.

**William G. Ruff** currently serves as the coordinator for the Educational Leadership program at Montana State University. In addition to working on the Voices 3 project, he served as director for Indian Leadership Education and Development, a multimillion-dollar series of projects sponsored by the U.S. Department of Education, and authored or coauthored 10 peer-reviewed articles in a variety of education and educational leadership research journals, including *Educational Administration Quarterly*.

**Rosemarye T. Taylor** has distinguished herself, during her 11 years as a faculty member at the University of Central Florida, with numerous journal publications and six books on leadership for second-order change to improve student achievement, literacy leadership, and creating systems to improve learning. She regularly speaks nationally and internationally as well as consults on leadership to improve learning. Before becoming a faculty member at the University of Central Florida, she served as an administrator at the school and district levels in both Georgia and Florida.

**Debra J. Touchton** is an associate professor and program director for Educational Leadership graduate programs at Stetson University. Her research interests are in the areas of leadership and organizational development, women in leadership, and the effects of poverty on teaching and learning.

**Tony Townsend** is the leader of the Professional Learning and Leadership Research and Knowledge Transfer Group at the University of Glasgow. Prior to that he worked at Florida Atlantic University and Monash University in Australia. He has published extensively in the areas of school effectiveness, school improvement, and leadership and is the editor, with John Macbeath, of the *International Handbook on Leadership for Learning* (Springer, 2011). He has been a visiting professor or conference presenter in more than 40 countries.

**Kathryn S. Whitaker** has been a professor of Educational Leadership and Policy Studies at the University of Northern Colorado for 23 years. Prior to that, she was a K-12 teacher, assistant principal, and principal. Her research interests have included principal burnout, restructuring schools, public school and university partnerships, and the superintendency. She has published in journals such as the *Journal of School Leadership*, the *Journal of Educational Administration*, and *Planning and Changing*. She is author or coauthor of several books and book chapters. Dr. Whitaker recently retired and is currently professor emeritus in the Educational Leadership and Policy Studies department.

CPSIA information can be obtained at www.ICGtesting.com
Printed in the USA
BVOW012215041112

304621BV00004B/1/P

9 781617 358982